# RETHINKING
# SOCIAL DEMOCRACY
# IN WESTERN EUROPE

# RETHINKING
# SOCIAL DEMOCRACY
# IN WESTERN EUROPE

*Edited by*
## RICHARD GILLESPIE
## AND
## WILLIAM E. PATERSON

## FRANK CASS

*First published 1993 in Great Britain by*
FRANK CASS & CO. LTD
Gainsborough House, Gainsborough Road,
London E11 1RS, England

*and in the United States of America by*
FRANK CASS
c/o International Specialized Book Services, Inc.,
5804 N.E. Hassalo Street,
Portland, Oregon 97213–3644

**British Library Cataloguing in Publication Data**
Rethinking Social Democracy in Western
Europe. – (West European Politics Series,
ISSN 0140–2382; Vol. 16, No. 1)
  I. Gillespie, Richard
  II. Paterson, William E.   III. Series
320.5

ISBN 0–7146–4525–7 (hardback)
ISBN 0–7146–4098–0 (paperback)

**Library of Congress Cataloging-in-Publication Data**
Rethinking social democracy in Western Europe / edited by Richard
  Gillespie and William E. Paterson
    p. cm.
  Includes bibliographical reference and index.
    ISBN 0–7146–4525–7 : $37.50. – ISBN 0–7146–4098–0
(pbk.) : $24.00
    1. Socialist parties – Europe.  2. Socialism – Europe.  3. Europe –
–Politics and government – 1945–1989.  I. Gillespie. Richard, 1952–
  . II. Paterson, William E.
  JN94.A979R48   1993
  320.5'315'094–dc20                                        93–6515
                                                              CIP

This group of studies first appeared in a Special Issue on 'Rethinking Social
Democracy in Western Europe' of *West European Politics*, Vol. 16, No. 1
(January 1993), published by Frank Cass & Co. Ltd.

Typeset by Florencetype, Kewstoke, Avon
Printed in Great Britain by
Antony Rowe Ltd, Chippenham

# Contents

# Reprogramming Democratic Socialism

## WILLIAM E. PATERSON

Socialism is what a Labour Government does.

This view of socialism, often attributed to Herbert Morrison,[1] was regarded as a curious British joke by democratic socialists on the European mainland. There, programmes and programmatic activity have been at the centre of party life and activity since the foundation of socialist parties in the last quarter of the nineteenth century.

### THE ERFURT MODEL

The status, character and role of programmes in these parties was set by the Erfurt Programme (1891) of the German Social Democratic Party(SPD). The Erfurt Programme provided both a long-term Marxist analysis of society and a series of short term political demands to be realised within the capitalist system and was seen to fulfil several crucial functions. Externally, it provided the basis of electoral appeal. For the party members the programme served to mobilise, to integrate and act as a blueprint for action should governmental status be attained. Its electoral function has meant that programmes have been subject to continual revision, a revision which has affected not only the short-term goals but also the analysis intended to underpin them.

The Erfurt Programme was challenged within a decade of its adoption by Eduard Bernstein (1850–1932) who not only wanted to change its short-term political goals but disagreed fundamentally with the analysis of capitalism embedded in the Programme. Bernstein was concerned to point to the unlikelihood of constructing an electoral majority on the basis of the proletariat and the need for the party to secure allies. This necessitated changing the party's view of capitalist development since the Erfurt Programme incorporated Marx's immiseration thesis in which the old middle class would shrink and its displaced members would then join the ranks of the proletariat and the unemployed. This challenge set off prolonged factional struggles inside the SPD between, on the one hand, those who wanted radical political goals to complement the radical analysis, and on the other hand the revisionists, like Bernstein, who wanted to bring the analysis into line with the rather moderate goals pursued by the party. The party leadership, for symbolic and integrative reasons, preferred to stick to the Erfurt recipe of radical analysis and moderate practice since even an electoral majority would not have brought them into government in Imperial Germany.

The programmatic orientation that characterised the continental social democrats was never really adopted by the British Labour Party. Identity in the Labour Party was defined organisationally rather than theoretically. The key test was not whether a member accepted some specific statement of socialism but the absence of membership in some other political organisation. In that sense it bore a striking resemblance to the Anglican Church which has never emphasised doctrinal purity. Theoretical questions were transformed into organisational questions and the characteristic leadership response to a challenge was not to engage in a theoretical debate but to expel the dissidents, a response still very marked in the Militant episodes of the 1980s.

## BAD GODESBERG AND PROGRAMMATIC REFORM

The central position of the SPD in the adoption of party programmes was retained in the widespread revision of party programmes that occurred at the end of the 1950s. The sustained economic boom of that decade and dissatisfaction with the residual Marxist legacy were common factors throughout a Western Europe that was closely linked to the United States. Pressure for programmatic change was particularly strong in Germany given the negative associations of many traditional aspects of socialism as a result of the establishment of the deeply unpopular German Democratic Republic (GDR). Three successive electoral defeats underlined these handicaps and programmatic changes offered a route to power by making the SPD an acceptable coalition partner for one of the bourgeois parties – a failure to engage in programmatic reform would have confronted the SPD with the prospect of permanent opposition. The resulting Bad Godesberg Programme of 1959 disavowed the Marxist heritage of the SPD and embraced liberal pluralism and the market economy.

One of the most interesting features of the Bad Godesberg Programme was the manner in which it acted against Prezeworski and Sprague's view that social democratic parties were bound to lose in the trade-off between securing more middle class allies by moderating their appeal and losing working-class support. The banning of the West German Communist Party and the association of socialism with the GDR meant that the SPD could increase its support among the middle class without losing working-class support. The weakness of communist parties meant that it was also a relatively cost free undertaking for other parties in the traditional social democratic heartlands of Scandinavia and Austria.

The example of the SPD was widely copied among other West European parties. The major exception was the British Labour Party where Hugh Gaitskell's attempt to outflank Clause 4 and its commitment to public ownership (incidentally, a part of the party's constitution rather than an element of its programme) by a wider statement of aims was defeated by a coalition of powerful trade unionists. Despite this defeat, most of the revisionist positions were adopted in practice in the 1960s and 1970s.

## PROGRAMMATIC RENEWAL IN THE 1980s AND 1990s

The burst of programmatic change which characterised the late 1950s recurred three decades later. The present volume is a product of a conference supported by the Friedrich Ebert Foundation designed to throw light on some central questions about the present phase of programmatic renewal. Our first concern was to identify the orgins of the current process of programmatic renewal and the manner in which it has unfolded, paying especially close attention to the view that it is a response to electoral decline and the ideological challenge of neo-Conservatism.

Within the social democratic parties in the 1970s and 1980s there had been a strong demand for more participative practices and structures and a second central question therefore related to the role of the party leaderships and the degree to which they initiated and controlled the process.

Programmatic change within the social democratic parties was accompanied by the decline and collapse of communism. The most innovative and far-reaching responses to this crisis came from the Italian Communist Party (PCI), the largest communist party in Western Europe, which already had been moving in a social democratic direction for some time. In important respects the new programmatic strategies of the Italians anticipated those of the East European parties. Social democracy remains extremely weak in central Europe, but if it has a future there it is likely to be one that is influenced by the initiatives of reform communists in the west. For this reason we were particularly grateful that Gianfranco Pasquino was able to contribute to this volume.

In the 1950s there was a great deal of mutual learning from the experience of other parties, sometimes facilitated by figures like

Benedikt Kautsky who were influential in both the Austrian and German debates. The inter-connections appeared less obvious in the 1980s.

Three explanations suggest themselves. The common experience of exile and wartime contact was still important in the 1950s. The universe of social democratic parties had expanded beyond its northern European heartland with a consequent attenuation of relationships; and the party press and party theoretical journals had largely disappeared. It remained possible, however, that foreign examples were important.

The emergence of environmentalism and feminism as major political issues had placed considerable strain on these parties in the 1980s and part of the programmatic renewal project was to attempt to integrate these issues at a programmatic level.

An attention to the genesis and development of the process of programmatic renewal was bound to tell us much about the dynamics of intra-party and inter-party relationships but would be incomplete without including two further questions. Has it led to the emergence of a distinctive set of new programmatic ideas especially on the central area of the management of the economy? And how helpful has it been to these parties electorally?

### NOTE

1. Although often cited, it is almost certainly apocryphal. It remains however a very accurate summary of Morrison's views.

# The Politics of Programmatic Renewal: Postwar Experiences in Britain and Germany

## CARL CAVANAGH HODGE

*The reform efforts of postwar British and German social democracy resulted in very different outcomes. The absence of a legislative record in government was only the most obvious reason why the German party showed greater flexibility. Widely different reasoning about the likelihood of electoral success and the need to pursue a creative coalition strategy also invigorated the cause of programmatic change. At the same time, the personalities and tactics of party reformers; the formal constitution of domestic politics; and the roles played by Britain and the Federal Republic in Cold War Europe further diminished or enhanced the chances of programmatic change.*

PROGRAMMING THE FUTURE, COMMEMORATING THE PAST

The 1950s marked the beginning of a period of adjustment for the forces of social democracy in Western Europe. The sudden reorganisation of European affairs around the ideological polarities of Washington and Moscow began an extended effort of self-examination and internal struggle by political parties that for so long had been at the centre stage of debate on the evolution of advanced economies. Scarcely a single domestic political issue was not influenced by the American-led revival of West European capitalism, on the one hand, and the Soviet threat to liberal-democratic government, on the other.

As the inheritors of bourgeois-radical, Fabian and Marxist traditions of the nineteenth century, social democrats had always seen themselves as a force for fundamental socio-economic and political change. At the same time, they remained more sentimental about their parties' intellectual heritage than their conservative or liberal rivals. Because the society they sought to create had for so long been an object of speculative and theoretical debate, socialists had acquired the habit of 'rededication', that is, of defining political goals for the future through constant reference to the commitments of the past. Rededication was more than the drafting of political blueprints. What Henry Drucker has written of the British Labour Party, namely that its sense of the past 'is so central to its ethos that it plays a crucial role in defining what the party is about to those in it',[1] is valid as well for Labour's continental counterparts.

A comparison of Labour's postwar politics of revision with those of German Social Democracy, however, demonstrates that the status of party programmes varied according to national context and political circumstance. For both parties, the 1950s began a process not only of reappraisal but also a depreciation of programmatic thinking overall. There was a diminishing sense that past commitments could be applied to the present and an increasing disinclination to articulate political goals in a systematic way. Many social democrats looked for a new suppleness in their approach to political struggle, either to consider new ways in which modern capitalism might be reformed to social ends; to redefine socialism's place within the political spectrum; or to seek governmental power as an end in itself without the claim that democratic socialism any longer implied fundamental change in the socio-economic order.

While programmatic debate within Labour and the SPD (*Sozialdemokratische Partei Deutschlands*) was so often driven by similar concerns, British and German social democrats arrived at altogether differing conclusions about future priorities. Overall, the Labour Party's programmatic heritage retained in the 1950s the kind of symbolic value for a majority of its members that went missing among a generation of German Socialists. The reasons for this divergence were numerous, ranging from differing expectations about the ability to achieve political power to the personalities and tactics of reform-minded party leaders, from the formal constitution of domestic politics to the realities of national circumstance in Cold War Europe.

SUBSTANCE AND SYMBOLISM IN DOMESTIC POLICY

Both Labour and the SPD included in their post-1945 objectives a mixture of planning, welfare-state and nationalisation proposals for the ultimate transformation of capitalism, but public ownership was of incomparably greater importance to the British party. And for very good reasons. Nationalised industry was at the core of what Labourites had understood as 'socialist' ever since its inclusion in Clause IV of the party's 1918 constitution. During Labour's decade in the wilderness during the 1930s it acquired the status of party writ and emerged, alongside progressive taxation, Keynesian economics and comprehensive social services, at the fore of the party's post-1945 agenda.[2]

On the strength of the massive parliamentary majority held by Labour between 1945 and 1951, the Attlee government of 1945–51 made the nationalisation of the country's key industrial sectors critical to the most radical reorganisation of the British economy to date. Samuel Beer has rightly observed that 'to an extent unprecedented in British political history the legislation of a Government was dictated by a party program'.[3] For party members and MPs who had known the interwar decades, nationalisation represented political fulfillment. Hugh Dalton, who as Chancellor of the Exchequer introduced four Labour budgets, had witnessed 'physical control' of the economy during the war and retained an unshaken faith in its importance to 'the socialist advance'.[4]

Nevertheless, the seed-time of doubt was brief. Tony Crosland's contribution to the *New Fabian Essays* of 1952 – with its call for a redefinition of socialist goals and a refinement of the institutional tools of transformation consistent with the 'managerial revolution' of modern capitalism – represented the first formal reformist salvo of the 1950s. Crosland turned to the electoral nub of the matter the next year at Labour's annual conference: 'If we are to go to the country pressing to nationalise an industry, we must convince the ordinary floating voter that this industry will clearly do much better under nationalisation than under private enterprise.'[5] For many who took up the defence of industrial nationalisation, the electoral appeal and economic utility of public enterprise were secondary considerations on which to base a critique. Nationalised industry was perforce socialist, as Kenneth Morgan expresses it, the proof that 'a vital step had been taken in the displacement of the old order'.[6] Returned to opposition, the party was in search of a way forward, but Crosland was apparently happy to leave a good deal of the existing industrial order in place and instead oil individual self-interest with higher public spending in pursuit of overall prosperity and reduced social rigidity.

So much of what Crosland said in the early 1950s prefigured the cultural upheaval of the following decade. When he warned that the road to progress could be blocked by people of the best intentions but 'lacking only in grace and gaiety', he protested against the grey inheritance of Fabianism and its obsession with efficiency and austerity. Still, Crosland was remarkably rough on party and national sensibilities. For him, the United States represented a 'progressive and revolutionary system' relative to those in Europe still 'bedeviled by the consciousness of class'; from Labour, he suggested, more flexible policies for progress were needed, because 'the easy and spectacular things have all been done'.[7]

The prevailing sentiment in Labour was that more of the 'easy and spectacular' was needed to construct a socialist Britain, though the speed and target of future nationalisations was open to debate. In the early 1950s opinion on public ownership clustered around two persuasions, the fundamentalist stance led by Aneurin Bevan, (as Minister of Health and Housing, a principal architect of postwar policy) and the 'consolidationists', represented foremost by Herbert Morrison. For Bevan public ownership was an intrinsically 'correct' policy. Britain could not approximate a socialist society so long as 80 per cent of the economy remained in private hands and the whole public sector was 'poisoned by the miasma of private enterprise'.[8] Morrison, by contrast, did not oppose further nationalisations in principle but was concerned with preserving Labour's 1945–51 legislative work and worried, like Crosland, 'that a Labour programme fervently committed to more extensive nationalisation was a recipe for electoral disaster'.[9] Labour's programme of 1953, *Challenge to Britain*, with its vague reference to a substantial degree of nationalisation, represented a temporary truce over the issue.

It was Hugh Gaitskell whose electoral ambitions for Labour brought the debate on public ownership and programmatic revision to a head. Gaitskell's position on nationalisation, spelled out in *Socialist Commentary* just prior to the conference which elected him leader of the party, was initially less radical than Crosland's. Even when the 1955 electoral post-mortem concluded that Labour's *Challenge to Britain* – with its emphasis on state intervention and control – had been a handicap, Gaitskell avoided open debate on the subject and managed both a healthy measure of party unity as well as peace with Bevanism between 1955 and 1959. In the meantime, both Crosland and Gaitskell proclaimed a 'social-democratic' future, even as the Labour left called for planning and a greater emphasis on equality.[10]

With Labour's third consecutive election defeat in 1959, the truce dissolved. Given the high quality of Labour's publicity and organisation during the campaign, the conclusion that something more fundamental than cosmetics must be amiss was logically respectable. It was encouraged as well by press analyses listing nationalisation as among the 'unusually unattractive albatrosses' in Labour's programme.[11] At this point Gaitskell abandoned discretion and turned against Clause IV of the 1918 constitution and the historic goal of 'Common Ownership of the Means of Production'. In so doing he crossed a threshold, because the elevation of the issue to a constitutional level necessarily involved the party in a review of fundamental values. Clearly, his assertion that contention over public ownership was not a question of principle but of 'presentation' was little more than wishful thinking.

Nor was Gaitskell's cause furthered by the pre-emptive tactlessness of fellow revisionists such as Douglas Jay, who combined demands for an outright ban on further nationalisations with recommendations for a change of the party's name, with a mind to escaping its working class image. It was one thing to debate the 'shopping list' of nationalisations at successive party conferences, but quite another for a middle-class intellectual to blush at the legacy of labour representation while challenging the legitimacy of an item so central to party tradition that it belonged, in Stephen Haseler's words, 'to the dimension of sentiment and inspiration'.[12]

It is not at all certain that the Gaitskellite position would have enjoyed a much better reception, even if it had been put forward with more stealth. Clause IV revisionism failed not because an older generation of Labourites frustrated the good intentions of upstart social-liberalism but because it confronted a broad coalition of forces for whom the Clause IV issue cut too closely to the party's identity. Admittedly, there were MPs such as Michael Foot on the Labour left who sought to unseat Gaitskell over this or any other issue, but more numerous were moderate trade union leaders who agreed with Transport and General Workers' Secretary Frank Cousins that:

> . . . we have all accepted in the past that, whilst we can have nationalisation without socialism, we cannot have socialism without nationalisation. Those who make any other form of approach are doing a disservice to the Labour movement.[13]

Labour's internal conflict over public ownership so poisoned the water of programmatic debate that the party developed no new and explicit programmatic alternative to the policies of successive Conservative governments. Between them, Tories and Labourites conducted an exercise in electoral posturing over details rather than in the fundamentals of public policy, while the decay of private sector industrial competitiveness accelerated Britain's slide to secondary status in the European economy.

If revisionism failed in the Labour Party of the 1950s, why did it triumph among German Social Democrats? The SPD's advocacy of public ownership, after all, went all the way back to the Erfurt Programme of 1891, which made Marxism official party doctrine, and it was reiterated by the Heidelberg Programme of 1925. Yet only one year after senior party member and economic expert Heinrich Deist identified nationalisation as 'the very kernel of the socialist conception'[14] the SPD made a break with the past in precisely the manner Labourites could not. What made the difference?

Only one factor is immediately obvious. The SPD of the 1950s had no legislative record in national politics. Assumed by its adherents to be the natural governing party of a post-Hitler Germany, the SPD was thrice beaten so badly by Konrad Adenauer's Christian Democratic Union (CDU) that by 1957 the chances of electoral victory were remote. These defeats, furthermore, were the result of a comprehensive miscalculation of postwar politics. Under the leadership of Kurt Schumacher the SPD invested in three assumptions about the trajectory of economic and political affairs in Germany. The first was an updated version of the orthodox Marxist faith in 'capitalist collapse', according to which the social-market capitalism of the CDU government was to suffer a terminal crisis. Social Democrats also expected a wave of nationalism to grip sections of an occupied populace and counted, lastly, on an early resolution of the Cold War division of Germany. In each instance they were wrong. Neither nationalism nor social unrest rocked the provisional republic. Wage-earners took their growing pay packets home to domestic and familial preoccupations. Increasingly, national reunification was discussed in the hypothetical.[15]

Though these errors were on matters of substance, the SPD of the early 1950s is notable for its concern with 'image'. From the start, SPD revisionism differed from the Labour variety, in that the publicity given to party reform was often deemed as important as the content of programmatic revisions themselves. Because the public perception of the SPD placed it far to the left of its actual policies, it was logical to conclude that what the party really needed was an intensive effort in improved public relations.[16]

The *Aktionsprogram* of 1952 is noteworthy for having begun a process of programmatic change involving a significant de-emphasis of public ownership. The document was, no doubt, influenced by the Adenauer government's 1951 Codetermination Law, which afforded labour representation on the supervisory boards of the iron, coal and steel industries, and thereby undermined the salience to German workers of the whole issue of industrial nationalisation. It contained, moreover, a contribution to its economic section by Karl Schiller (who, as SPD Economics Minister, later applied Keynesian demand-management to the 1966–67 recession) calling for competition and free consumer choice as integral to 'elastic forms of a free socialist policy'. Criticism of the programme was neither widespread nor especially vigorous.[17] Part of the reason resided in the fact that SPD revisionism in economic policy included the question of public ownership but did not focus upon it or any other single theme. From the start, concern with the party's image made the project of reform more ambiguous in content and diffuse in appeal.

After the election defeat of 1953, revisionism entered a new phase, in which the federal distribution of power in the Bonn republic became a key factor. It was at this point that the party's '*Bürgermeister*' faction (SPD heads of government in the city-states of Berlin, Bremen and Hamburg) became more forthright, recommending that a party programme in the traditional sense of the word was simply not necessary. The special status of this group, namely the ability to win electoral office when the national party could not, enhanced the legitimacy of its arguments for SPD rank-and-file members and youth groups, who joined in greater numbers the call for new programmatic departures.[18]

Symbolic of the progress in opening the party to more ambitious renovations was the lengthy applause given Willi Eichler's carefully-crafted speech to the 1954 conference, wherein the SPD's Marxist heritage was treated as one of several intellectual traditions informing the party's past and present. By now the development of an entirely new programme proceeded, according to Schellinger's interpretation, by way of a constantly shifting focus from one policy realm to another that rarely offered its critics a concrete position to defend.[19] Throughout, a stream of articles published in party journals such as *Vorwärts* and the newly-founded *Neue Gesellschaft* kept the broader membership abreast of the latest ideas of the leadership and policy consultants. Programmatic renewal was neither a principled crusade nor a reckoning with history; it was a bureaucratic and semantic enterprise.

By 1957 the enthusiasts of programmatic reform were well-positioned to exploit the sense of frustration following that year's Bundestag elections, in which the Adenauer-CDU became the first party in German history to garner an absolute majority of the vote. Early in 1958 Carlo Schmid recommended a formal 'opening to the right' of SPD policies and platform. In substance Schmid was suggesting a series of policy adjustments to entice the parliamentary caucus of the liberal Free Democratic Party (FDP) away from its long-time alliance with the Christian Democrats and toward an alternative left-centre formation with the SPD – a project furthered by Herbert Wehner's discrete but constant labours to strengthen contacts with the FDP. The effort was well-timed, for the Free Democrats were themselves doubting the wisdom of continuing a centre-right coalition.

In this respect, the electoral ambitions of the SPD's reformers were more modest than Labour's Gaitskellites, because they centered on the desire to construct a social-liberal coalition with the FDP rather than an outright parliamentary majority. Even if the electoral results of 1957 were particularly depressing, SPD reformers never assumed that the party could aspire to a governing majority on its own strength, especially given that the Federal Republic's system of proportional representation in elections awarded no bonuses to a party taking a plurality of ballots. Consequently, discussion of ways to attract new voters was more relaxed and, compared to Labour, free of the worry that success at the polls necessarily proceeded at the expense of programme. Inevitably, coalition government with the FDP would involve compromises and revisions to any legislative agenda worked out at party conferences.

The Godesberg Programme, upon which the SPD constructed the social coalition that elected SPD-led governments in the 1960s and 1970s, was remarkable firstly for what it did not include. Its statement of general economic policy named 'the constant growth of prosperity and a just share for all in the national product' as its goal, but public ownership was to have all but no role in the achievement thereof. Nationalisation was demoted to the status of a last resort policy, to be applied only when 'economic functions vital to the community cannot be carried out in a rational way except by excluding competition'.[20]

The programme's principal author, Heinrich Deist, noted elsewhere that in Britain Labour's nationalisations had not ended the bondage of the wage-earner and that a 'free order' prospered only under 'pluralism, decentralisation and autonomy'.[21] No substantive programmatic objectives took the place of the discarded tools of public ownership, planning and worker control, while Keynesian demand-stimulus and full employment policies penetrated the SPD only in the wake of the Godesberg reforms. With the creation of the European Economic Community and the full convertibility of the Deutschmark in 1958, the programmatic overhaul introduced a suppleness to SPD economics that prefigured subsequent legislative breakthroughs, such as the SPD-sponsored and Keynesian-inspired Stability and Growth Law of 1967.[22]

Viewed from this perspective, Godesberg reforms represented a repudiation of programmatic thinking and qualified as a doctrinal reconstitution of German Social Democracy itself. Klotzbach's magisterial treatment of the reforms locates their historical significance in the forthright commitment 'to preserve and build upon the intellectual and institutional edifice developed by the liberal democratic tradition for self-fulfillment of the individual and the progress of society.'[23] It is worthwhile stressing as well that the programme secured an easy passage – drawing 324 ballots against only 16 dissenting votes – because the SPD was commonly held to be overripe for a second founding. Whereas Gaitskell's case against Clause IV fell to a massive trade union veto, the

SPD conference of 1958 listened calmly while a future chancellor, Helmut Schmidt, stressed the need for the party to cover its electoral flanks over the unsavoury issue of public ownership.[24]

## THE HARD CHOICES OF COLD WAR

In Britain and Germany debate on domestic policy was subject to a counterpoint of internal division over defence, European and international issues under the pressures of the Cold War. For the postwar Labour government international affairs represented such a distant second priority to domestic affairs that by 1953 *Challenge to Britain* committed barely a page to the American/Soviet confrontation and 'Overseas Responsibilities'. True, the Attlee government had presided over the granting of independence to four Asian colonies and the reconstitution of Britain's relationship to its African territories,[25] but vision on matters closer to home was sadly lacking. The question of Britain's disposition toward the fledgling European Communities ran afoul of Europhobes such as Ernest Bevin (Foreign Secretary, 1945–51) and Hugh Dalton. Later, the European option competed unsuccessfully with Gaitskell's quaint notion of a 'special relationship' with the United States and his Fabianist emphasis on stronger ties to the Commonwealth.[26]

On the broader front, pressure within Labour for a 'socialist foreign policy', which would express in international relations the ethical thrust of the party's domestic programme while maintaining great power prestige, produced some jarring contradictions. Originally, the Attlee government was prepared to take on the expense of developing a British nuclear weapons capacity to avoid dependence on the US atomic arsenal. Yet by 1957 a majority of Labourites favoured reduced reliance on the whole concept of nuclear deterrence, when only a year earlier the annual conference had endorsed a call for an end to national service. How these positions were to put substance into Labour's declared ambition to make Britain a 'Third Force', holding the balance of power between East and West, went unexplained.[27]

Labour's denunciation of the Eden government's incompetent handling of the Suez crisis in effect set aside any nuanced consideration of what British interests were in fact at stake in the Middle East and how, short of the force used, they might have been secured.

In this and other instances Labour's progressive internationalism substituted 'a fine flourish of moral indignation' for any systematic critique of the folly of the government's actions; it represented not so much an alternative foreign policy as a self-satisfied claim to moral superiority, in the verdict of one critic 'the mentality of a superannuated nanny'.[28]

The repudiation of power politics in the international arena, furthermore, ultimately became entangled with existing left-right divisions over the domestic programme and Clause IV. When after the election defeat of 1959 the party committed itself, against Gaitskell's opposition, to the scrapping of British nuclear weapons, the vote had as much to do with attacks on Gaitskell's leadership, and the revisionist threat to Clause IV, as with defence policy itself.

In Germany, meanwhile, the interplay of changes in the SPD's foreign and defence policy with new departures on the domestic front took on a completely different dynamic. The first reorientations in foreign policy, in fact, were in many ways the thin end of the revisionist wedge. It was one of the *Bürgermeister* faction, Ernst Reuter, who in the early 1950s not only cautioned the party against the hallowed illusion of 'capitalist collapse' but also warned against a primitive anti-Americanism that dulled a full appreciation of the Soviet threat.[29] In reality, Reuter touched upon something more fundamental than anti-Americanism. The Schumacher SPD, however, was a landmark in the German Socialist tradition in its unqualified 'yes' to the German national state. The SPD's insistence on a quantum of self-respect for an occupied people was deemed critical to the party's legitimacy in the eyes of the postwar electorate. To the extent that Schumacher's demand for national self-determination was at odds with the Federal Republic's *de facto* subordination to the interests of the Western occupation powers,[30] however, adopting a neutralist stance with nationalist overtones was not only badly-timed but also typical of a foreign policy programme that left the SPD on the loser's side of a series of questions: reunification, rearmament, NATO, the European Community.[31]

Simultaneously, a highly selective internationalism served all too often as the party's alibi of choice. When Schumacher's successor, Eric Ollenhauer, spoke in 1952 on the European Defence Community (EDC) before the Bundestag, he struck upon the dead letter of German self-determination yet advocated a more comprehensive, international collective security system, rejecting the EDC 'out of responsibility to Europe'.[32] Philosophically, internationalism was readily embraced, but those designs of European defence and economic integration which actually had a chance of fulfillment were dismissed as '*kleineuropäisch*' and unworthy of the SPD's singularly high standards. After the failure of the EDC Carlo Schmid and Fritz Erler applied a similar logic to their promotion of a neutralist position on defence which climaxed in opposition to NATO membership.[33]

Still, by 1955 practical experience of transnational and inter-party contacts, along with a recognition of the measure of legitimacy afforded the Federal Republic through Community politics, had brought a good many Social Democrats to see European integration as an unfolding opportunity. A slow but relentless abandonment of all-or-nothing internationalism, in favour of the promotion of a broader, multi-sectoral integration, got underway. As German membership in NATO pushed the issue of reunification toward an even more distant future, the change of position on the European Community tied revision of the SPD's domestic programme, because of its relationship to social justice and working class prosperity, to the acceptance of *Westbindung* in foreign policy.

Symbolic of the latter in particular was the promotion of Willy Brandt through the party's upper offices to the position of chancellor-candidate, based not least of all on a concern to demonstrate the SPD's foreign policy reliability to Washington. It cannot be overemphasised, however, that the goal of a reunited Germany was not thereby betrayed. On the contrary, the SPD's subscription to West European integration and its loyalty to the North Atlantic alliance provided the basis of legitimacy for the *Ostpolitik* of the first SPD-led governing coalitions. By the late 1960s the SPD's foreign policy was in many ways more realistic than that of the CDU, 'not because it lessened the Federal Republic's strategic dependence on the United States or allegiance to NATO, but because Bonn's readiness to accept the territorial *status quo* tackled German security problems at their roots'.[34]

In this sense revisions to the SPD's European and foreign policy were complementary to the domestic Godesberg reforms. Whereas the interplay of foreign and domestic policy only complicated the already problematic cause of programmatic reform in the Labour Party, in Germany the two worked more or less in tandem to make the SPD of 1959 an altogether different party to that led by Kurt Schumacher.

REVISION IN RETROSPECT

In comparing the experience of social democratic programmatic renewal in postwar Britain and Germany, it is tempting to conclude that, above all, the existence of the 1945–51 legislative record kept Labour from making the kind of reforms embraced by the SPD in 1958 – that the debates of the 1950s were in essence not about Britain's future but about Labour's past. The passionate defence of public ownership, certainly, came from a satisfaction with the recent achievement of historic goals. German Social Democrats simply had no such record to defend or reassess; the existence of the CDU's codetermination laws, in fact, undermined the relevance to German workers of any 'common ownership of the means of production'.

The contrast between British and German social democracy in the 1950s, however, is more complicated than this. Whereas Labourites after 1951 could aspire to a parliamentary majority – because they had already had one – a decade of electoral failure opened the SPD leadership and rank-and-file to fundamental change in order to escape the electoral ghetto. If the SPD made ideological peace with liberal capitalism at Bad Godesberg, the altogether pragmatic goal of a governing coalition with the Free Democrats influenced every step of the process. In a doctrinal and tactical sense, the SPD abandoned Marxism for social-liberalism.

It is just possible, furthermore, that Labour revisionism might have been more successful, if the crucial issue of public ownership had been handled more adroitly. Hugh Gaitskell not only attacked it head-on; he tied it to a revision of the 1918 party constitution. In so doing, he enhanced its symbolism to the party conference, where trade unionists employed in the public sector were well-represented, and stiffened the resistance of party members for whom Labour's record in this realm gave meaning to its claim on socialism.

Programmatic reform in the SPD, meanwhile, featured no all-important point of contention nor a single figure within the party with whom the revisionist cause was identified. Though Godesberg did to some extent represent the 'coming out' of a younger wave of Social Democrats, a list of those who contributed something to the party's second founding – Ollenhauer, Erler, Eichler, Wehner, Schmidt, Reuter, Deist, Brandt – cut across the generations. Because programmatic change was not identified with a Crosland or Gaitskell and was thus relatively separated from personal rivalries, the jettisoning of Marxist doctrine along with its programmatic baggage involved little in the way of personal defeats or humiliations.

At the same time, the project of reform enjoyed points of entry into the SPD which were not available to the Labour Party. The federal constitution of the Bonn republic meant that Social Democrats who held power at a local or regional level, when the national SPD remained in opposition, could use their prestige to further programmatic reform on a broad front. Gaitskell, by contrast, could either sell revisionism, modest or ambitious, at Labour Party conferences, or give it up. The fact of German membership in the European Community added yet another dimension to programmatic renewal, to the extent that the European integration of market economies fuelled the prosperity of the German working-class and gave legitimacy to the Bonn republic, even as it eroded the very idea of national sovereignty in economic policy.

Fundamental differences of national circumstance underpinned the divergence of choices in foreign and defence policy. The forthrightly subordinate status of the Federal Republic within the Western alliance removed a host of issues from meaningful debate within the SPD. On the other hand, it is safe to say that postwar Labourites originally shared with Conservatives, in a watered-down version, great power illusions about Britain's role in the world, as evidenced by the 'Third Force' concept. When in the late 1950s Gaitskell defended Britain's retention of a nuclear deterrent, his position on Clause IV specifically, and programmatic reform generally, was in further jeopardy. The SPD's acceptance of *Westpolitik*, NATO and the EEC, by contrast, amounted to the recognition of newly-established but inalterable realities imposed by Germany's peculiar role in Cold War Europe.

A by-product of the Godesberg reforms was that the SPD had by 1959 significantly deemphasised the value of a party programme of any variety. The party paid a price for this. Far-left radicalism during the 1960s was in part a function of the SPD's armistice with capitalism, while the Green/Alternative movement of the 1980s prospered in part through its indulgence in a pedestrian version of neo-Marxist *Theoriebildung* of the kind that the Godesberg SPD had cast aside.

The end of the Cold War necessarily poses new questions for social democracy in a Europe free from the polarities of the US-Soviet rivalry. This is especially true of the SPD, since national reunification has made the Federal Republic more sovereign, officially at least, than ever before. The Labour Party of a post-Thatcher Britain, however, also faces a daunting task of readjustment, in government or in opposition. With so much in flux, from Single Market Europe to Western European Union, the politics of programmatic renewal would seem to be more relevant to social democracy now than at any time since the 1950s.

## NOTES

I wish to thank Dick Geary, Richard Gillespie, Willy Paterson, Gordon Smith, Jonathan Story and Anthony Wright for their helpful comments on an earlier draft of this essay.

1. H.M. Drucker, *Doctrine and Ethos in the Labour Party* (London: Allen and Unwin, 1979), p. 25.
2. R. McKibbin, *The Evolution of the Labour Party, 1910–1924* (Oxford: OUP, 1974), p. 96. E. Durbin, *New Jerusalems: The Labour Party and the Economics of Democratic Socialism*, (London: RKP, 1985), pp. 214–18, 263.
3. S.H. Beer, *Modern British Politics: Parties and Pressure Groups in the Collectivist Age* (London: Faber, 1965), p. 179.

4. K.O. Morgan, *Labour People: Leaders and Lieutenants, Hardie to Kinnock* (Oxford: OUP, 1987), pp. 126–7, 129. Ben Pimlott, *Hugh Dalton*, (London: Cape, 1985), pp. 450–75.
5. Labour Party, *Report of the 52nd Annual Conference, 1953*, p. 117; C.A.R. Crosland, 'The Transition from Capitalism' in: R.H.S. Crossman (ed.), *New Fabian Essays*, (London: Turnstile, 1952), pp. 33–68.
6. K.O. Morgan, *Labour in Power, 1945–1951* (Oxford: Clarendon Press, 1984), p. 140.
7. C.A.R. Crosland, *The Future of Socialism*, (NY: Schocken, 1956), pp. 355–6; idem., 'The Transition From Capitalism', pp. 54–5, 68.
8. W.H. Greenleaf, *The British Political Tradition* (London: Methuen, 1983), II, pp. 466–75; Labour Party, *Report of the 49th Annual Conference, 1950*, p. 132.
9. Ibid., p. 474.
10. K. Middlemas, *Power, Competition and the State: Britain in Search of Balance, 1940–1961* (London: Macmillan, 1986), p. 225; Hugh Gaitskell, 'Public Ownership and Equality', *Socialist Commentary*, 19 June 1955, pp. 165–7.
11. *The Economist*, 10 Oct. 1959, p. 117.
12. Stephen Haseler, *The Gaitskellites: Revisionism in the British Labour Party, 1951–1964* (London: Macmillan, 1969), pp. 175–6; David Howell, *British Social Democracy, A Study in Development and Decay*, (London: Croom Helm, 1980), pp. 222–3.
13. Labour Party, *Report of the Annual Conference, 1959*, pp. 122, 131.
14. Richard Breitman, *German Socialism and Weimar Democracy* (Chapel Hill, NC: Univ. of N. Carolina Press, 1981), pp. 114–30; Deist quoted in: David Childs, *From Schumacher to Brandt: The Story of German Socialism, 1945–1965*, (Cambridge, MA: Harvard UP, 1965), p. 85.
15. F.H. Tenbruck, 'Alltagsnormen und Lebensgefühl in der Bundesrepublik' in R. Löwenthal and H-P Schwarz (eds.), *Die zweite Republik: 25 Jahre Bundesrepublik Deutschland – Eine Bilanz*, (Stuttgart: Seewald, 1974), pp. 289–310.
16. U.W. Kitzinger, *German Electoral Politics: A Study of the 1957 Campaign* (Oxford: Clarendon Press, 1960), pp. 129–30.
17. H.K. Schellinger, *The SPD and the Bonn Republic: A Socialist Party Modernizes* (The Hague: Martinus Nijhoff, 1968), pp. 72–3.
18. Douglas A. Chalmers, *The Social Democratic Party of Germany: From Working Class Movement to Modern Political Party* (New Haven, CT: Yale UP, 1964), pp. 59–60.
19. *Protokoll der Verhandlungen des Parteitages der Sozialdemokratischen Partei Deutschlands, 1954*, pp. 149–69. Schellinger (note 17), p. 46.
20. Schellinger (note 17), pp. 47–9; *Basic Programme of the Social Democratic Party of Germany, 1959*, p. 9, p. 11.
21. Heinrich Deist, 'Gemeineigentum in der freiheitlich geordneten Wirtschaft', *Neue Gesellschaft* 6/1959, p. 356.
22. Christopher S. Allen, 'The Underdevelopment of Keynesianism in the Federal Republic of Germany' in Peter A. Hall (ed.), *The Political Power of Economic Ideas: Keynesianism Across Nations* (Princeton UP, 1985), pp. 273–5.
23. Kurt Klotzbach, *Der Weg zur Staatspartei: Programmatik, praktische Politik und Organisation der deutschen Sozialdemokratie, 1945 bis 1965* (Berlin/Bonn: J.H.W. Dietz, 1982), p. 452; Klaus Lompe, 'Zwanzig Jahre Godesberger Program der SPD', *Aus Politik und Zeitgeschichte*, B46, 11 Nov., 1979, p. 9.
24. *Protokoll der Verhandlungen der Sozialdemokratischen Partei Deutschlands, 1958*, p. 218.
25. Labour Party, *Report of the 52nd Annual Conference, 1953*, pp. 61–80; Morgan (note 4), pp. 188–231.
26. Morgan, *Labour in Power*, p. 256; Denis Healy, *The Time of My Life* (London: Penguin, 1990), pp. 88–9, pp. 210–11. On Britain's rejection of the Schuman Plan see Alan Bullock, *Ernest Bevin, Foreign Secretary 1945–51* (London: Norton, 1983), pp. 779–90, p. 818.
27. Ibid, pp. 394–6; Haseler (note 12), p. 137.

28. Robert Skidelsky, 'Lessons of Suez', in R. Skidelsky and V. Bogdanor (eds.), *The Age of Affluence, 1951–1964* (London: Macmillan, 1970), p. 174, pp. 181–2.
29. Klotzbach (note 23), p. 289; Ernst Reuter, 'Flucht in die Selbsttäuschung', *Der Monat* 5/50 (Nov. 1952), pp. 155–7.
30. V. Stanley Vardys, 'Germany's Postwar Socialism: Nationalism and Kurt Schumacher', *Review of Politics* 27/2 (Summer 1965), pp. 237–8; Wolfram F. Hanrieder, *Germany, America, Europe: Forty Years of German Foreign Policy* (New Haven, CT: Yale UP, 1989), p. 143.
31. W.E. Paterson, *The SPD and European Integration*, (Westmead: Saxon House, 1974), pp. 49–58; Rudolf Hrbek, *Die SPD, Deutschland und Europa: Die Haltung der Sozialdemokratie zum Verhältnis von Deutschlandpolitik und Westintegration* (Bonn: Europa, 1972), p. 109, pp. 156–7; G. Wettig, *Entmilitarisierung und Wiederbewaffnung in Deutschland, 1945–1955* (München: R. Oldenbourg, 1967), pp. 523–6; G.D. Drummond, *The German Social Democrats in Opposition, 1949–1960: The Case Against Rearmament* (Norman, OK: Univ. of Oklahoma Press, 1982), pp. 44–8.
32. See, e.g.: Federal Republic of Germany, *Verhandlungen des Bundestags, Stenographische Berichte 14*, 242 Sitzung, 5 Dec. 1952, p. 114.
33. Carlo Schmid, 'Germany and Europe', *Foreign Affairs* 30/4 (July 1952), pp. 531–44; idem, 'Die Aussenpolitik des Machtlosen', *Aussenpolitik* 3/1 (Jan. 1953), pp. 11–19.
34. Susanne Miller, 'Die SPD vor und nach Godesberg', in Löwenthal and Schwarz (note 15), p. 394; Hanrieder, p. 99; Hrbek (note 31), pp. 288–9; Paterson (note 31), pp. 130–1.

# The German Social Democrats; A Redefinition of Social Democracy or Bad Godesberg Mark II?

## STEPHEN PADGETT

*The SPD's programme review was part of a wider attempt to modernise all aspects of party life. In particular it set out to reconcile the traditional values of social solidarity with the individualism and achievement orientation of large sections of the electorate. This study examines the structural and attitudinal characteristics of the SPD which conditioned the drafting process. It will focus on the conflict between the forces of modernisation and the orthodoxies of the social democratic tradition. It is argued that the ultimate failure of the exercise reflects the profound disorientation of the party in the face of social and economic change.*

Programme review in the German Social Democratic Party (SPD) was conceived in very ambitious terms. Its remit included radically reappraising and reformulating the basic values of the seminal 1959 Bad Godesberg programme. The objective was to redefine social democracy in order to regain the ideological hegemony which the SPD had lost at the beginning of the 1980s. Five years of intensive progammatic activity culminated in 1989 in a new Basic Programme. A survey of the exercise, however, reveals a wide gulf between the objective and the achievement. The first phase of the programme draft was characterised by a lack of purpose which reflected the party's strategic disorientation. Intiatives were taken in certain policy areas, notably a new emphasis on detente in defence and security, and the modernisation of the economy on environmentally safe lines. This latter initiative was the centrepiece in the new programme's first draft issued in 1986. Generally, however, the attempt to steer between competing strategic perspectives, and to reconcile conflicting political tendencies, meant that the draft programme lacked clarity and force.

The second phase of programme drafting was more purposeful. It focused on the value conflict between social solidarity and individual achievement which forms the crux of the social democratic dilemma in late industrial society. The SPD had concluded that whilst the traditional social democratic ethos of social solidarity still commanded a resonance among the socially deprived, it was alien to the achievement orientation of the 'affluent majority'. Programmatic activity now centred on the attempt to reformulate the values of social democracy in response to economic modernity and mass affluence.

Two interventions stand out from the second phase of programme drafting. The first was chancellor candidate Oskar Lafontaine's introduction of a radically new concept of the labour market and the labour process. The content of these proposals and the provocative way in which they were introduced into the debate deliberately challenged party and trade union orthodoxy in an attempt to modernise the party's identity. Lafontaine's initiative met widespread resistance in the party and was only partially successful. The second intervention came from the economics ministers in SPD governed states, advocating a more positive appraisal of the market economy and a willingness to embrace structural economic change. The new programme met their requirements in large part. However, the result was to reaffirm the principles of Bad Godesberg rather than genuine innovation. In short the Basic Programme opened up new questions and challenged some old orthodoxies. Its emphasis was on the humanisation of a dynamic, competitive market economy. However, the search for a new value orientation was largely fruitless and the central prescriptions of the Godesberg programme were left untouched. Launched in December 1989 at the height of national fever over German unification, and with the SPD in disarray over its response to unity issues, the new Basic Programme was almost entirely eclipsed. The SPD's disastrous performance in the December 1990 election was indicative of the failure of the programme to make any positive impact.

PROCEDURE

The formal starting point for programmatic renewal was the Essen *Parteitag* (Party Congress) of May 1984, at which it was resolved at the proposal of the *Parteivorstand* (Executive) to establish a *Programmkommission* (Programme Commission) with the brief of 'working out on the basis of the fundamental principles of the Godesberg Programme, a new Basic Programme'. The drafting process was to take place in two phases. The Commission established at Essen was given responsibility for the preparatory work which was to culminate in a first draft in 1986. After a break to accommodate the campaign for the Bundestag election of January 1987 the draft would be subjected to debate at all levels of the party and a new commission set up to amend and supplement the draft and to finalise the new programme.

The chairman of the Commission (Willy Brandt) and three deputy chairmen were elected by the Congress while the remaining 13 places were filled by nominees of the Executive. The political balance was somewhat asymmetrical; including Brandt nine of its members could be broadly identified with the left or centre left, five were identified with the right and three had no clear factional identification. The Commission first convened in August 1984. Plenary sessions were held more or less monthly, outside of which proceedings were devolved into working groups around the central themes of programme building, and consisting of Commission members and advisers. Close contact was maintained with the party's standing commissions for specific policy areas. Periodically, bulletins on particular themes were issued by the commission. Participation in the party at large was restricted at this stage to the publication in party organs of 'Perspektiven 2000', an invitation for contributions on a wide range of policy themes identified by the Commission. The first draft was published in June 1986. Overshadowed by the mounting election campaign it made little impact either in the party or in public.

Phase two was initiated at the *Ausserordentlichen Parteitag* (Special Party Congress) of June 1987 which established a new Programme Commission. Of its members, nine were nominees of the Executive whilst 24 were put forward by the *Bezirke* and *Landesverbände* (regional party organisations). Members of the first Commission who lost their full status in this reshuffle were given non-voting seats on the new body. In terms of political balance the second Commission was broadly similar to its predecessor, although it was significant that several figures with a strong ideological identification now occupied the non-voting places. The Commission leadership was also altered, reflecting changes in party leadership. Having replaced Brandt as Party Chairman, Hans-Jochen Vogel stepped into Brandt's role as Commission Chairman. Oskar Lafontaine's introduction as *Geschäftsführenden Vorsitzender* (Business Manager Chairman) reflected his elevation to the top party leadership. Lafontaine had concealed neither his ambition to head the Commission, nor his desire to impart a new direction to the programme-drafting exercise.

This second phase of the exercise had a much higher public profile. In September 1987 a major conference was staged in Munich under the title '*Wir Denken weiter*' (further deliberations) bringing together leading figures in the Programme Commission and party along with scientists, philosophers, trade unionists, and representatives of the business

*Verbände*, the churches and cultural establishment.[1] Similar events were held at *Unterbezirke* (district) and *Ortsverein* (local) level. They were calculated to give the impression that the programme drafting exercise was taking place in a broad and open political atmosphere and to emphasise the SPD's character as a *Volkspartei* open to all sections of society. It was also intended to open up debate within the party at large. However, at the local level the programme drafting exercise still failed to make a great impression.

As in the first phase the Commission broke up into working groups which maintained contact with the appropriate standing policy commissions. In October 1988, however, it became apparent that fragmentation on these lines was leading to a loss of coherence. Moreover, political differences were seriously impeding the drafting exercise. A new 'Super-Commission' was established, bringing together the standing policy commissions for economics, finance and taxation, environment and energy, and social policy. Its brief was to formulate a coherent policy for 'the ecological and social renewal of industrial society'.[2]

Postponements plagued the second stage of the exercise. Originally the timetable envisaged the completion of drafting by November 1987 and endorsement of the new programme at a special congress in spring 1988. For a variety of reasons it proved impossible to adhere to this schedule. Disarray in the party following the Bundestag election of January 1987, and a change in party leadership in spring, meant that the second Programme Commission was not constituted until June. At this stage the schedule was extended, allowing until April 1988 for completing the draft, with a party congress for its approval early in 1989. Dissatisfaction with the Irsee Draft, however, and the introduction of some new and explosive issues into the debate prolonged the process still further. The deadline for completion was now extended until December 1988 with the Congress now scheduled for August 1989. Even this elongated timetable proved difficult to fulfill and in January 1989 with key sections of the programme still some way from agreement a further posponement threatened.[3] However, in a series of hurried compromises a draft was agreed by the Programme Commission on 12 January, ratified by the Executive two weeks later, and published in March 1989. Minor amendment and editorial refinement followed, before the new Basic Programme was formally adopted by a special Programme Conference in Berlin, on 19–20 December 1989.

Whilst the Programme Commission and the standing commissions for specific policy areas were the centrepiece of the programme drafting process, policy formulation was not confined to these bodies. Throughout the process, numerous interim policy papers drafted by the standing commissions were submitted for approval by the Executive and sub-sequently for endorsement at party congresses. Approval was by no means always a formality. Occasionally, policy drafts were returned by the Executive for amendment. Even drafts approved by the Executive were occasionally amended by the *Antragskommission* (Resolutions Commission) responsible for drawing up the congress agenda. This procedure for approving interim policy drafts inevitably broadened the scope for participation, enabling the *Bundestagsfraktion* to enter the arena and creating openings for factional mobilisation in opposition to policy statements emanating from the commissions.

PHASE ONE 1984–86

Drafting began from the premise that the new programme would be an extension of, not a departure from, Godesberg. The triad of basic principles – freedom, justice, solidarity – on which the earlier pro-gramme had been built, was to remain unchanged except in one respect. The report of the Basic Values Commission which prepared the ground for programme review stated that 'although no member. . . . asked to replace justice with equality there were intensive discussions over the connection between the two values'.[4]

It was also generally accepted that the Godesberg Programme com-mitment to the market economy would be reaffirmed, although the commitment's terms were subject to discussion. The Basic Values Commission had recommended that the section on the economic and social order required radical revision. It was no longer realistic, for instance, to 'expect that unemployment can be overcome through econ-omic growth, the beneficial effects of which were taken for granted in 1959'.[5] However the Commission was either unable to reach consensus here, or unwilling to pre-empt the continuing debate within the party.

Indeed, this debate continued into the spring of 1986, when Fried-helm Farthmann, Fraktion leader in North-Rhine/Westphalia (though not a member of the Programme Commission) issued a policy paper which heavily criticised the free market economy. His intervention undermined the attempts of Wolfgang Roth, chairman of the Economic and Finance Policy Commission, to draft a consensual economic policy programme. Farthmann later disassociated himself from the views ex-pressed in the paper and in May Roth was able to rally support for maintaining the party's longstanding commitment in principle to the market economy.[6] However, it was tinged with ambivalence, hedged about with qualifications, and overlaid with a heavy dose of interventionism.

Economic policy was an area in which the SPD had experienced some difficulty in establishing a direction after entering opposition. Its early initiatives were very heavily marked by a Keynesian perspective, and the orthodoxies of the Social-Liberal coalition were amended only in piecemeal fashion, without an overall concept. The only significant new development was the Economic and Finance Policy Commission's formulation of a strategy for coming to terms with the environmental limits to growth by reconciling economic growth and environmental protection in a formula for 'qualitative growth'. The concept had initially been developed by the SPD economist H. J. Krupp of the German Institute for Economic Research in Berlin.[7]

Its attraction for the SPD was that it was entirely consistent with the party's belief in state intervention in the market economy for the attainment of social goals. It involved the stimulation of research and investment in a new technology of environmental protection. The 'ecological modernisation of the economy' would simultaneously create a dynamic growth sector with an export and job creation potential, *and* serve environmental needs.[8] This formula subsequently became one of the party's front line programmes, presented as the centrepiece of 'a social democratic reform programme for the rest of the century'.[9]

In defence and security policy the drafting process proceeded from decisions at the Cologne and Essen Congresses of 1983 and 1984. The Cologne resolution had condemned the deployment (then imminent) of Cruise and Pershing II missiles on German territory. The Essen Congress also reflected the ambivalence of sections of the party towards NATO. The Executive's resolution attempted to reconcile conflicting perspectives on security policy, reaffirming the party's commitment to the Alliance, but going on to call for a new NATO strategy based on a 'security partnership' between the power blocs and a new European peace order in which East/West rivalries could be contained. The resolution charged the Security Policy Commission with the task of formulating these principles into a concrete programme.

Under the chairmanship of Andreas von Bulow, former state secretary in the defence ministry, the Security Policy Commission subsequently drafted a policy paper which advocated major reforms in NATO strategy, organisation and weaponry, a more limited role for the Federal Republic in the Alliance and a radical restructuring of the West German armed forces.[10] It was anticipated that by the year 2000 'Europeans in East and West should be able to defend themselves at least in the area of conventional arms'. The paper unleashed a storm of protest particularly amongst the Atlanticists in the *Bundestagsfraktion*. It was rejected by the Executive and had to be hurriedly redrafted. The new draft was much more muted and cautious in its advocacy of NATO reform, balancing the previous document's emphasis on European security interests with a firm commitment to the United States and the 'basic value system' which it represented.[11]

It is significant that Oskar Lafontaine's suggestion that West Germany should leave NATO was never even discussed in the Commission. Moreover, the paper rejected the unilateral renunciation of intermediate nuclear force weaponry, instead linking the withdrawal of American missiles to the Soviet withdrawal of SS-20s. In other respects, though, the Commission advocated what might be described as a non-nuclear policy. The paper endorsed the 1982 Palme Commission report's advocacy of a nuclear weapon-free zone in central Europe. It rejected the strategic NATO concepts of 'Air Land Battle', 'Land Battle 2000' and 'Follow on Forces Attack'. The 'security partnership' theme was extremely prominent.[12] Confidence building and the renunciation of the use of force between East and West Germany were important parts of the security partnership, and the paper explicitly placed the concept in the tradition of *Ostpolitik*. The 'second phase of detente' however, went further in its implications, envisaging the ultimate dissolution of the alliance blocs. 'When the peaceful order in Europe advocated by the Social Democrats has become a reality, the alliances will have lost their significance and served their purpose'.[13] A defence policy on these lines was accepted by the Executive, and subsequently endorsed by the Nürnberg Congress of 1986.

The first phase of the programme drafting exercise was characterised by caution and a reluctance to break decisively with the past. Compromise prevailed on most issues, facilitated by the strong internal cohesion within the SPD elite. However, this gave the first phase of programme drafting a closed and secluded character. The reluctance to open up major issues of the party's identity and purpose inevitably curtailed the scope of programmatic renewal in the first phase. Perhaps not surprisingly, given the highly developed sense of pragmatism in the SPD, programmatic activity was geared to immediate electoral horizons. After the state election successes of 1985, which persuaded many of the possibility of victory in the impending Bundestag election, this instrumentalism was accentuated at the expense of a genuine policy regeneration and reappraisal of the party's objectives.[14]

THE IRSEE DRAFT

One respect in which the first draft differed from previous SPD programmes (including Godesberg) was its emphasis on abstract principles, the absence of which from party thinking had been a common complaint of the left intelligentsia. Represented in the Programme Commission by Erhard Eppler, Johano Strasser and Thomas Meyer, they were able to impose a heavy overlay of abstraction in the opening sections of the draft. The preamble consisted of a lengthy analysis of 'the world in which we live' which was notable chiefly for the resounding pessimism of its tone, typified by the statement that 'for the first time in human history the survival of the species is endangered'.[15] It went on to what one of its author's described as a 'political anthropology' of the human state[16] – a miniature treatise on man as a natural, individual and social being. The preamble also made a lengthy excursion into the history of the social democratic movement, ranging from the 1848 revolutions to the SPD's role in postwar reconstruction.

Another feature which distinguished the draft from previous programmes was the underlying ambivalence towards market capitalism: 'Democratic socialism aims not only to improve capitalism but to put in its place a new social and economic order'.[17] There were also references to the 'excessive influence in society and in the firm of the owners of capital and managers', and to 'breaking the power of capital over working people'. Ambivalence towards market capitalism was reflected in an unusually strong emphasis on interventionism. 'Where political decisions are concerned . . . what should expand and what should contract . . . the economy must have clear framework conditions set out for it.'[18] Other prescriptive measures were formulated in terms of fiscal policy and a reform of taxation and social security systems geared to employment promotion and environmental protection. Concerning the overall level of taxation, however, and the balance between private and public consumption, the draft was deliberately non-commital. 'For us the state's share is not a dogma . . . the touchstone is whether quality of life is best served by an increase in private consumption or by an improvement in the performance of the state.'[19] Conveying no clear conception of the relation between state and market, the draft vacillated between interventionism and a reiteration of the SPD's traditional commitment to the 'dynamic of the market'.

An emphasis on the failure to meet social requirements was reiterated elsewhere in the draft. The section entitled 'Through social justice towards social solidarity' underlined the obligations implied by the 'social state' provision in the Basic Law and reaffirmed the classical social democratic principles of social citizenship. Reviving these principles in state social policy entailed a structural reform of social security and the health system, and the reorientation of economic and finance policy towards social objectives. The vocabulary of social solidarity permeated this section with references to 'a revival of the spirit of comradeship', and 'the culture of collective human life'. The ethos of solidarity was embodied in the concept of 'pacts' between the employed and the unemployed and between the generations (over pensions). However, there was no semblance of a political formula on which to build social coalitions of this sort. Rather the programme was formulated in terms of an appeal based on humanist ethics.

Humanist ethics also permeated the section on new technology. Its analysis of the relationship between technological innovation and progress betrayed the profound scepticism in the SPD's 'new left' concerning technological development. Juxtaposing the potential benefits of new technology with its perils and with the emphasis on the latter, the draft stated that 'technical innovation must be consciously guided, its dangers recognised and guarded against.'[20] Incipient conflicts between technological and human values were repeatedly underlined. Heavy emphasis on the relationship between scientific freedom and responsibility gave the unmistakable impression of mistrust. The draft explicitly distanced the SPD from its earlier 'fascination' with the nuclear promise. Nuclear power was only acceptable as a short term, transitional energy source. The implied commitment to phase it out foreshadowed the categorical renunciation of nuclear energy at the Nürnberg Congress.

In defence and security policy, the basic principles agreed at Nürnberg – common security, restructuring the Western Alliance on defensive lines and introducing nuclear weapon-free zones – were incorporated (much condensed) in the Irsee Draft of the new programme. The compromises on which the policy stood were relatively successful and in the second phase of programme drafting defence and security was not to be a major issue, although it is worth noting that Andreas von Bülow, author of the paper which so incensed the Atlanticist wing of the party, lost the chairmanship of the Security Policy Commission.

Subsequently, the Irsee Draft was subjected to some very heavy criticism from within the party. The philosophical tone of the document and its overwhelming sense of pessimism attracted criticism from the right and the trade union wing. It was written in the style of a papal encyclical with ethical pronouncements replacing combative political propaganda.[21] With its graphic catalogue of impending dangers and threats, the draft was not sufficiently inspirational. Insufficient emphasis had been placed on the achievements of social democracy and its capacity for overcoming present and future problems. Its ambivalence towards capitalism and generally negative appraisal of new technology further detracted from the force of the programme.

Economic liberals like Karl Schiller questioned the qualifications attached to the market economy principle in the draft. The corporatist tone of references to 'framework planning' was difficult to reconcile with the basic commitment to the market. Schiller also warned against the inclination towards outdated formulas of Keynesian economics, and against going too far towards a full employment policy.[22] However, representatives of the labour wing resisted the retreat from full employment, reiterating the right to work as a moral principle which was independent of whether or not Keynesianism was still functional as an economic philosophy.

Another major criticism concerned the programme's failure to address the 'affluent majority'. There were references to the 'unprecedented affluence which has freed a great many of our citizens from material want', but the focus was on *Angst*, social deprivation, and failure. The emphasis on social security was allowed to obscure the dimension of economic performance, and the prominence of the theme 'social solidarity' overshadowed that of individual opportunity. The party's analysis of the 1987 Bundestag election drew attention to this problem.

> It is important for . . . the SPD to be in a position to reconcile performance with social security and scope for individuality with solidarity instead of counterposing them as opposites . . . So long as important sections of the electorate do not trust the SPD for the tasks of economic modernisation, but only for ensuring that social safeguards are maintained, it will be very difficult to build a majority.[23]

PHASE TWO

Whilst the first phase of the programme draft had largely been a policy review working over old ground, the second phase saw some genuinely innovative initiatives and a much greater willingness to question party orthodoxy. The trend was associated with a group which had emerged shortly after the break up of the Social Liberal coalition. Centred on Brandt, but consisting of relatively young, left-oriented upcoming leaders of the party in the *Länder*, the group became known as Brandt's *Enkel*. After the election, and after Brandt's replacement as party chairman, Oskar Lafontaine assumed the leadership of the circle. Although they had come from the left, their initiatives broke quite radically from the traditions of left politics in the SPD. Indeed, the debate which they precipitated cut across orthodox left/right divisions, as the old left, the labour wing and the right combined to oppose the attack on tradition from the 'new revisionists'.

The revisionists deliberately flouted long-standing party taboos. Beginning from the premise that in economic and social policy many of the SPD's prescriptions were antiquated, they argued that more attention had to be given to economic success and the 'achievement-oriented' sections of society and that technological development had to be seen in a more positive light. They also sought to introduce a new *glasnost* into internal party debate, and to break down the *unter uns gesagt* (between ourselves) mentality which dominated the upper echelons of the SPD.

> Internally it has been conceded for some time that the party must open up these ideas more energetically, but in public . . . the arguments are carried on in the old tried and tested ways . . . The *unter uns gesagt* mentality which ultimately means only that one does not represent to the outside world what one has freely accepted internally, must be overcome.[24]

The trade unions were the revisionists' major target, since they symbolised traditional party orthodoxy. Attempting to distance the SPD from the unions, the revisionists asserted that the party was not merely a 'sounding board' for the unions; 'it had to be responsive to the whole of society, and that meant entrepreneurs, professionals and higher grade clericals as well as trade unionists'.[25] The revisionists warned the *Deutscher Gewerkschaftsbund* (DGB-German Trade Union Federation that they had no veto over the programme review and could not be allowed to stand in the way of party reorientation.

Conflict centred on the longstanding trade union demand for a reduced working week, originally conceived as a measure to redistribute work in an attack on unemployment. The demand had been at the heart of the lengthy and bitter IG Metall strike of 1984. The SPD had endorsed the demand and supported the metalworkers' action. On the crucial question of wage compensation, party and unions had maintained a rigid unity, refusing to countenance pay concessions in return for reduced working time. This position was incorporated in the first programme draft. Employers were to bear the cost of the 30-hour working week. They would be compensated by increases in productivity and by tax incentives. The burden on the state would be offset by savings in unemployent and social security payments.

The revisionists' proposals breached the principle of full compensation. High income groups might lower their pay expectations in return for reduced working time. Moreover, they were explicit in linking the reduction of worktime to the introduction of flexible work practices. This attack on the symbols of trade unionism was part of an attempt to introduce a new openness into the thinking of both unions and party. It was conceived of by some as an initiative for the full-scale reorientation of social democracy.

> The European left has at its disposal, if only it can grasp the opportunity, a concrete Utopia which can move millions; a shortening of worktime, not only as a technocratic instrument but as a human idea capable of integrating and binding together different strata in society . . . bringing work and leisure into a new balance.[26]

Introduced into the programme discussion at the eleventh hour, however, the initiative had little chance of success. The revisionists' failure to intervene earlier reflected their lack of standing in the party. Most of them were relatively new to the upper echelons of the party elite and lacked a strong power base. The *Enkel* had acquired a collective identity only after the Bundestag election of January 1987.

The weakness of the revisionists' position was exposed in the build-up to the Munster *Parteitag* of August 1988. Union accusations of a 'stab in the back' had increased the pitch of the debate, and in April a peace summit was held between party leaders and the DGB in an unsuccessful attempt to heal the breach.[27] It was against this background that Wolfgang Roth's Economic Policy Commission drafted the congress resolution on the issue. Entitled 'A solidaristic policy on working time' it reiterated party orthodoxy – the reduction of working time with the costs carried by the employers and the state – but included an important concession to Lafontaine's proposals. Compensatory cuts in real wages were 'not unthinkable' for higher income groups. (*Frankfurter Allgemeine*, 13 June 1988). Roth's 'bridge to Lafontaine' was immediately accepted by the Executive in spite of the opposition of both the trade union-aligned *Seeheimer Kreis* and the *Frankfurter Kreis* on the left.[28]

Subsequent developments underlined the multiplicity of opportunities for factional mobilisation during policy formation in the SPD. They also highlighted the obstacles to reforms which infringed entrenched orthodoxies across the spectrum of party opinion. A heterogenous coalition drawn from the circles of both right and left succeeded in amending Roth's compromise formula in the *Antragskommission* (Congress Resolutions Commission). All but the remotest traces of Lafontaine's ideas were expunged from the draft resolution.[29] Moreover, the mixed response to Lafontaine's speech and the reduced margin of his re-election as party vice-chairman, reflected the lack of support for the revisionists' position.

An intervention from a quite different quarter came in November 1988 with a letter to Vogel from the economics ministers of the SPD-governed *Länder*. SPD Business Manager Anke Fuchs has characterised the programme review as follows: 'To begin with it was a case of SPD against trade unions, then Oskar against the rest of the world; only now have we come to address the issues.'[32] At the end of the drafting process an attempt was made to increase the emphasis on issues with the creation in October 1988 of a 'Super-Commission' for economics, finance, taxation, and social and environmental policy. In addition to sharpening the focus on issues, the new Commission also accelerated the final stages of the programme review. It was argued by some that more time was needed to pursue issues opened up relatively late in the process. However, with an important round of state elections and a Bundestag election due in 1990, it was decided to adhere to the time-table and conclude the review. A draft was approved by the Party Executive in January 1989. Protracted amendment and editorial refinement followed before the programme was finalised at the Berlin Congress of December 1989.

THE NEW BASIC PROGRAMME

The new programme contained no more than fleeting references to the ideas of the revisionists. The commitment to the 30-hour week was formulated in terms of trade union orthodoxy, without compensatory pay reductions. The only evidence of Lafontaine's initiative was contained in the statement that 'the reduction in working time means that a just distribution of income is even more important. Wage and salary increases should be differentiated according to income group'. The concept of a more flexible work regime appeared only in passing, and was also very heavily hedged around with qualifications: it had to be employee-oriented and subject to 'collective safeguards'. The deregulation of work practices was explicitly rejected.[33] In no sense did the prescriptions for a shorter working week amount to the front line policy innovation which had been proclaimed by the revisionists.

In contrast to the new revisionists' failure to make a major impact on the new Basic Programme, the intervention of Roth and the economics ministers was quite dramatically successful. They were able to neutralise the influence which the left had exerted on the 1986 draft. The rhetorical hostility towards capital was notably absent. The attribution of unemployment to capital's failure to meet its social responsibilities was omitted in favour of the blander prescription that 'it is the task of a democratic and social *Rechtsstaat* to make provision for full employment'.[34] The new Programme went far towards meeting the requirement that the relationship between the state and the market should be clarified. It contained a categorical commitment to the principle of the competitive market. Indeed it reiterated the leitmotif of Bad Godesberg, 'competition in so far as possible, planning in so far as necessary'.[35] The finalised Programme contained hardly any references to the role of the state in the economy. Inasmuch as it appeared at all it was limited to setting the 'framework conditions' within which 'the autonomous decisions of entrepreneurs would be taken.'

Roth's initiative on structural economic change was included in the Programme. However, significant changes had been made between the March 1989 draft and the final document. The March draft had endorsed the principle of structural change in resounding terms: 'A dynamic economy manifests itself in a continual process of structural change, which promotes competitiveness and can enhance the conditions of work and life'.[36] The final version of the Programme was much more qualified, drawing attention to the negative social consequences of structural change. These had to be mastered through structural and regional policy programmes.

The Basic Programme of 1989 reflected continuity with the Godesberg Programme in many respects. It restated the Godesberg triad of principles – freedom, justice and solidarity[37] – and is based on the same philosophical foundations of humanism and political pluralism. However, there is considerably more emphasis on *solidarity* in the 1989 Programme, with a lengthy section entitled 'through social justice to the solidaristic society'.[38] Moreover, the new programme endows the humanist perspective with some new dimensions. The most prominent of these is the concept of social equality between men and women,[39] a theme which runs throughout the programme. The humanisation of the working environment, technology, education and culture adds further dimensions.[40] Political pluralism is also expanded to include critical dialogue between elected representatives and citizens, and within certain limits, the use of referenda.[41]

The most striking innovations however, are in the area of ecology. The 'ecological modernisation of the economy' was one of the earliest initiatives to emerge from the programme review, and is one of the centrepieces of the Programme.[42] An environmentalist perspective is evident throughout. Another of the concepts carried over from the 1986 draft is the 'common security framework',[43] which has derived additional force from the conclusion of the Cold War.

A notable change from the 1986 draft was the elimination of the undertone of 'cultural pessimism'. The new document had a much more positive 'future orientation' reflecting the 'progress only with us' formula which the party had launched in 1988. On the other hand, the 1989 Programme has not overcome the tendency towards abstract formulation which was a characteristic of the earlier draft, and which reflects the SPD's academic character at all levels. In summary, it could be said that the Programme contains a few genuine innovations, but that there are no historic ideas capable of changing the destiny of the party. In terms of political realignment, the programme represents the gradual but progressive drift of the SPD during the 1980s towards the new left.

CONCLUSION

Programmatic renewal is part of the process by which parties undertake a reorientation of strategy and values in order to maintain their relevance in the face of socio-economic and political change. It is clear that the SPD undertook its programme review in these terms. Experience indicates, however, that success depends in large measure on the realisation of a strategic reorientation *prior to* undertaking the programme review. The SPD set out on the Godesberg course well before embarking on the formal process of drafting the new programme. In effect the programme revision at the end of the 1950s simply recognised a reorientation that had already taken place in response to clearly recognisable changes in economic and social life. The reformers who led the way down the revisionist road in the 1950s had a very clear strategic orientation. The pluralist ethos which they embraced was geared to the electoral expoitation of a rapidly-growing new middle class, and the replication of the *Volkspartei* model pioneered by their rival. In terms of coalition strategy, SPD leaders in the 1950s also had a clear objective. Several of them had come to the view that a grand coalition with the Christian Democrats offered the key to government. Programme revision thus proceeded from a prior reorientation of strategy in a way that it could not in the 1980s.

The lack of direction and purpose which characterised the 1980s programme review underlined the absence of any sense of strategic orientation. Indeed the party's posture was one of profound disorientation. Kurt Sontheimer has identified the source of this disorientation.

The decision to embark on the programme review was taken in a situation in which it is extraordinarily difficult to arrive at a clear picture of developments in the world and in society. That is the dilemma in which the party finds itself. It knows that in these changing times, a reorientation appears necessary but change itself makes reorientation hard to accomplish. Science offers no diagnosis of the age (*Zeitdiagnos*)) no common understanding of what is happening and what future developments will be. It is very difficult to draw decisive and firm conclusions on the basis of uncertain evidence. Therefore there is a succession of problems in the programme review which it is very difficult to rectify.[44]

In the face of these difficulties, programmatic renewal did not match the full scale reorientation undertaken in the 1950s. It is clear that the Bremen programme will not supersede Bad Godesberg in the sense of redefining social democracy. It will, however, serve to update and supplement the values and prescriptions of the previous programme, in a new formulation of the old model – a Godesberg Mark II. It could be argued that this is not an inconsiderable achievement, and is as much as could reasonably have been expected. Indeed, despite the rhetoric of 'redefining social democracy' an analysis of the exercise shows that it was conceived from the outset in these terms.

The most far-reaching initiatives were introduced in the second phase of programme drafting. Not surprisingly, those of the new revisionists around Lafontaine came up against powerful internal party interests and entrenched modes of thought. It should, however, be added, that the rhetorical resonance of the reformers was not wholly matched by the coherence and substance of their proposals. The most successful initiatives were those like the 'common security' policy on defence, or the 'ecological modernisation of the economy' formula, which had spent some time in a painstaking process of policy formulation and gestation.

The 'deliberative' style of the drafting exercise was typical of a party and a party elite attuned to compromise building. The success of Roth's prescriptions for a more positive perspective on structural change was due to the exercise of a wilful drive to force issues to the forefront of the drafting agenda. It is worth noting, however, that the impetus came from outside the top party leadership. Throughout the programme review, Vogel interpreted his role much more as a broker between conflicting interests than as an initiator.

The successful mobilisation of the party's labour wing to defeat the Lafontaine initiative on flexibility in the labour market was indicative of its continuing ability to exercise a veto over reform which struck at union orthodoxies. However, on other issues of economic modernisation – the 'ecological renewal of the economy' and the Roth formula for structural change – the trade unions were less inflexible. Their attitude here stemmed from a mutual recognition that in order to preserve the historic ties between social democracy and the labour movement, party and unions had to keep in step with each other and with social progress.

For the most part, the SPD's basic values were left untouched by the programme review. From the outset, the party right had staked out its ground in defence of the Godesberg values and it appears that they have been able to defeat the attempt by sections of the left to revert to the *dirigisme* of the pre-Godesberg era. The search for a new value orientation was largely fruitless and it is doubtful whether the new programme will meet the challenge identified by the 1987 *Wahlanalysekommission* – the reconciliation of the values of social solidarity with the ethos of individual achievement.

Coinciding with the collapse of the GDR and the first steps on the road to German unification, the conclusion of the new Basic Programme was robbed of all impact. The Programme Conference of December 1989 was switched from its original venue to Berlin in recognition of the new focus of political life. Inevitably it was dominated by the unification issue, especially as the SPD had not at that stage formulated a coherent response on the new Germany. Lafontaine's position was particularly ambivalent, emphasising the primacy of social justice over abstract models of national unity. Subsequently, attempts were made to establish linkages between the modernity theme of the new programme and the tasks of reconstruction in the former GDR. Under the title, *Der Neue Weg*, (the New Way), the programme for the all-German elections of December 1990 drew heavily on the Basic Programme. However, the social tensions arising out of unification intensified the value conflict between social solidarity and individual achievement which the programme had failed to resolve.

On the evidence of the Bundestag election of 1990 and of subsequent state elections in is clear that the SPD's new programme does not contain the key to an electoral renaissance. The Bundestag election indicated a shift in the electoral centre of gravity of the party. The loss of around one million votes to the right, combined with gains of around half a million from the Greens suggests that sociologically and psychologically the SPD is becoming identified with the new left. Its inability to attract manual workers in the five new *Länder* and the devastating loss of manual worker strongholds in the heavily industrialised Ruhr region underlines this shift. These results and those of Land (state) elections in 1992 also suggested that the SPD has yet to come to terms with the post-unification issues – distributing the burdens of unity, and control over the influx of economic migrants and asylum seekers. Indeed, these issues merely underlined the incongruence between traditional social democratic values and the new political landscape.

The values of social solidarity represent the residue of the origins of social democracy in the class politics of industrial society, and are symbolic of the parties' relationship to their core working class clientele. In wide swathes of the electorate, economic modernity and mass affluence have eroded the relevance of these values. However, the German experience indicates that attempts to update and modernise basic values can weaken still further the ties between the parties and their hard core electorate. This is the central dilemma of German social democracy.

## NOTES

1. *Suddeutsche Zeitung*, 19 Sept. 1987.
2. *Frankfurter Rundschau*, 18 Oct. 1988.
3. *Westdeutsche Allgemeine*, 6 Jan. 1989.
4. SPD *Parteivorstand, Materialen; Godesberg Heute: Bericht der Grundwertekommission zum Godesberger Grundsatzprogramm*, (Bonn 1984).
5. SPD *Parteivorstand, Godesberg Heute*.
6. *Nürnberger Nachrichten*, 12 May 1986.
7. *Frankfurter Rundschau*, 6 Jan. 1981; *Nullwachstum 1981*.
8. SPD *Parteivorstand*, 'Die Wirtschaft okologisch und sozial erneuern'. Entwurf der Kommission Wirtschafts- und Finanzpolitik beim Parteivorstand der SPD, *Politik: Informationsdienst der SPD* 10 (Nov. 1985).
9. SPD *Parteivorstand*, 'Fur eine okologische Modernisierung der Volkswirtschaft – Chance fur eine sozialdemokratische Reformpolitik der 80er Jahre', *Politik: Aktuelle Informationen der Sozialdemokratischen Partei Deutschlands* 7 (July 1985).
10. *Suddeutsche Zeitung*, 10 Sept. 1985.
11. SPD *Parteivorstand, Friedens– und Sicherheitspolitik; Beschluss des Parteivorstandes der SPD vom 28.4.1986, Politik: Informationsdienst der SPD* 5 (May 1986).
12. Ibid.
13. Ibid.
14. Stephen Padgett, 'The West German Social Democrats in Opposition, 1982–86', *West European Politics* 10/3 (July 1987), pp. 333–56.
15. SPD *Parteivorstand, Entwurf fur ein neues Grundsatzprogramm der Sozialdemokratisches partei Deutschlands* (Bonn 1986).
16. Thomas Meyer, 'Grundwerte – idealistisch und nutzlos? Grundsatzfragen im Irseer Entwurf', *Die Neue Gesellschaft; Frankfurter Heft* 2/1988, p. 175.
17. SPD *Parteivorstand, Entwurf fur ein neues Grundsatzprogramm*, 1986, p. 7
18. Ibid., p. 25.
19. Ibid., p. 27.
20. Ibid., p. 21.
21. Dieter Hoffmann, 'Kleine Schritte sind nicht zu wenig; Zum Irseer Programmentwurf', *Die Neue Gesellschaft; Frankfurter Heft* 1/1988, pp. 35–8.
22. Karl Schiller, in SPD *Parteivorstand, Materialen; Wir denken weiter; Programm in der Diskussion; Eroffnung des Dialogs zum neuen Grundsatzprogramm der SPD im Munchener Kunstlerhaus* (Bonn 1987), p. 18.

23. SPD *Parteivorstand, Analyse und Konsequenzen; Auswertung der Bundestagswahl 1987* (Bonn 1987).
24. *Wirtschaftswoche*, 29 April 1988.
25. Ibid.
26. Ibid.
27. *Suddeutsche Zeitung*, 25 April 1988.
28. *Frankfurter Rundschau*, 27 June 1988.
29. *Die Zeit*, 19 Aug. 1988.
30. *Frankfurter Rundschau*, 6 Jan. 1989.
31. *Die Zeit*, 19 Aug. 1988.
32. Ibid.
33. SPD Parteivorstand, *Grundsatzprogramm der Sozialdemokratischen Partei Deutschlands* 1989, p. 25
34. Ibid., p. 24
35. Ibid., p. 42
36. SPD Parteivorstand, *Das neue Grundsatzprogramm der Sozialdemokratischen Partei Deutschlands; Entwurf März 1989*, p. 44
37. SPD, *Grundsatzprogramm*, p. 6.
38. Ibid., pp. 31–4
39. Ibid., pp. 17–19
40. Ibid., pp. 25–6; 39–40; 27–31.
41. Ibid., p. 47
42. Ibid., pp. 37–9
43. Ibid., pp. 12–13
44. Kurt Sontheimer, in SPD Parteivorstand (ed.), *Wir Denken Weiter; Programm in der Diskussion; Eröffnung des Dialogs zum neuen Grundsatzprogramm der SPD im Münchener Künstlerhaus* , p. 5.

# The Swedish Social Democrats and the Legacy of Continuous Reform: Asset or Dilemma?

## DIANE SAINSBURY

*Programmatic renewal has rarely been considered as a contributing factor to the long reign of the Swedish Social Democrats; yet an intriguing pattern of innovation and continuous reform has evolved since the party came to power in the early 1930s. This analysis addresses the issue of whether such a pattern emerged during the formulation of the party's most recent programmes. It outlines the Social Democrats' current ideological stance – focusing on their vision of the good society and the major goals and policy recommendations for the 1990s. The concluding section discusses the intellectual and tactical implications of the renewal process and the resulting contradictions.*

The longevity of the Swedish Social Democrats (*Sveriges socialdemokratiska arbetareparti*, SAP) as the party of government has intrigued many observers, and they have attributed the party's dominance to a variety of factors. Among the factors singled out as major explanations are class structure, mobilisation of the working class, the configuration of party competition (especially the fragmentation of the non-socialist opposition), the electoral system, party policies, and party strategies.

Notably few analysts have directly addressed the issue of ideology and programmatic renewal as a factor contributing to the SAP's dominance.[1] In fact, as Tim Tilton has pointed out, the conventional picture of the Swedish Social Democrats as eminently pragmatic has tended to block consideration of the party's ideology as a contributing factor to its success. Yet looking at the SAP's period in office from the early 1930s onwards, we find a pattern of innovation and renewal which has arguably aided the Social Democrats in perpetuating their long reign.

In attempting to understand recent ideological developments within the SAP, the concept of programmatic renewal provides a useful point of departure. This concept has the advantage of integrating what have tended to be two separate paths of enquiry, and in some instances the paths have been viewed as opposites. The first is the study of ideology in terms of the philosophical foundations and values of political parties. However, the idea of programme also implies specific proposals and policy alternatives. In other words, programmatic renewal is more than the study of principles and ideals; it also contains a policy dimension. This diverges from a conceptualisation of ideology which separates theory and practice. A further advantage is that programmatic renewal focuses attention on content, on the actual ideas and proposals of a programme, whereas ideology conjures up associations having to do with the attributes of the ideas, often negative associations.[2] To illustrate, ideology is often equated with either radical or conflictual ideas, and 'ideologisation' is synonymous with radicalisation and polarisation respectively.

A final asset is that programmatic renewal suggests innovation and political creativity – not simply accommodation to existing circumstances. The significance attached to innovation and creativity is particularly important when examining and comparing the programmatic development of socialist parties, because many studies have been preoccupied with patterns of radicalisation where both socialism and radicalism have been equated with public ownership and extensive state controls. This fixation has diverted attention away from an equally important area of analysis, the study of innovation. The experiences of the SAP in the 1930s and 1950s demonstrate the shortcomings of this preoccupation. During these two decades the common interpretation at the time was that the ideological position of the party had undergone far-reaching deradicalisation, and this perception overshadowed the fact that the Social Democrats had launched major innovative reforms. In view of the party's perceived rightward shift in economic matters in the 1980s, such an interpretation and neglect of possible innovations once again seem particularly imminent.

This study examines the recent programmatic renewal of the Swedish Social Democrats – from 1980 onwards with major emphasis on the programmes drafted for the 1990s. Initially it sketches the context of renewal in an effort to identify important factors shaping the process. Special attention is devoted to the SAP's legacy of continuous reforms since a major question posed here is: has a pattern of renewal and innovation typical of earlier decades emerged during the 1980s and early 1990s? This discussion also sets recent developments in a historical perspective. Subsequently the formal process of renewal with respect to programme formulation is briefly described. The essay then outlines the broad contours of the SAP's present ideological stance. The concluding section speculates on the outcome of programmatic renewal. It attempts to assess the impact of the current renewal process as well as its limitations.

## THE CONTEXT OF RENEWAL: CONTEMPORARY CHALLENGES AND HISTORICAL INFLUENCES

Programmatic renewal during the past decade has taken place within the context of a twofold ideological challenge – the simultaneous rise of neo-liberalism and Green values. As a result, the situation differed in complexity from earlier decades when the challenge came largely from either the right as in the 1950s or from the left as in the late 1960s and 1970s.

This twin challenge has been augmented by pressing problems related to environmental deterioration and a changing economy. Globalisation of the economy has led to a restructuring and shrinkage of the industrial sector, faltering international competitiveness, and dwindling Swedish shares in the world market. Sluggish economic growth and high labour market participation rates tend to preclude a continued expansion of the tax base; at the same time public commitments require enormous resources, with Swedish public spending in the 1980s amounting to roughly two-thirds of the GDP.

The changing economy has produced a new class arithmetic altering the preconditions of electoral success for the Social Democrats. The restructuring of the economy has entailed a decrease in working class occupations, and economic dislocations have weakened traditional identities and communities. The size of the working class and the incidence of class identification among workers were previously major sources of strength for the SAP; but in the 1980s class identification became less widespread, and the decline in working class identification largely corresponded with changes in occupational structure.

These difficulties constitute common challenges confronting socialist parties in Western Europe, although the degree of their severity has varied. Interwoven with these shared elements are influences specific to the individual parties, which also mould the renewal process. In the case of the SAP three circumstances have provided a distinctiveness to its programmatic renewal: the sequence of office-holding, the procedures of programme formulation, and the legacy of continuous reform and innovations.

From the mid-1970s onwards the cycle of office-holding for the Swedish Social Democrats has deviated substantially from several other northern European socialist parties which were in office during the late 1970s but one by one lost power, frequently remaining in opposition during most of the 1980s. By contrast, after six years in opposition, the SAP returned to office in 1982 and was the party of government with minority administrations during the rest of the decade. Thus the renewal process occurred with the Social Democrats at the helm, allowing them to take the initiative and to be in a less reactive role. Furthermore, the domestic challenge of neo-liberalism was less forceful.

Second, the actual process of programmatic formulation and revision seems quite distinctive. Programmatic renewal has been a labour movement affair, not confined to the party; and it is by no means limited to revising the statement of basic principles, what is termed the party programme here. Especially important is a tradition of party-union collaboration in drafting programmes of action which was established with the formulation of the 1944 *Postwar Programme of Swedish Labour*. Since then the drafting committees of action programmes have invariably included trade union representatives. Independently of the party, the trade union movement has also produced a series of programmes over the years, and several of them have been major sources of policy innovation. Uniquely, the current renewal process resulted in three major programmatic statements: the 1990 Party Programme, an action programme for the 1990s, and a new trade union programme.

In addition, the process of programmatic revision displays more regularity and continuity compared to many other socialist parties. This regularity is witnessed in the fairly frequent major revisions of the party programme (1911, 1920, 1944, 1960, 1975, 1990) which has probably eased the traumatic nature and controversies surrounding revision. The nature of the process has also softened discontinuities. Revisions have involved rewording the previous version of the programme, and this procedure extends back to the original 1897 programme.[3] Thus, the SAP has never written a completely new statement of principles; instead large sections of the previous programme have remained intact.

It should also be noted that the formulation of election manifestos has gradually lost its former importance as a programmatic activity of the party. Until the mid-1930s the party congress adopted the election manifesto; subsequently the national committee (*partistyrelsen*) assumed this task. The manifesto remained the central document of election campaigns, being distributed to all households into the 1950s, but it was eventually eclipsed with the advent of TV elections. Instead programmatic activities of the party congress have intensified since the mid-1960s through adopting action programmes and/or policy guidelines.

Third, assuming that politics involves learning, the SAP's legacy of continuous reforms and innovation suggests itself as a crucial determinant in programmatic renewal. In any event, an interesting series of innovations has emerged during each decade since the Social Democrats came to power in the 1930s – from an acclaimed unemployment programme to combat the Great Depression to the highly publicised wage-earner funds introduced in the early 1980s.

The unemployment programme of the 1930s, which broke with economic orthodoxy, was basically a Keynesian economic policy (predating the publication of Keynes' major theoretical work). It aimed at stimulating *both* production and demand, and the most controversial innovations were deficit spending and paying market wages to workers employed in public works projects. The justification for regular wages was that they would boost demand together with cash benefits provided by social reforms, such as unemployment insurance, improved old age pensions, paid vacation legislation, and family policy measures. The latter in themselves constituted an additional complex of innovative policies which were introduced to cope with the serious decline in the birth rate. The most unusual measures were legalisation of abortions, maintenance allowances for single parents, and prohibition against firing women because of marriage, pregnancy, and childbirth.

During the subsequent decades of their lengthy period in office, irrespective of whether the spirit of the times was conservative as in the 1950s or radical as from the mid-1960s to the mid-1970s, the Social Democrats proposed numerous inventive reforms. Although contemporary observers in the 1950s interpreted programmatic developments within the SAP as an ideological retreat compared to the mid-1940s,[4] in retrospect and in comparison to other socialist parties, five innovations stand out. The first was the steady expansion of the welfare state, where as distinct from the continent, expenditures were devoted to both social insurance benefits and *public facilities and services*, laying the foundations of the 'social service state'. The second was the introduction of an active labour market policy which emphasised vocational training, mobility allowances, and stand-by job programmes. Third the solidaristic wage policy was established to reduce wage differentials. The fourth accomplishment was the supplementary pension reform (ATP) which created a universal state occupational pension scheme and huge pension funds in the public sector, thus altering the extent of private dominance over the capital market. Fifth, the decade constituted a period of experimentation paving the way for an integrated school system. All of these achievements – with the exception of the supplementary pension reform – can be traced to the aspirations of the 1944 Postwar Programme.

In contrast to the conservative mood of the 1950s, the mid-1960s onwards witnessed a radical upsurge which was eventually reflected in the SAP's programmatic activities, culminating with the adoption of the 1975 Party Programme and the 1976 trade union report on wage-earner funds. The Social Democrats' initial ideological response, however, was embodied in three programmes whose combined effect was a stronger advocacy of state intervention in the economy, the reassertion of equality as a major party goal, and the call for greater employee influence. The three programmes had an enormous impact in shaping the reforms legislated in the 1970s.

The first document, *Programme for an Active Industrial Policy*, adopted by the 1968 party congress, resurrected the demand for greater democracy in the economy, although largely through a statist approach. It proposed regional planning and industrial location policies and increased involvement of the state in research and development, environmental and land utilisation planning, investments, and economic planning (steering and co-ordination). A larger role for state enterprises was also envisaged.[5] Among the novel features of the second programme, *Towards Equality*, adopted by the 1969 party congress, were the view that equality signified more than equal opportunities, an expanded participatory stance, and emphasis on gender equality. Several proposals were put forward to promote equality between the sexes: individual taxation of spouses' earnings, labour market measures tailored to women, a pre-school reform expanding public day care facilities, and family law reforms to ensure equality and economic independence of spouses.[6] Third, *Industrial Democracy*, a trade union (LO) programme, signalled a major reorientation on co-determination in management. LO advocated workers' representation on company boards in combination with expanding the unions' powers of negotiation.[7]

The leftward shift of the Social Democrats peaked in the 1975 programme revision and the report on wage-earner funds, both of which assigned key importance to economic democracy. According to the 1975 Party Programme, *economic democracy* was the Social Democrats' third historical project building upon the first – *political democracy* – the introduction of universal and equal suffrage and the second – *social democracy* – the extension of social rights through the construction of the welfare state. The 1975 Party Programme envisaged economic democratisation as a process of extending the influence of the individual *cum* citizen, employee and consumer. The most important innovation was the emphasis on co-determination of employees and their participation in capital formation, implying employee rather than government ownership.[8] The LO report on wage-earner funds, whose chief author was Rudolf Meidner, can be viewed as a solid expression of the idea of employee ownership.[9]

In conclusion, continuous reforms have been largely dependent upon the ability of the SAP to retain its position as the party of government. However, it seems equally true that continuous reforms and innovation have underpinned the party's long dominance in office. As recently pointed out, one crucial component of party dominance is control of the public policy agenda,[10] and the past record of the SAP shows a sustained effort at programmatic renewal. This is not to argue that all the programmes, or all planks of the programmes, produced by the SAP have entailed a tactical or electoral advantage. For example, the radical points of the 1944 Postwar Programme and the wage-earner funds were more of an electoral liability than an asset. Nor do I want to suggest that the reforms initiated by the government occurred in a vacuum or were the single-handed accomplishment of the Social Democrats.

During most of these years the SAP did not command a majority of its own in parliament. Moreover, in many instances the party's programmatic stands have been responses rather than initiatives. What is important, however, is the ingenuity of the responses and the SAP's continuous endeavours to formulate programmes for the future and thereby shape the policy agenda. To what extent was this tradition carried on into the 1980s? Before turning to the issue of innovation in recent efforts at renewal, let us look briefly at the formal process itself.

THE FORMAL PROCESS OF RENEWAL: WIDESPREAD CONSULTATION
AND LEADERSHIP DOMINANCE

The large-scale involvement of the labour movement in programmatic formulation at the end of the 1980s is perhaps best viewed as the culmination of a decade of programmatic activity. The action programme for the 1990s incorporated earlier changes during the 1980s, and sought to maintain the momentum in the quest for renewal. Already in the debate following the 1985 election which resulted in a slippage of votes for the SAP,[11] several party influentials voiced the need for programmatic renewal. Ingvar Carlsson, then deputy prime minister, expressed the conviction that reformism and equalisation policies must not be limited to bread and butter issues. He concluded, 'We cannot be content to find new means to achieve old objectives. We must strive toward completely new goals.' As examples, he mentioned environmental policy, public sector reform, educational policy, a working life contributing to personal growth, and shorter working hours. In a similar spirit, the president of the youth organisation, Anna Lindh, called for the party to 'leave the 1960s' and 'prepare for the 1990s!'.[12]

The decisions leading to the formulation of new programmes did not occur until the late 1980s. Initiative came from the party leadership but the process involved considerable activity by party organisations, and was even extended to circles outside the party and trade unions. In 1987 the national committee recommended to the party congress that it decide to revise the 1975 Party Programme with the aim of adopting a new programme at the next congress in 1990. In its recommendation the national committee noted that 15 years was the usual life span of a party programme, and that a revision was appropriate in view of the coming 100th anniversary of the SAP (in 1989) and a new decade in the offing. It further specified that since the ideological posture of the party had not undergone major change, a far-reaching revision was not necessary but modernisation and clarifications were in order.[13]

After the 1987 congress decision, the programme commission, headed by party leader and prime minister, Ingvar Carlsson, embarked upon revision. In the spring of 1988 the commission asked numerous party notables and outside intellectuals for their views on the party programme. The first formal step followed in the autumn when party organisations were encouraged to set up study circles dealing with the party programme and send in reports of their deliberations to national party headquarters by early 1989. The reports were structured by a series of study questions,[14] and a major purpose of the circles was to tap grassroots sentiments.

Although not especially impressive in number (258) this initial wave of comments represented a cross-section of the party – the auxiliary organisations, local unions, and branches. The comments emphasised the need for a revised class analysis, and the Women's Federation pointed out that a class analysis had to be complemented by a feminist perspective. Concern was expressed about the growing concentration of power in the private sector during the 1980s. Some reports criticised the term 'planned economy', but opinions were overwhelmingly in agreement about the role of economic planning in the sense of co-ordination of economic activity and framework legislation to guarantee the attainment of national goals. The comments distrusted the market's ability to meet social needs; they rejected privatisation of public sector services but were positive toward user influence and decentralisation.[15]

Armed with the views of the party organisation, the commission drafted a proposal for a new programme, which was then sent out to the local branches for their comments. The branches and individual members were entitled to propose amendments in the form of resolutions to the party congress. On the basis of the comments and resolutions, the commission revised its proposal, incorporating many suggestions and points in the resolutions. In this way, the programme became a collective document. The major changes traceable to the resolutions consisted of a stronger feminist orientation; an elevation of the role of popular movements and co-operatives; and a series of statements emphasising a more traditional ideological stance.[16] The revised proposal was subsequently adopted by the 1990 party congress with virtually no changes.

The decision to draft an action programme for the 1990s was taken in the autumn of 1988, on the heels of the general election and when the Swedish economy appeared restored to health. The national committee appointed a high-powered work group, dubbed 'the '90s-Group', which was headed by Anna-Greta Leijon, a former minister and member of the party executive committee. Other members were finance minister, Kjell-Olof Feldt; the president of LO, Stig Malm; one of the vice-presidents of LO, Rune Molin; and the general-secretary of the party, Bo Turesson. The national committee's directives stressed that the group should devise an integrated strategy and identified four dilemmas which needed to be addressed: (1) how to combine full employment, low inflation, and improved real wages; (2) how to renew the public sector through increased citizen involvement and greater freedom of choice without jeopardising equality and security; (3) how to invigorate the political work of the labour movement as working conditions and employee influence are altered by new technologies, new class relations, and higher levels of education; and (4) how to protect and improve the environment and simultaneously attain the traditional goals of the labour movement.[17]

The working procedures of the '90s-Group bear several resemblances to those of the programme commission. The group organised a series of seminars to discuss the challenges of the coming decade; its strategy was to include diverse and opposing opinions. These discussions set the stage for writing *The 1990s Programme (90-talsprogrammet)*, a draft document to stimulate debate in the labour movement.[18] Both party and union organisations participated in this debate, submitting nearly 1,600 reports to the party national headquarters. The overall effect of the comments was to tone down proposals and arguments generating disagreement within the labour movement.

In a comparative perspective, some aspects of the SAP's revision process are worth noting. During the postwar period, the party leader and prime minister has headed the programme commission, giving its deliberations a special status. Each of the programme revisions has thus been closely associated with the party leader at the time, the 1960 programme with Tage Erlander, the 1975 programme with Olof Palme, and the 1990 programme with Ingvar Carlsson.

Although extensive consultation occurs, the actual drafting of programmes remains the prerogative of quite a small sector of the party – the commission or a special drafting committee, with the head secretary vested with the task. There is little reliance on outside think-tanks or party research units to draft proposals. Nor have opinion polls or attitude surveys been consulted in the process.[19] Perhaps this is due to the marginality of the election manifesto in the programmatic activities of the SAP. Also, the party programme is conceived as an enduring document, making its drafters more impervious to opinion polls. Equally important is how the party views its role in opinion formation. The SAP sees itself as shaping opinion by formulating its positions and then winning support for them.

The specialisation in types of programmes may have contributed to the relatively smooth functioning of the revision process and the ability of the SAP to meet its timetable. Factionalism is not as extensive as in many other parties, but various groupings seeking to influence the content of renewal crystalised. These groupings coalesced on certain issues and recombined on others. For the sake of convenience they can be labelled the feminists, the 'economists', the decentralists, and the traditionalists.[20] All of these tendencies left their mark on the current programmes.

PROGRAMMATIC RENEWAL IN THE 1980S AND 1990s

In certain respects the current project of programmatic renewal resembles that of the 1950s. In both instances conservative forces claimed they provided a more appealing vision of the future society, which enshrined individual initiative and freedom of choice. An additional parallel was the challenge posed by an analysis of societal change pointing to a supposedly inevitable erosion in the support for socialist parties. In the 1950s it was predicted that growing prosperity would cause affluent workers to desert socialist parties. In the 1980s and early 1990s post-industrial society and the resulting shrinkage of the industrial sector, it was held, would deprive socialist parties of their natural base. As in the 1950s, the SAP responded by emphasising individual freedom and seeking solutions involving the public sector.

In other respects, however, the project has been strikingly different. Renewal in the past consisted of devising and launching new reforms which entailed additional expenditures. However, in the early 1980s when public spending constituted such a large share of the GDP, opinion within the SAP was divided on both the advisability and feasibility of increasing expenditures. In other words, the prime solution underlying programmatic renewal during past decades was no longer an attractive option, and some party influentials did not even regard it as an option.

The rise of the Greens further complicated programmatic renewal since they pose a different challenge through their image as a progressive party with a futurist orientation. The Social Democrats, because of their defense of earlier reforms, have had to deal with a status quo image, and at a time when public finances have left few resources for future reforms – which have been the essence of the SAP's progressive profile.

Part of the SAP's response was to underline that it represented an alternative to neo-conservatives and neo-liberals: its programme constituted a 'third way'. Toward the end of the decade the party put greater emphasis on ecological concerns. The principal features of the third way and the SAP's current ideological stance, as reflected in its three programmes for the 1990s, are described below. Special attention is given to the party's vision of the good society and the policy recommendations contained in the action programme, *90-talsprogrammet*, to achieve the four major goals for the decade: a good living environment, an enriched working life, a renewal of the public sector, and a strong economy.

## The Good Society

The Social Democratic vision of the good society, as spelled out in the 1990 Party Programme and its predecessors, is a classless society – 'a community of people cooperating on the basis of freedom and equality'. The abolition of the class society has a timeless quality in the good society envisaged by the SAP, extending back to the first official party programme. However, recent Social Democratic pronouncements suggest a possible acknowledgement of the enormous difficulties in achieving a classless society. Now a more limited ambition was to introduce the quality of 'classlessness' into certain areas of social life; that is, the goal is to create areas in society where class distinctions and social status are neutralised. The main instrument for achieving this is the public sector.

More dramatic has been the change in the party's analysis of classes over time. A new element in the class analysis of the recently adopted programmes was the attention given to the impact of post-industrial society and the emergence of a new set of cleavages based on knowledge, higher education, and professional status conferring job autonomy. Among the groups negatively affected by the new cleavages are industrial workers, poorly paid women in routine white-collar jobs, and service workers in the care sector. The crucial point of the SAP's analysis is that, contrary to most post-industrial and post-materialist theorists who claim that the new class divisions are replacing the old, the party underscores the co-existence and frequently reinforcing nature of materialist and non-materialist class cleavages. Accordingly the Social Democrats called for measures to combat both sorts of cleavages, but their energies were directed to attacking the new class differences. The most concrete proposals focused on meaningful employment and stimulating work, discussed below.

Finally there has been a tendency in recent Social Democratic discourse to fall back on anti-utopias, that is, presenting a picture of the undesired society. At times during the past decade anti-utopias have overshadowed visions of the good society. The anti-utopia in the action programme was a 'two-thirds society' where two-thirds of the population enjoy a high standard of living and can choose their own lifestyle and one-third are substantially worse off with little opportunity for personal growth.[21]

*The Goals for the 1990s*

*Meaningful Work.* Although demoted during the 1990 programme revision, work as a value in itself has occupied a central position in Social Democratic ideology. In terms of policy prescriptions, its importance is reflected first in the work principle (*arbetslinje*) and second in the strong focus on working life.

The work principle has exerted a persistent influence on policy and policy prescriptions. In the initial formulation of the third way, the Social Democratic crisis programme, 'The Future for Sweden' (*Framtid för Sverige*), adopted in 1981, the formula for extricating Sweden from the economic recession was to save and *work*. In certain respects this formula harked back to the policy of the 1930s and the Postwar Programme by stressing insufficient demand and measures to promote employment. The major departure was that in the past insufficient demand had been bolstered by a combination of public investments and measures to strengthen purchasing power, whereas the 1981 crisis programme exclusively recommended intensifying public investments (in energy, transportation, construction and later research).

To a large extent, the work principle has also been the foundation of employment policy. The principle prescribes providing work rather than compensation to the jobless. The result has been a unique labour market policy which assigns priority to active measures – such as placement services, training, and rehabilitation – so as to aid as many people as possible to find and keep a regular job. Conversely unemployment benefits play a minimum role. Upon returning to office, the Social Democrats pumped substantial resources into active labour market measures, and Swedish levels of unemployment were much lower than the OECD average during the entire 1980s.

The action programme for the 1990s called for a radical extension of the work principle. Besides underscoring the individual's right to employment and the ensuing benefits, the extension of the work principle was held up as a possible way to improve the financing of social insurance schemes. The aims were to reduce sickness absences and early retirement, to introduce a flexible pension age to allow persons over 65 to continue working if they so desired, and to increase the proportion of women in full-time employment.

The strong focus on working life recurred in the action programme for the 1990s and LO's draft programme *Det utvecklande arbetet* (Enriching Work). The action programme designates an enriched working life as one of the four major goals for the 1990s. This goal is to be achieved by eliminating hazardous jobs, improving educational and job training opportunities, flattening the job hierarchy and wage differentials, along with removing differences in status and privileges distinguishing 'salaried employees' (*tjänstemän*) from 'workers' (*arbetare*). For the most part, this equalisation was to occur through securing these advantages for LO-affiliated workers who are manuals and lower level nonmanuals.

These proposals were summed up as a 'solidaristic working life policy' because of the thrust to seek improvements for workers whose conditions were worst. One of the most interesting proposals bears resemblance to the solidaristic wage policy. It advocated a strategy of dealing with the worst job environments first and increasing the costs so that monotonous and hazardous jobs were priced out of existence. Such a strategy is reminiscent of the solidaristic wage policy which assigned priority to wage improvements of the most poorly paid workers and through higher wages forced the least profitable enterprises out of business.

In conclusion, two features concerning policy prescriptions with respect to working life stand out. First, the quest for equality was more sharply formulated in this area compared to other policy areas. In addition, the programme underlined the reinforcing nature of measures to achieve equality and efficiency, especially with respect to educational measures. Second, a stronger individualistic orientation was also reflected in the action programme. It called for the empowerment of the *individual* wage-earner. Moreover, it stated that changes in ownership, as shown by the public sector, will not solve the problems of powerlessness and a sense of futility among workers, which are the result of authority relations and subordination. The action programme and the LO report also note that the focus on the individual worker differs from efforts in the 1970s which concentrated on strengthening the position of unions in the workplace.

*The Environment.* One of the most profound reorientations in 1980s policy prescriptions concerned the environment. The action programme for the 1990s elevated a good environment to one of the four major goals for the decade. This reorientation was ushered in at the 1987 party congress with the adoption of the environmental policy guidelines in 'The Environment – Our Common Future' and the subsequent launching of the 'fourth project'.[22]

The reorientation can be summed up in three points. The first was the central place assigned to the goal of a good environment by likening it to the party's major projects and policy achievements.[23] As the 1988 election approached the Social Democrats went all out to present themselves as an ecology party. They designated a good environment as the fourth project and gave it the same standing as the fight for universal suffrage, efforts to combat unemployment, and the construction of the welfare state. In a similar vein, the action programme proclaimed that environmental policy has the same position as full employment policy, and that environmental considerations must pervade the decision-making process in its entirety and all areas of policy.[24]

Second, the reorientation featured a wide array of policy recommendations. In several instances the party dressed up earlier proposed measures but was more emphatic about their urgency. The main innovations were a tougher stand on dismantling nuclear power, especially the decision to phase out two reactors earlier than originally planned,[25] the call for an initially 'clean' technology rather than attempting to clean up afterwards, the formulation of national emergency plans with specific targets to reduce dangerous emissions and eliminate toxic substances in production, emphasis on individual responsibility in adopting an environmentally sound lifestyle, the introduction of surcharges and fees, the revenues of which would be used for investments necessary for a cleaner environment, and the development of a national accounting system which would include effects on the environment – a green GDP. A final shift, and possibly the most important if translated into action, was the abandonment of the holistic perspective (*helhetsperspektivet*). Previously in making decisions on environmental policy, ecological considerations were to be weighed together with social and economic concerns. The new programmes declared that ecological requirements must be the basis for environmental legislation – not what is technically or economically reasonable.[26]

The third facet was an attempt to integrate ecology concerns with traditional ideological tenets. Accordingly, the 1987 guidelines explicitly declared that environmental issues were ideological. Their ideological character stemmed from the fact that the solution to environmental problems involves the right to determine production; a strong ecology stance thus impinges upon corporate power over the economy and private ownership. The party's ideological heritage can be further detected in the heavy emphasis on the environment as a public good and a human right, the stress on the necessity of collective solutions entailing state intervention, the imperative that the people's interest and well-being take precedence over private profits, and the fusion of environmental issues with the longstanding aspirations of equality and solidarity at a national and global level.[27]

The new central place of the environment also required the party to address the relationship between economic growth, technology and the environment. On this score, the SAP did not alter its positive view of economic growth. The party continues to see growth as a prerequisite for its reformist redistributive policies and an ambitious environmental policy. The Social Democrats argued against the view that economic growth per se results in environmental degradation; instead the type of technology was at fault. Both growth and technology could provide the solutions, and new environmentally-friendly technologies can furnish jobs. The action programme exuded a technocratic enthusiasm with regard to the environment and put much faith in a more effective administration and proper steering mechanisms (both controls and incentives in the form of rewards and sanctions). The programme's recommendations were alluded to as a third way between a free market which fails to include environmental destruction in its calculations of costs and the central planning of command economies.

*Renewal of the Public Sector.* In the area of social policies, the Social Democrats have outlined two tasks for the future: to safeguard the universalist welfare policy and to renew activities in the public sector. The SAP remained firmly committed to public provision of services – day care, education, employment placement and job training, health and medical care, and personal social services – based on universalism in the form of equal access for all citizens and residents, according to need, irrespective of income and status. Privatisation of services involving basic needs was ruled out, although in the case of technical services, along with auxiliary services, such as cleaning, laundry, and food services, the Social Democrats contemplated contracting out on the basis of competitive bids. An additional universalist aspect defended by the SAP was the financing of public services largely through taxation rather than relying on user fees or individual insurance contributions. The party rejects substantial reliance on user fees in such areas as education and hospital services, but it accepted increases in user fees for technical services, like banking, postal and telecommunication services.[28]

The task of renewal of the public sector amounted to a bold reorganisational scheme which the Social Democrats presented as a 'third way' between bureaucratic and market solutions. Renewal was necessary because of legitimate demands for higher quality services and more variety in their provision, elimination of bureaucratic rigidities and inefficiencies, and uneven services.[29] Equally if not more important, renewal required substantial organisational changes in the public sector because of one feature of the 'third way's' economic policy: a stabilisation of public expenditures. The fundamental line of reasoning was that the public sector was already generously funded.

The first organisational change is decentralisation – moving the sites of decision-making closer to the citizens, the users of services, and employees delivering services. This entailed trimming the size and functions of central administrative agencies, such as the National Board of Education and the National Board of Social Welfare, and reallocating tasks which were the responsibility of central or regional authorities to the municipalities. At the municipal level, because of local government amalgamation reforms, decentralisation also involved assigning tasks to a new local level of decision-making. Administratively, budgetary and operational responsibility was to be located at the point of delivery of services whenever possible.

The second was deregulation in the sense of eliminating detailed directives and introducing new steering mechanisms, such as users' preferences, evaluation studies, quality standards to measure performance, and cost controls. More crucially a stricter division of responsibilities was advocated, first, between politicians and administrators and, second, between public authorities paying for services and those supplying services. The latter was a prerequisite for creating 'internal public markets' where both production and distribution took place in the public sector, but market effectiveness was introduced in the form of competition, while avoiding the worst aspects of private markets, such as segregation and 'creaming off' effects.

The third feature of renewal was the increased direct influence and involvement of citizens as users and employees. The programme called for users' involvement (*brukarmedverkan*) and the participation of those utilising the services: pupils, parents, patients, pensioners, and relatives. The influence of users was viewed as a means of achieving greater effectiveness by allowing them to choose between suppliers of services but also to enable a ranking of suppliers according to quality. Direct influence also included citizen involvement or self-administration and the formation of service co-operatives by employees or voluntary and idealistic organisations. This form of organisation was heralded as offering small-scale solutions and being a third alternative to bureaucratic centralist arrangements and solutions based on private profits.

In summary, the implementation of the SAP's proposals would signify a major restructuring of the Swedish welfare state, a restructuring which attempts to retain an ambitious universalism – public social services available to all through communitarian funding – but would scale down the central bureaucracy and presumably lead to cuts in other areas of government spending. The reallocation of responsibilities from the central and regional levels to the municipalities would mean that local governments would face hard choices in determining priorities in their budgets.

*A Strong Economy.* Recommendations to achieve the fourth goal of the 1990s action programme – a strong economy – were generally vague, and much of the discussion summarized the accomplishments of the third way until the late 1980s.[30] With regard to the future, the programme concentrated on spelling out the central objectives of the SAP's economic policy: full employment, expanded collective savings to reduce the public sector's dependence upon private capital, lower inflation rates, and increased international competitiveness. It also identified certain problems, like wage determination, low household savings, and the funding of future pensions, especially state occupational pensions (ATP). The LO report was more specific concerning savings and pensions. As a means to promote savings and limit the concentration of private wealth, the report called for the conversion of the ATP scheme into a premium reserve system with 10–20 pension funds in the public sector.[31]

The reorientation embodied in the third way left its mark on the new party programme's view of the economy. References to a planned economy (*planmässig hushållning*) as the type of economy desired by the SAP have been stripped from the programme, and more explicitly than in previous party programmes, a mixed economy was promulgated. The role of planning and state controls as policy instruments has been toned down. On the issue of collective ownership the 1990 party programme retains the former socialisation clause, loaded with ambiguity: 'Natural resources, credit institutions or private enterprises are to be transferred to public ownership or public control in cases necessary to secure major common interests.' But its only specific justification for introducing co-operative and public forms of ownership is to promote diversification and competition.[32] More to the point, the new programme declares 'it is the right of determination over production and distribution . . . which is central, not the right of ownership'. This statement, however, is a codification – not a modification – of the SAP's position.

## THE IMPACT AND LIMITATIONS OF PROGRAMMATIC RENEWAL

In assessing the impact of renewal it is useful to consider both the intellectual and tactical functions of programmes.[33] Very briefly, the intellectual functions involve diagnosis (definition and explanations of the situation or current problems) and prescription (goal specification and policy recommendations). These functions are crucial in establishing ideological hegemony and in shaping the policy agenda. They are also essential in maintaining the party's self-confidence and sense of purpose. The tactical functions refer to integration and mobilisation of support; they are intimately bounded up with the strategic goals of parties – party cohesion and maximisation of votes.

A central motive of programmatic renewal, especially in the case of the action programme, has been to specify the major goals of the 1990s, and thus take the lead in formulating the policy agenda for the decade. In a wider perspective, current renewal constitutes an intellectual response to the claims of neo-liberalism and the Greens. It also represents an endeavour to re-establish the historical project of Social Democracy.

In responding to neo-liberalism, the SAP emphasised the third way as an alternative, which involved both traditional policies and departures. The main departures were tax reforms eliminating progressivity, pruning and stabilising public expenditures, and 'privatising' state corporations – stances which seem to pre-empt the neo-liberals. Despite similarities, the policy outcomes differ from those the neo-liberal project. The tax reforms lowered the marginal rates of the national income tax, but to finance these cuts other taxes were increased. Estimated government revenues for 1990–91, after the first phase of the tax reform, indicated only a small decline, hardly in accordance with neo-liberal aspirations. The Social Democrats pruned government expenditures but not social spending, which has been a prime target of neo-liberal retrenchment efforts. 'Privatisation' of state enterprises generally took the form of issuing new shares with the government retaining control over the corporations.[34] Possible future ventures were envisaged to create resources to invest in collective projects, like renewal of the infrastructure, mass transit systems, renovation of public housing, energy systems, and cleaning up the environment.

The response *vis-à-vis* the Greens has involved an effort to combine materialist and post-materialist themes and values. On the one hand, the party's materialist bent is clearly revealed in the weight attached to the economic basis of freedom, the argument that a materialist foundation is a prerequisite for the realisation of spiritual or post-materialist values, the celebration of a growth philosophy, an optimistic faith in rationality, technology and expertise, and the work principle. In the SAP's vision of the future there is no freedom from work, the challenge is to enrich work. On the other hand, post-materialist influences can be seen in the 'greening' of the party by virtue of assigning a central place to the environment, along with the growing scepticism and opposition to nuclear energy; the new prominence of cultural, moral and spiritual values; the participatory stance accentuating self-administration and citizen involvement; and the emphasis on self-development, and on diversity and pluralism as values in themselves. In particular, an individualist orientation stands out in the recently adopted programmes: in working life the empowerment of the individual worker through the improvement of resources, in the environment by emphasising individual responsibility for one's lifestyle, in the renewal of the public sector through the individual's ability to influence services directly.

Despite the imaginative nature of these responses, limitations became apparent as the tide of events quickly overtook the programmatic renewal of the Social Democrats. An economic downturn in the late 1980s continuing into the 1990s altered the rosy assessment of the third way's economic policy and its claims of success. Second, the collapse of communist regimes and the introduction of market economies transformed the 'third way' into a misnomer. Third, the process of goal formulation failed to deal with one of the major issues of the 1990s – Sweden's relationship to the European Community. A few months after the adoption of the programme's, the SAP was in the process of putting EC membership on the agenda and propagating a socialist strategy for Europe.[35]

With respect to the integrative function, internal discussions concerning the party programme's purpose have stressed that subscription to the statement of principles serves to unify party members. Through its consultative nature, the revision process of the party programme attempts to enhance integration. Furthermore, members of the revision commission viewed an essential part of their task as clarifying the distinctive nature of social democracy.[36]

Nonetheless, the final versions of the party programme and the action programme contained a series of contradictions, producing uncertainties and undermining party cohesion. One source of tension was between the party's altruistic tradition emphasising motives of human behaviour related to neither self-interest nor private gain and the economistic reasoning in the action programme stressing economic incentives. This clash was also manifested in the idea that competition and economic incentives offer solutions to the problems of the public sector versus the view that the task of the public sector is to provide goods and services determined by human needs, not profits as in the market. Potential strains also existed in the new emphasis on diversity in relation to the universalist construction of social policies characterised by equal access and benefits. Similarly, decentralisation and local solutions can easily come in conflict with the goal of equality. A further contradiction was found in extending the work principle and voluntarism into user involvement in the provision of services.

In terms of mobilisation of support and maximisation of votes, the current renewal process appears contradictory in its effects as reflected in the mixed record of the SAP in the last four elections. During the 1980s the party's polling strength averaged nearly 45 per cent of the vote,[37] but in the 1991 elections the Social Democrats experienced one of the worst defeats in their history, declining to 37.6 per cent compared to 43.2 per cent of the vote in 1988. In the elections of the 1980s the 'third way' with its emphasis on employment aided the SAP by reinforcing one of its main trumps in winning votes: the electorate's positive perception of the party in maintaining full employment. The SAP's reorientation with respect to the environment also appears to have been an asset in the 1988 election. The Greens entered the Riksdag, but not at the cost of a socialist majority.

In the 1991 election the SAP initially attempted to convert the four goals for the 1990s into major campaign issues.[38] However, as economic difficulties mounted, the state of the economy and its future direction became a prime focus of the campaign, and the party was put on the defensive in explaining its record. An additional source of the Social Democrats' defensive stance was that party popularity in opinion polls dropped to an unprecedented low of around 30 per cent in early 1991, and past supporters became hesitant about their party choice. As a result the party emphasised traditional demands, and new aspriations for the 1990s found little room in the campaign.

To what extent was this decline in support related to the renewal process? The sagging popularity figures in opinion polls followed a pattern of sharp losses coinciding with the introduction of tax reforms and austerity measures – suggesting a close association with the issues of taxation and running the economy. The tax reforms eliminated progressivity, whilst many party voters subscribed to the view that people in high income brackets should not receive tax cuts – which is exactly what happened. The decline during 1989 was clearly related to disenchantment among the leftist voters for the party,[39] and renewal has been perceived as a reorientation to the right. The ambiguities and tensions of renewal may also account for voters' widespread hesitancy.

Although maximisation of votes in individual elections is a crucial measure of mobilisation of support, the long-term aggregation of different sections of the population, enabling the party to forge viable coalitions of voters in the future is decisive. The current renewal process suggests that the SAP has been grappling with two strategic considerations. First, it is essential that renewal aggregates the 'old' and 'new' left, preventing the development of a cleavage along the lines of materialist and non-materialist values. By combining materialist and post-materialist concerns in its new programmes the SAP seems to have sought to avoid such a schism. Second, a possible coalition of the future, implied in the party's class analysis, is an alliance based on women's increased labour market participation. In view of women's less favourable position in the labour market, a 'solidaristic working life policy' potentially could aggregate industrial workers and working women.

In conclusion, a major test of the success of the renewal process is the degree to which conflicts between the intellectual and tactical functions of programmes are resolved or kept to a minimum. Ironically, the Social Democrats may have exerted major influence in shaping the policy agenda for the 1990s but in the process seriously damaged their electoral support, at least in the short run. The long-term outcome, however, remains to be seen as the decade unfolds.[40]

## NOTES

1. A major exception is Tim Tilton, *The Political Theory of Swedish Social Democracy*, (Oxford: Clarendon Press, 1990). Cf. Nils Elvander, *Skandinavisk arbetarrörelse* (Stockholm: LiberFörlag, 1980), pp. 219–55.
2. For a discussion of the attributes associated with ideology and the resulting difficulties, see Diane Sainsbury, 'The End of Ideology Debate Revisited: An Appraisal of Definitional and Theoretical Issues', *Scandinavian Political Studies* 9/2 (Spring 1986), pp. 111–128.
3. For an analysis of the successive changes in the wording of the 1897, 1911 and 1920 programmes, see Herbert Tingsten, *The Swedish Social Democrats; Their Ideological Development* (Totowa, NJ: Bedminister, 1973), pp. 167–245.
4. For the 1940s, see Diane Sainsbury, *Swedish Social Democratic Ideology and Electoral Politics 1944–1948* (Stockholm: Almqvist & Wiksell International, 1980).
5. *Program för aktiv näringspolitik, Näringpolitiska kommitténs slutrapport* (Stockholm: SAP, 1968).
6. See *Towards Equality, The Alva Myrdal Report to the Swedish Social Democratic Party* (Stockholm: Prisma, 1971). This publication is an abridged version of *Jämlikhet* (Stockholm: Prisma, 1969).

7. *Industrial Democracy*, Programme adopted by the 1971 Congress of the Swedish Trade Union Confederation (Stockholm: LO, 1972), pp. 5–13.

8. *The 1975 Party Programme*, pp. 20–1, 34.

9. Rudolf Meidner, *et al.*, *Employee Investment Funds* (London: Allen & Unwin, 1978).

10. T.J. Pempel, 'Introduction', *Uncommon Democracies, The One-Party Regimes* (Ithaca, NY: Cornell UP, 1990), p. 4.

11. For a brief account of the 1985 election, see Diane Sainsbury, 'The 1985 Swedish Election: The Conservative Upsurge is Checked', *West European Politics* 9/1 (April 1986), pp. 293–7.

12. Ingvar Carlsson, 'Ett nytt uppdrag för socialdemokratin!', *Tiden*, 1985, pp. 486–90 and Anna Lindh, 'Lämna 60-talet – förbered 90-talet!', *Tiden*, 1985, pp. 557–9.

13. *Programkommissionens förslag om programrevision in Partistyrelsens utlåtande och övriga förslag till socialdemoraternas 31:a kongress*, P9, pp. 19–20.

14. *Partiprogrammet 1990. Studie- och diskussionsmaterial inför programrevisionen* (Stockholm: SAP, 1989).

15. For a discussion of these comments, see Anne–Marie Lindgren, 'Klassisk socialdemokrati', *Tiden*, 1989, pp. 354–63.

16. Cf. *Programkommissionens reviderade förslag till nytt partiprogram, Häfte: Pl and Programmotioner, Häfte: Ml*.

17. *Partistyrelsens utlåtande över nittiotalsprogrammet och förslag till riktlinjer, Häfte: P3*.

18. Interview with Klas Eklund, Head Secretary of the '90s-Group, 21 May, 1991 and the special issue on the programmatic debate of the labour movement from the 1940s to the 1990s, *Arbetarhistoria, Meddelande från Arbetarrörelsens Arkiv och Bibliotek* Nos. 53–54 (1990), p. 33.

19. Interview with Enn Kokk, Head Secretary of the Programme Commission, 16 May, 1991.

20. Cf. Rune Premfors 'The "Swedish Model" and Public Sector Reform', *West European Politics* 14/3 (July 1991), pp. 83–95.

21. Anti-utopian themes were also prominent in the crisis programme of 1981.

22. To get some sense of the change, cf. the national committee's proposal concerning the guidelines for environmental policy at the 1984 party congress, *Partistyrelsens förslag till riktlinjer för miljöpolitiken, Motioner 18, Miljö. Jordbruk* (Stockholm: SAP, 1984), pp. 57–9 and *Miljö – vår gemensamma framtid. Miljöpolitiska riktlinjer antagna av Socialdemokraternas 30e partikongress 1987* (Stockholm: SAP, 1988).

23. The environment has been a programmatic issue since the late 1960s, and it was incorporated into the 1975 Party Programme (The 1960 Party Programme did, however, mention protection of natural resources and conservation measures.) Environmental planning was an important recommendation in the industrial policy programme, and special programmes on environmental policy were adopted in 1968 and 1972. Subsequently, the environment was eclipsed by other issues – social policy reforms, economic democracy, and the wage-earner funds. Furthermore, in environmental policy, attention was riveted on a single issue from the mid-1970s onwards – energy policy – and the SAP's pro-nuclear energy position damaged its previous image as a progressive ecological force. In the 1980s environmental policy was crowded out by issues concerning the economy until 1987.

24. *90-talsprogrammet*, pp. 62–3, 68, 81.

25. Dismantling nuclear power was written into the 1990 Party Programme. This stand contrasts with the 1960 Programme's clause 'the expansion of nuclear power under state auspices' and the SAP's position in the early 1970s which advocated nuclear energy in preference to oil with the eventual development of breeder reactors. See *Miljöpolitik. Förslag till nytt socialdemokratiskt miljöprogram* (Stockholm: Prisma, 1973), p. 37.

26. For statements on the holistic perspective see *Miljöpolitik*, p. 50 and the 1975 Party Programme, article 12, p. 37. Cf. *Programkommissionens reviderade förslag till nytt partiprogram*, article 11, and *90-talsprogrammet*, p. 112.

27. See esp. *Miljö – vår gemensamma framtid. Miljöpolitiska riktlinjer antagna av Socialdemokraternas 30e partikongress 1987* (Stockholm: SAP, 1988), pp. 4–8.
28. *90-talsprogrammet*, p. 205, p. 181. See also *Fackföreningsrörelsen och välfärdsstaten* (Stockholm: LO, 1986) and Lars Anell and Ingvar Carlsson, *Individens frihet och framtidens välfärdssamhälle* (Stockholm: LO, 1985), pp. 23–31.
29. For a discussion of public sector reforms in the 1980s and the resulting dissensions within the SAP, see Premfors (note 20).
30. For a summary of the results of the third way, see *The Economist*, 7 March, 1987, pp. 19–24.
31. *Det utvecklande arbetet*, 1990, pp. 345–54.
32. By contrast, the 1975 Party Programme was punctuated with recommendations for public ownership: the production and distribution of energy, public measures to promote collectively owned enterprises, co-operative and non-profit enterprises in housing, and the production of textbooks and teaching materials.
33. For this distinction, see Sainsbury, *Swedish Social Democratic Ideology* (note 4), Ch.1.
34. For more details see Jonas Pontusson, 'The Triumph of Pragmatism: Nationalisation and Privatisation in Sweden', *West European Politics* 11/4 (Oct. 1988), pp. 129–140.
35. See, e.g., *Politisk platform antagen av partistyrelse och LOs landssekretariat den 24 januari 1991*.
36. Anne-Marie Lindgren, 'Livsvillor och värderingar: Förslag till nytt socialdemokratiskt partiprogram', *Arbetarhistoria*, Nos. 53–54 (1990), p. 24.
37. For election trends in the 1980s, see Diane Sainsbury, 'Swedish Social Democracy in Transition: The Party's Record in the 1980s and the Challenge of the 1990s', *West European Politics* 14/3 (July 1991), pp. 31–57.
38. As note 35.
39. Sören Holmberg, 'Socialdemokraternas opinionras 1989', in idem and Lennart Weibull (eds.), *Medier och opinion i Sverige* (Gothenburg: Dept. of Political Science, Mass Communications Unit, 1990), pp. 69–79.
40. Fourteen months after the 1991 election the opinion poll ratings of the SAP had bounced back to 45 per cent. See 'Partisympatiundersökningen November 1992', *Statistiska meddelanden* Be 60 SM 9202 (Stockholm: SCB, 1992).

# The Norwegian Labour Party: 'En Attendant l'Europe'

## KNUT HEIDAR

*The Norwegian Labour Party revised its programme of principles in 1981. This marked the beginning of a decade of ideological reorientation, if not so much programmatic change. Through the internal 'Freedom Debate' the leadership sanctioned views on the state, the markets, the identity of the party itself and Labour's relations with the trade unions underwent change. Triggered by the electoral defeat of 1981 and influenced by tendencies in international social democracy, individualism and social pluralism became ideologically accepted concepts of analysis for the 'modernised' Labour Party. Traditional left groups within and outside the party presented little opposition; the loudest protests came from a handful of trade union leaders.*

> My party's called Liberal, but it's basically quite socialist.
> With these Europeans, it's the other way around.[1]

The search for ideology as well as identity has been an integral part of labour movement history since its beginning as an organised force. In autumn 1985 the Norwegian Labour Party (*Det norske arbeiderparti*, DNA) again found itself discussing identity. Who 'owned' the party? Did the trade unionised, metal-working section of the traditional bedrock working class and their representatives have any special 'rights' to the party? Or had they lost those rights to the new 'public class', the salaried employees created by Labour's very own project: the welfare state. When Gro Harlem Brundtland formed her second government (1986–89), deals had to be made in the Storting with the 'bourgeois' centre parties. From the left there were hints about a sellout of the family silver. (In the old days an inappropriate metaphor!) But during the 1980s new terms and themes had found their way into Labour's vocabulary: privatising industry; rethinking the welfare state; liberalising the economy. What was happening to the 'party soul'?

In this essay I shall discuss the changing character of the Norwegian Labour Party in the 1980s. First, by presenting the main programmatic changes and the new tendencies in party debates. Second, by surveying the 'traditionalist' response to the party 'modernisers'. And finally, by looking at the changes in the organised framework for party decision-making. The point being that the changing character of a party cannot be identified by programmatic changes alone.

MODERNISING LABOUR: PROGRAMMATIC CHANGES

Labour was – apart from three weeks – continuously in government from 1945 to 1965. During these 20 years the policies of the Labour government changed from active reformism in its early years to a more laid-back administrative approach in its later period.[2] Programmatic debates sprang very much from the immediate problems of rebuilding Norway after the war. At the same time it was a political necessity to keep some bridges to the interwar rhetoric of the party. The contrast was nevertheless stark to the interwar period when party debates originated in the great questions of West European socialism. In so far as ideological borrowing took place after the war, it was from Keynesian economics and Swedish social engineering. The days of discussing the socialist classics had gone. Ideological discussion proper – in the sense of searching for a coherent set of ultimate goals and the means of getting there – was left to a few intellectuals devoid of political influence.

During these 20 'postwar' years the party presided over the Norwegian branch of the 'you-have-never-had-it-so-good' era. In a modified version Labour became in deeds if not always in words the local proponent of 'keine experimente' – meaning 'no bourgeois government'. It must be added though that this primarily holds for economic policies, not for the social and cultural policy sectors. In education, for example, Labour set in motion a massive expansion and transformation of schools and universities. With an expanding economy, the government had the resources to build a 'social democratic society' with 'equal opportunities' at its core and education as its main tools. By the early 1960s the reformist 'new-society' spirit of the early postwar years had subsided. Party leaders dared to speak clearly: 'Old dogmas give few answers'. The new answers were to be found in systematic research, and the 1965 election manifesto demanded 'more research' in most fields.

A centre-right coalition of the bourgeois parties entered government following the 1965 election. Six years later it broke down over the European Community issue. The debate over EC-membership and the referendum in 1972 changed Norwegian politics and radicalised the Labour Party. The Labour governments from 1973 to 1981 were all minority governments – supported by the Left Socialist Party in the Storting. To regain the initiative on the left, Labour introduced several reforms. Oil revenues were used to finance shorter working hours and a lower pension age. A new state company – Statoil – was given a prominent place in the growing Norwegian oil industry. Laws were passed on industrial democracy and the improvement of the work environment. Those were all ideologically based reforms, strongly criticised from the right. This was also the case with Labour's proposal to restrict grading in the schools. But most strongly attacked was the law intending to implement 'bank-democracy' which placed public representatives on the policy-making assemblies of the banks.[3]

## The 'Freedom Debate'

The political climate changed as Norway entered the 1980s. Labour was out of power from 1981 to 1986. The bourgeois coalition headed by a conservative prime minister, Mr Kaare Willoch, followed the international trends in their policies to 'roll back the frontiers of the state'. Reaganism and Thatcherism were forceful inputs to the general debate and the government played the 'dynamic tax-policy' card, arguing that lower taxes would fuel the economy and in the end give increased public revenues. They also started to deregulate the credit market. Private interests were invited to enter into education, into the health sector, nurseries, etc. And although this was conceived on a small-scale basis, the direction was clear. Private local radio-stations were allowed and the government launched a programme to slim down public bureaucracy and make it more service-minded.

At its 1981 congress Labour adopted a new programme of party principles. This, however, did not arouse much controversy within the party. Still, the new principles were more than a rewrite. It was cast in an analytical sociological language. The party faced 'new challenges' which demanded 'new answers'. Socialism was 'not a condition, but a process'. The 1969 programme of principles had stated rather bluntly that the goal of the party was 'a socialist society'. Now this socialist 'process' was directed at particular goals. Three were emphasised: freedom, democracy and equality ('equal worth'). Later in the programme 'solidarity' – central to 'democratic socialism' – was added to the list. The important new twist to the 1981 programme was its strong emphasis on the labour movement as a 'freedom movement'. Freedom was linked to solidarity and equality as *the* main values guiding the social democratic project. Possible trade-offs between freedom and equality were brushed under the carpet. Politically this was directed at the argument contending these to be antithetical goals.[4] The new programme also left out the old demand to establish public control over banks and credit institutions. The party history describes the 1981 programme as 'a lot more pragmatic'.[5]

The internal party debate focused much on *international* issues. After the 1979 Nato's two-track decision, the question of deployment of new medium-range missiles in central Europe polarised Labour. The peace movement was active, and the missile debate was a favoured theme of the right parties in order to question how trustworthy the socialists really were when it came to national security. This rather turbulent debate was put to rest through a broad party compromise in 1984. As the 1985 election came closer the party adopted a traditional social-democratic opposition to the economic policies of the centre-right government. Growing unemployment, hospital queues and problems with financing the welfare state gave the Labour Party unity and mobilised its rank-and-file. Labour staged a successful election campaign and increased its vote from 37 to 40 per cent. But the party did not achieve a parliamentary majority, even when including the Left Socialist Party.

Shortly after the election the Labour leadership announced plans for a broad internal party debate labelled the 'Freedom Debate'. Politically, they were reacting to the policies of the bourgeois government since 1981, in particular to the increased prominence gained by 'private solutions' in the general debate. The main purpose of the campaign was therefore to 'recapture' the concept of 'freedom' for the labour movement. And organisationally the debate was planned to culminate in the formulation of the 1989 election manifesto. What was the content of the 'Freedom Debate'? Six themes were singled out for special discussions in local study groups from 1986 to 1988:

1. *Politics for freedom.* The focus here was to be on the relationship between individual freedom, collective welfare and the public sector, that is, the need to strike a balance between the private and the public in a mixed economy.

2. *Time for each other.* This theme addressed the trade-offs between a lower pension or shorter working day and how to ease the problems for new groups – like women – when they entered the work-force.

3. *Schools for the future.* How to adjust education to the changing social patterns – with both parents working outside the home. And how to provide equal opportunities in a changing society based on 'new' technology.

4. *Common environment.* This theme laboured the point that 'freedom from' a dangerous and unhealthy environment – inside industry as well as elsewhere – implies restrictions on the individual 'freedoms to'.

5. *Freedom and housing.* Rising housing costs and particularly the

high interest rates were discussed alongside the consequences of
the liberalisation of the housing market in the 1980s. The discussion centred on the right balance between freedom and
regulations.
6. *Economic democracy.* The Swedish wage-earners' funds were –
according to the 'theme manual' – *not* the way to extend economic
democracy in Norway. The discussion relevant to Norway was how
to extend public control over banks and credit institutions as well
as to increase the influence of the employees over their own firms.

It is difficult to assess how successful the campaign was in
organisational terms: how many party members took part in the study
groups, how much debate – public as well as at party meetings – was
generated. But even if not a great mobiliser of grassroot activism, the
campaign is still indicative of political thinking at the party centre. All
themes raised – from different angles – the question of the proper
balance between state and markets, between the public and the private.
The aim was to promote discussions on what was a proper social
democratic answer – relevant for the 1980s.

To achieve this the party leadership set out to challenge two Labour
traditions: The rooted belief in the *public sector* and the close ties with
the *trade unions*. During the 1970s and early 1980s an expanding public
sector with detailed regulations and a growing bureaucracy had – as the
electorate's belief in state intervention dwindled – become increasingly
troublesome parts of the social democratic project. The state-bashing of
the bourgeois parties no doubt found fertile soil in strategically important sections of the electorate. And the Labour leaders considered this a
threat both to the party and to the welfare state. They prepared for a
counter-offensive by presenting two general points on party policies to
its grass roots. First, the choice of policies should be made on the basis
of what benefited *the consumer*, that is, not the producers in the trade
unions. Second, Labour had to come to terms with more *variation* in
policy approach. Centralised policies treating everyone alike would not
necessarily give the best solutions.

The Freedom Debate also raised the question about what *kind* of
party Labour ought to be. Here the question of the future relationship
with the trade unions was central. The dilemma was that the party
needed to be a party for more than trade unionists but at the same time
should keep in close contact with the unions. The party secretary – in a
speech at the 1987 congress – predicted a rising level of tension as
Labour had to appeal to a growing non-unionised electorate. In the
same speech the secretary also invited more ideological debate on the

political platform of the Labour Party. To stimulate that debate he announced a new party journal devoted to ideological questions. Ideological debate, he argued, was necessary to capture the new voters – less tied to established interest groups and not entrenched in traditional cleavages. The message from the party leadership to the activists wrapped up in the Freedom Debate was loud and clear: in order to survive electorally, Labour policies had to adjusted significantly.

Why this campaign after the successful 1985 election? The reasons were many – but 'it would be stupid to deny', the deputy leader said at the 1987 congress, 'that our debate has also been marked by the conservative challenge'.[6] Behind the call to recapture the ideological hegemony was the fear of future electoral decline. A recurring theme in the presentation of the Freedom Debate, was the necessity of making adjustments to 'new circumstances' so that Labour would remain a '40 per cent party'. Declining support among youth since the 1970s, shrinking of the so-called bedrock electorate in traditional industries and weakening of socio-political ties made change imperative to long-term party survival.

### Environment and Gender: New Policies for the 1980s?

In the 1970s green politics had been mostly about hydroelectric development projects and the protection of natural reserves. During the 1980s, however, debates increasingly turned towards general industrial and economic issues. While the 1969 election manifesto asked for the public's unhindered access to recreational areas, the 1989 manifesto argued for a stabilisation of the total energy consumption in Norway by the year 2000. In 1972 the Labour government set up a Department for the Environment headed by a cabinet minister. Environmental questions were also raised in the new programme of principles from 1981.

During the 1970s there were heated debates within the Labour party over several hydroelectric projects – debates which partly followed the division established in the European Community debacle of 1972. In many of these fights the party's youth movement faced powerful trade unions and district interests – it was 'environmentalism' against 'electrification socialism'. At the 1985 party congress the issue of growth v. protection came out with the highest 'conflict potential' in a delegate survey.[7] With the rise in unemployment after 1988 the trade unions have been increasingly on guard against environmental policies which could hinder the creation of new jobs.[8] Mrs Brundtland, who started her political career as a Minister for the Environment and later headed the UN Commission on Environment and Development (1984–87), has had to balance the party line between these different tendencies. The

Labour voters, however, were found in the 1989 election study to be below average in judging the importance of environmental issues.[9]

Neither was the gender issue new to the labour movement in the 1980s. Labour had its own women's movement, and although this has declined in organisational strength since the late 1960s, its influence has nevertheless increased. Issues put on the agenda by new feminist groups forced the political parties to address them. To the fury of the party leadership – who feared the loss of voters – a proposal from the floor at the 1969 party congress committed Labour to a women's right to abortion policy. Again, in 1981 the congress adopted a motion from the party women to make the 6-hour working day the long-term goal of Labour – against stark warnings. The party established in 1983 a quota system with at least 40 per cent of either sex in all party assemblies. Two years before the first woman, Mrs Gro Harlem Brundtland, was elected chairman ('leader' after 1983). This took place only a few months after she had become the first woman prime minister of Norway, and although elected uncontested the incumbent was forced to step down. In 1986 Mrs Brundtland set a new standard in Norwegian politics when 8 out of 18 cabinet positions went to women. In Labour's Storting group of 1989–93 a majority of the MPs are women.

Parliamentary politics and not electoral gains brought Labour back into government in April 1986. The right wing Progress Party voted with Labour against the government's proposal to increase taxes on petrol, and Mrs Brundtland subsequently formed her second government. But Labour needed the support of the Agrarian or the Christian Peoples Party to survive in parliament. A complex parliamentary situation and the need for tight economic policies after the spending spree of 1984–85 absorbed the energy of the Labour elites. The party had to compromise in the Storting and to talk the trade unions into wage restraint at the same time. The government partly paid the unions off by introducing wage laws (1988 and 1989) which prevented all other groups from getting more than the trade union members.

In the aftermath of the Freedom Debate and the moderate 1986–89 government there was some public debate about the general direction of Labour policies. This was also fuelled by a steep rise in the unemployment figures. But at the spring 1989 party congress there was only a meek, almost a symbolic opposition. Economic set-backs made chances bleak for expensive reforms, and the leadership had its way with a moderate election manifesto for the 1989–93 term. The manifesto put more jobs, more solidarity and improving the environment high on the agenda. A rebellion did come, however, in the election of a new deputy leader. The candidate favoured by the top leadership had to share the job with a former trade union leader, Mr Torbjørn Berntsen, who campaigned as a representative of the 'old groups' within the labour movement. The leadership also met defeat on a proposal to remove the collective trade union affiliations to the party. The 1992 party congress voted to phase out collective membership over a two-year period. These were minor obstacles, however. After the congress parliamentary business prevailed as usual, the important task being to keep the Conservatives out of power.

The 1989 election brought the centre-right coalition back to power – but only for a short period. The Conservative led government of Mr Jan P. Syse fell after one year – the three parties were unable to agree on the negotiations on the *European Economic Area* between EFTA and the EC. In November 1990 Mrs Brundtland formed her third minority government. The European issue had by now again become central, having been 'exiled' for 17 years from Norwegian politics. Still, the 'ghosts' from 1972 reappeared. To Labour in the shape of a fear of splitting the party – this time possibly bringing its electoral following down to the 20 per cent range. The left socialists and the agrarians were ready and eager to pick up the slack if the Labour leadership went too quickly ahead in its pro-EC policies. To play it safe Labour's May Day slogan of 1990 was 'One Democratic Europe' – to cope with challenges in both East and West.

## THE TRADITIONALIST REACTION

Opposition to the new ideological signals of the Freedom Debate was scattered. Even though Gallup poll figures in 1989 showed that 25 per cent of the Labour voters thought Labour had moved too much to the right 'these last years',[10] there was not much internal opposition. The deputy party leader (1981–89), Mr Førde, later summed up his experience: 'The Norwegian Labour Party is one of the least idea-oriented social democratic parties I know.'[11] Possibly the critics held back not to harm the minority Labour government 1986–89. This had not silenced the left wing in the past though, so perhaps it had more to do with the general decline in party activism. The grassroots did not turn out in great numbers to discuss the Freedom Debate – they rather enjoy their individual freedom in front of the television. Nor did the youth movement – traditionally the guardians of ideological causes – fly the red flag. In contrast to the late 1970s when the Labour government made compromises to the left *and* experienced a viable left opposition, the Labour left had by the late 1980s faded under the impact of a new international climate and the domestic electoral 'right wave'.

A few critical voices nevertheless addressed publicly what they judged to be a scrapping of traditional values within the party. Just after the 1985 election Mr Torbjørn Berntsen (the deputy leader from 1989) had complained that he, with his trade union and industrial background, was not given a sufficient influential position within the parliamentary party group. This outburst triggered the 'identity-debate' presented at the beginning. In policy terms, the leader of the Municipal Workers Union, Mrs Liv Nilsson, was predictably outspoken in her criticism of the signals in the Freedom Debate opening for 'private solutions'. Nilsson was a member of the Labour Party's central committee and had already offended party culture by arguing that she was the *representative* of her union within that committee.[12] The public quarrel came over how to create new nurseries. The Labour manifesto for the 1987 council elections emphasised the need for more places for pre-school children, and the question was if this should be the exclusive task of the councils or whether one should encourage the creation of private and 'cooperative' nurseries. No doubt Mrs Nilsson held the traditional view of social democrats that a public sector solution had a value *in itself* which could not be reduced to a question of cost and expedience. And at the 1987 congress she argued strongly that a 'de-ideologisation of the means very well can lead to the goals not being achieved'.[13]

Although publicly a meek opposition, the internal concern was widespread. The old party leader, Mr Steen, who was often considered a protector of the left, had – in a private telephone conversation – the following description of the kind of society sought by the 'modern' right wing within the party: 'A welfare society for the affluent middle class . . . It will be a kind of mini-America. Where the Conservatives and Labour compete for power, without anybody being able to notice much difference between them.'[14] Steen had lost the leadership contest in 1981, and the new leadership of Mrs Brundtland along with electoral trends and a new international climate pacified the old party left.

*The Academic Left: An End to the 'Social Democratic State'?*

Opposition to the new party line had, however, some backing from the old academic left. In 1988 a former MP of the Left Socialist Party, Professor Ottar Brox, published a book defending 'traditional social democracy'.[15] Brox, however, had the rhetorical problem that he was on file as fairly critical of 'traditional social democracy' in its alleged golden age.

From within the party, Professor W. M. Lafferty argued that the new party discussion on 'freedom' was to enter 'bourgeois territory'.[16] Lafferty agreed with the critics from the right that there *was* a conflict between freedom and increased pluralism on the one side and solidarity/

equality on the other. And he feared that the Labour leadership by 'stumbling into the desert of instrumental materialism' ran the danger of replacing the ethical basis of social democracy with 'technique'.[17] In Lafferty's view the 1975 to 1981 period with a minority Labour government supported by the Left Socialist Party, had seen the culmination of the 'social democratic state'.[18] This was the time when Labour in practical politics came closest to the 'social democratic idea' which was about uniting classical socialism – meaning equality in property and status – with democratic decision-making within all spheres of society.

In a response to Lafferty, Mr Einar Førde argued that Lafferty was right in seeing the 1980s as a time for change of course for Labour, – but it was a change of means, not of basic values.[19] The changes, according to Førde, was in line with international trends within social democracy: upgrading markets, downgrading state solutions. And in fact the 1980s had been an important ideological phase in the history of Labour – being closer to 'real ideological debate than almost at any time in our history'.[20]

## DISMANTLING DEMOCRATIC CENTRALISM

Today little is left of what used to be Labour's 'special character' – with a mass membership and committed activists. The vitality at the grassroots is no longer impressive. Its members – like other parties' – prefer television at home to political education in the town hall. Party culture is, however, still marked by old traditions. The prime minister remembers her days in the movement's children groups. Old labour songs are sung at meetings. Every party congress still – to some of the delegates' embarrassment – ends with the first verse of the International, although to their comfort they immediately change to the first verse of the national anthem.

In 1919 the Norwegian Labour Party joined the Comintern and adopted the principle of democratic centralism. The party left four years later, but centralism stuck. Factional struggles with left groups during the 1920s and 1930s and the revived competition with the Communist Party after World War II, maintained the centralised structure of the party well into the 1950s and 1960s. Ideology as well as historical legacy made unity and respect for party decisions an important party creed. And this creed was activated in full during the debate on the European Community in the early 1970s. The leadership was strongly in favour while members and voters were split. At the special party conference called in spring 1972 to make the final decision, there was laughter around the hall when the entire delegation from the northern county of

Nordland voted yes to membership. Everyone knew there was a massive stand *against* in that county – also among Labour members and voters.[21] The Labour government's defeat in the 1972 referendum and, even more, the massive set-back of the following year's Storting election shook the party and led to an opening up of the decision-making process.

## The Party Congress

The national congress is the party's 'highest authority'. This does not mean that the 300-strong body is where major decisions are generally made. Important decisions are, however, usually confirmed there – and everyone has to include the debates at the congress in their strategic planning. Occasionally important decisions have also been made at the congress itself. The decision to bring Norway into NATO in 1949 was *de facto* taken here. The 'atom-paragraph' – banning atomic weapons on Norwegian soil – entered the election manifesto in 1957. Proposed from the floor it created problems for the party leadership later. The same happened when Labour became an early proponent of free abortion at the 1969 congress.

Since 1967 the Labour congresses have been open to the media. The 'openness' in itself, however, did not mean much as the important editorial committees still met behind closed doors. The memoirs of key figures within Labour in the 1950s and 1960s give the impression of highly centralised decision-making. 'Some of us had been talking together' is an expression used by the prime minister and party leader Einar Gerhardsen. In his era the 'some-of-us' were the most trusted cabinet ministers, the party secretary, the leader of the trade union movement and the editor of the central Labour paper. But this tight control was lost in the 1970s. Old organisational values evaporated during the unruly debate over the European Community.

The exit of the wartime generation and the changing media also played a part. More important still was probably the general social changes. These are reflected in the composition of the 1985 congress: 57 per cent of the delegates were then public employees, only 12 per cent came from industry. And 46 per cent had education at university level.[22] The party secretary in 1985 explained the need for a more open policy process by pointing to a new kind of member who demanded respect for his or her points of view.[23]

The new openness was also reflected in the selection of the top leadership. In 1967 it sent shivers through the entire organisation when the old party leader, Mr Gerhardsen, confronted the powerful party secretary at the congress. At the 1975 congress internal conflict was more accepted. Still, a head-on collision between left and right was just avoided in the election of a new party leader. Only a compromise kept the peace. This gave the position of prime minister-in-waiting to the right's candidate while the party leadership went to the candidate of the left. In 1981 another open row over leadership positions arose. The incumbent leader was forced to withdraw when challenged by the new prime minister, Mrs Harlem Brundtland. Finally the congress in 1989 forced the party leadership to accept a joint deputy leadership accommodating both the 'left' and the 'right' tendencies.

## The Election Manifesto

A detailed election manifesto is adopted at the congress, and only in exceptional circumstances can the party elites depart from it. The 1985 manifesto did for example block the introduction of advertising on radio and television. But when the responsible minister later found the time ripe for a change, the party had go through the hassle of organising a special round with party counselling to legitimise the turn around.

The manifesto process evolves through three stages. First, a high-level committee is appointed by the central committee, often chaired by the leader/prime minister and composed of members from the main branches of the labour movement. A proposal is worked out in close co-operation with the party secretariat, the parliamentary spokesmen and the relevant ministers. Second, the proposal from the manifesto committee is discussed at branch level within the party. The party centrally also calls meetings with a broad range of special interest organisations – including for example the employer's association – and outspoken individuals to sound out opinions on the manifesto proposals. Third, there is the discussion at the congress itself where the remaining contested issues have to be resolved – if necessary by a vote. Two main changes have taken place during the 1980s. The initiative to let organisations *outside* 'the family' voice their opinions was introduced in 1984. In addition, the branch level has become more active in formulating policy alternatives. The number of branch proposals brought before the congress in 1989 was over 1,000, while during the 1970s they numbered barely 200.[24]

## Decline of Party?

In terms of nominal members Labour has had a mixed fortune during the 1980s – rising from 153,000 in 1980 to 176,000 in 1985 and then declining to 121,000 in 1990. In the 1970s the figures were around 150,000. A decline in Labour membership seems to have begun only in the later 1980s. The party entered government in 1986 just as organisational renewal was put on the agenda with the Freedom Debate. In 1989 the party secretary acknowledged, however, that Labour had not been able to combine government power with a 'lively and critical debate within the party'.[25]

The labour movement as a whole – trade unions, the co-operative movement, etc. – also faced problems. The decline if not the death of the traditional working class during the 1970s, removed the social glue necessary to hold 'the movement' together. Indicative were the quarrels with the public employee unions. The increased independence of the press owned by the labour movement also caused problems to the party. This has about 20 per cent of the national daily circulation and includes important regional strongholds. But during the last two decades the labour press increasingly operated on a professional basis and felt free to criticise and 'de-mask' Labour politics and politicians almost as much as the other media.[26]

The use of professional surveys had their breakthrough in the 1970s. Party headquarters increasingly used them to test public opinion, thus bypassing both the media and their own organisation. Labour and the Conservative Party were the only parties to subscribe to the *Norwegian Monitor*, a systematic (and expensive) effort to depict the political and market sentiments of changing socio-cultural groups within Norwegian society.[27] Labour has no doubt become a more 'open party' during the 1980s to paraphrase its 1987–88 organisational campaign. Openness, however, was not only a necessary adjustment to a new political context, but also an organisational benefit to be enjoyed by fewer and less involved party members.

## LABOUR'S 'NEW DIRECTION'

It is difficult to measure in any precise way how different the 1990s version of 'social democracy' is from that of the 1970s or the 1960s. The complex tapestry of ideological change cannot be neatly summed up in the accountant's ledger. Equally difficult is it to tell how instrumental this change has been in redirecting Labour Party *policies*. Still, Lafferty claimed that the Labour leadership had signalled a 'new direction' with its 'Freedom Debate'. But looking back on the interwar changes in party ideology, the programmatic changes alone during the 1980s look rather modest. More generally, there has not been *any* 'Bad Godesberg' in Labour's postwar history. Changes in policies and programmes have been gradual and generally with ideology lagging behind. Precious little of the old type 'socialization socialism' survived the 1950s. During the 1960s socialism came to be about growth, research, planning and educational standards. And at the 1990 party congress the secretary claimed social democracy to be the rightful heir to the liberal values that paved the way for democracy in the last century, giving substance to the views expressed by the Colombian delegate quoted in the beginning.[28] However, our main question is this: *what is new* in the Freedom Debate of the 1980s? That is, apart from a half-hearted sanctioning of ideological debate – which did not quite materialise.

Two departures from 'old social democracy' as it appeared in Norway up till the 1970s could be noted. *First*, a change of argumentative logic and, *second*, the group perspective. The arguments most forcefully presented in the Freedom Debate were the instrumental ones. As an example of how sensible the collectivist logic is, the sports-interested Mr Førde favoured the story of how *all* spectators watching athletics at Oslo's Bislet stadium were better off sitting down. If any one rose to get a better view, everyone would have to rise – and they would *all* be worse off. In other words: solidarity pays! Collective solutions are often the most sensible ones. It is not that solidarity is a fundamental value to be sought *even if* detrimental to particular individual goals. Through the Freedom Debate, to argue for individual interests was no longer bad language. It was considered a fact of life which the party had to come to terms with. Social democrats should in consequence pursue their goals with the help of, rather than against the markets – not only in the economy, but in other arenas of social life as well.

The second break with tradition could be found in the views on Labour's social base. New groups were to be courted in order to preserve the party's status as a '40 per cent party'. This was the perspective of the party secretary when he called for an 'open party'. In this campaign the party invited new groups to press for their particular demands *through* the Labour Party. Labour would aspire to be a 'governing instrument' which most groups could learn to play. But this of course would require a change in the special relationship with the trade unions.

Why this change of course during the 1980s? Any answer to this would have to be tentative. Three factors are no doubt relevant. First, the changes in 'external environment' – both in Norway and internationally. In Norway, 'de-industrialisation' and the growth of the 'new middle classes' along with the electoral 'right wave'. Abroad, the end of the Cold War and a changing European scene. Second, the situation in the Storting was different in the 1980s. During the 1970s Labour's minority governments had been supported by the left socialists. But in the late 1980s Labour had to reach an accord with the parties of the centre. The third factor is the international co-operation between the social democratic parties. Labour has always kept in close contact with the other Nordic parties, in particular the Swedish social democrats where a parallel debate evolved throughout the 1980s.[29]

Also the frequent contacts with the other West European parties made an impression. This is most clearly seen in the political manifesto of the party secretary, *My European Dream*, published in 1990.[30] On balance, the electoral defeat of 1981 made it clear to the party leadership that *something* had to be done, while the stimuli from the international debate gave the crucial input to *what* had to be done. Programmatic renewal in Norway was not a change forced upon the party leadership from below. All the way it was a process closely guided and directed from the top. And the 'grassroots' either agreed or chose to remain silent.

The spectre haunting the Norwegian Labour Party at the beginning of the 1990s is not, therefore, the Freedom Debate. Nor is it the old duel between 'left' and 'right' tendencies. It is rather the European Community issue which has returned to Norwegian politics after 17 years – re-activating the old cleavage between 'centre' and 'periphery'. In 1990 this toppled a centre-right government – just as it did in 1971. Again Labour had to take over to finish the negotiations with the European Community – this time via EFTA on an 'European Economic Area'. Any hopes the Labour leadership might have nurtured that public opinion would have 'matured' in the meantime, or that the Swedish and Finnish applications for membership would have softened electoral feelings about the Community, have not come true. The Labour Party seems to be heading towards the same debacle as in 1972, even though the leadership this time is doing everything in its power to avoid the internal feuding of the 1972 debate. From the outset (1989–92) the leadership played for time in a kind of waiting game. Internal discussion groups were to prepare for a decision at the party congress in November 1992. The congress voted with a ⅓ majority to apply for EC-membership. But the voters and the other parties were in no mood for waiting. Sceptical voters turned increasingly to the clear 'No!' parties. And the polls so far hold little hope for a Labour recovery in time for the 1993 Storting election.

These trends among the voters, however, have – by all indications – precious little to do with the process of the political renewal which took place in the Norwegian Labour Party during the 1980s. The re-emergence of the European issue is a sufficient explanation.[31] But of course no one knows how the polls would have looked like, or what the general shape of the party would have been, *without* these changes.

NOTES

1. Colombian delegate at the Stockholm 'centenary get-together' of the Socialist International in June 1989, *The Economist*, 30 Sept. 1989.
2. See K. Heidar 'The Norwegian Labour Party: Social Democracy in a Periphery of Europe' in W.E. Paterson and A.H. Thomas (eds.), *Social Democratic Parties in Western Europe* (London: Croom Helm, 1977), pp. 292–315. For a general political history of the party in this period, see T. Bergh, *Storhetstid 1945–65*, Arbeiderbevegelsens historie i Norge, Vol. 5 (Oslo: Tiden, 1987).
3. See J. Nyhamar, *Nye utfordringer 1965–1990*, Arbeiderbevegelsens historie i Norge, Vol. 6 (Oslo: Tiden, 1990), pp. 368–72.
4. The importance of 'freedom' was certainly not new to party programmes. The programme of principles from 1949 makes this very clear. However, the 1949 programme dealt more with freedom *from* than freedom *to*. See E. Lorenz (ed.), *Norsk sosialisme i dokumenter* (Oslo: Pax, 1970).
5. Nyhammar (note 3), p. 355.
6. E. Førde in *Protokoll fra DNA's 51. ordinære landsmøte 1987* (Oslo: DNA, 1988), p. 72.
7. K. Heidar, *Partidemokrati på prøve*, (Oslo: Universitetsforlaget, 1988), p. 76.
8. See, e.g., the LO leader Yngve Haågensen's strong stand on this in *Arbeiderbladet*, 28 Dec. 1991.
9. H. Valen, B. Aardal and G. Vogt, *Endring og kontimuitet. Stortingsvalget 1989*, Sosiale og Økonomiske studier 74 (Oslo: Statistisk Sentralbyrå, 1990), p. 17.
10. *Arbeiderbladet*, 27 Feb. 1989.
11. E. Førde 'Ideologi i Gros tid' in R. Hirsti, *Gro – midt i livet* (Oslo: Tiden, 1989), p. 44.
12. See, e.g., the discussion at her controversial re-election in 1987, *Landsmøteprotokollen 1987* (Oslo: DNA, 1988), pp. 191–3.
13. *Landsmøteprotokollen 1987*, p. 115.
14. The statement came in a secretly taped, private and very open-hearted telephone conversation in 1981, see V. Johansen og P.T. Jørgensen, *Edderkoppen* (Oslo: Aventura, 1989), p. 90.
15. O. Brox, *Ta vare på Norge!* (Oslo: Gyldendal, 1988).
16. Lafferty's views are expressed in W.M. Lafferty, 'Den sosialdemokratiske stat' i *Nytt Norsk Tidsskrift* 3/1 (1986) and idem, 'DNAs nye retning' in *Nytt Norsk Tidsskrift* 4 (1987).
17. Lafferty, 1986, p. 36.
18. Lafferty, 1986.
19. Førde, 1988, pp. 41–57.
20. Ibid., p. 47.
21. N.P. Gleditsch and O. Hellevik, *Kampen om EF* (Oslo: Pax, 1977), p. 81.
22. Heidar (note 7), pp. 45–63.
23. I. Leveraas at the 1985 Congress. Quoted in Heidar (note 7), p. 36.
24. In general, the programmatic activities at branch level increase when the party is in opposition. In other words: to be in government changes the direction and character of branch-based initiatives, see K. Heidar 'Landsmøtepolitikk: På verkstedgolvet i Det norske Arbeiderparti' in G. Djupsund and L. Svåsand (eds.), *Nordiske partier* (Åbo: Åbo Akademi, 1990), pp. 131–50.
25. *Dagbladet*, 25 Oct. 1989.
26. H. Østbye 'Media in Politics' in K. Strøm and L. Svåsand (eds.), *Challenges to Political Parties*, forthcoming.
27. Labour, however, has now dropped this.
28. T. Jagland, MS, DNA's landsmøte, Folkets Hus, Oslo, 9–11 Nov. 1990, p. 10.
29. D. Sainsbury 'Swedish Social Democracy in Transition: The Party's Record in the 1980s and the Challenge of the 1990s' in *West European Politics* 14/3 (July 1991), pp. 31–57.
30. T. Jagland, *Min europeiske drøm* (Oslo: Tiden, 1990), p. 12.
31. According to the polls in spring 1992, the voters were leaving the Labour Party because of the EC issue. See, e.g., *Aftenposten* 7/3 (1992).

# 'Programa 2000': The Appearance and Reality of Socialist Renewal in Spain

## RICHARD GILLESPIE

*Spain's experience of programmatic renewal was unusual in that it began in a period of unprecedented political success for the Socialist Party, the PSOE. The latter invested considerable resources in the renewal process, yet its programmatic outcome was disappointing. Its interest lies chiefly in what it reveals about the internal politics of the PSOE. Although some socialists sought to provide future strategic orientation for the PSOE, the whole process was overshadowed by factional rivalry within the party. This power struggle conditioned the whole debate about renewal, whose programmatic value became even more questionable in 1991 following a government reorganisation.*

In several respects Spain was an unlikely venue for socialist programmatic renewal in the mid-late 1980s. The long history of the Spanish Socialist Workers' Party (PSOE), stretching back over 100 years, had been largely barren of renewal, let alone ideological innovation and discussion.[1] A party that had experienced prolonged adversity under authoritarian rule, in a country which had known very few years of open representative democracy before the 1970s, had traditionally defended a set of fundamentalist programmatic ideas of Marxian derivation, and had seen pragmatic departures from them as strictly tactical. Some renewal occurred in the 1970s as the PSOE responded to, first, the possibility, and then, the reality, of Spain's transition to democracy, but the very proximity of this process was likely to reduce the pressures for further renewal in the 1980s.

Certainly, throughout the rest of southern Europe – where to differing degrees renewal processes were a feature of the late 1970s – the renovation of socialism had lost all momentum by 1983. Socialist parties emerged from renewal exercises much more pragmatic, and with undisputed leaders who were aware that further programmatic debate might constrain their room for manoeuvre in negotiations with existing or potential coalition partners. Having jettisoned Marxism and placed or confirmed charismatic leaders in positions of supreme authority, unhampered by internal party democracy,[2] none of the other southern parties showed an active interest in the mid-late 1980s European process of programmatic renewal.

Nor did the PSOE's landslide electoral victory in October 1982 augur well for programmatic renewal in Spain. Although recent Scandinavian experience shows that social democratic parties may engage in programmatic renewal while in office, a rather more common European pattern has been for renewal to be addressed when parties are in opposition, as a means of restoring a party's 'electability'. In Spain, not only has the PSOE been wedded to office since 1982: its electoral success has been so impressive that some observers have speculated about the possible emergence of a Sartori-type 'predominant' party system.[3]

Why then did the PSOE break with its own historical tradition and the southern European pattern, and in spite of its pre-eminent position in the Spanish party system, produce *Programa 2000*, supposedly as a programme to guide Spain's Socialists through the 1990s and into the next century?

There were various reasons and influences, both historical and contemporary, national and international. First, it is worth pointing out that, although the PSOE has never made an important ideological or programmatic contribution to the international socialist movement (and, conversely, the movement showed little interest in Spain before the 1930s), Spanish Socialists are acutely aware of this fact. Indeed, they have something of an inferiority complex in this respect,[4] which possibly helps explain the party's desire to join in the 1980s European renewal process, in the hope of belatedly acquiring an international standing.

Moreover, although party renewal was a recent experience for the PSOE, it is significant that the González leadership had emerged through that earlier process, with *renovación* as its programme and battle standard. In the early 1970s, the party's *renovadores* had finally overcome the resistance presented by the gerontocratic leadership around Rodolfo Llopis, whose outlook was still shaped decisively by the experiences of the Spanish Civil War.[5] The renewal current was a broad coalition that ranged from revolutionary Trotskyists to former Christian Democrats, but the eventual effect of its triumph was to provide the party with a younger, more dynamic leadership, whose radical rhetoric did not in fact prevent the party from becoming more pragmatic. The visceral anti-communism of the old party gave way to a readiness to ally with all the other anti-Franco forces, including the Spanish Communist Party (PCE); the PSOE's lingering 'catastrophist' perspective on the future of capitalism was replaced by recognition of the recent dynamism of the Spanish capitalist economy; and before long the party would recognise that reform elements within the regime had a positive role to play in the dismantlement,of Francoism.

Later in the decade, a debate that was supposedly about whether to retain the historical commitment to Marxism in the party programme was in fact less directly concerned with ideology than it was with turning the PSOE into a 'catch-all' party, by giving it a more moderate image and nullifying rank and file influence. From two congresses held in 1979, the party emerged with a uniform executive, devoid of left wingers, and dominated by the Andalusian duo Felipe González and Alfonso Guerra.[6]

It is important to note too that historically, even if more insular than several European socialist parties, in the national context the PSOE has been 'the least typically Spanish, the most European of Spanish parties',[7] Europe having served as a key source of ideas and models for the party. Prior to the 1940s, this 'Europeanism' did not translate into strong practical links with sister parties in Europe, but thereafter the Spanish socialist exile of the Franco years helped bring about closer inter-party relations, which the PSOE later capitalised upon during Spain's transition to democracy. The need for solidarity led the Spanish party to join the new Socialist International in 1951 and to subscribe to its original Frankfurt programme, notwithstanding its own more radical programme.

Since the 1960s, the PSOE's identification of national progress and modernisation with Europe has been reinforced by the crucial role of foreign investment in Spain's economic development and European Community support for Spanish democratisation. The new PSOE leadership that emerged during the 1970s was a product of a new university-educated generation of socialists that had been profoundly affected by these trends. It is no surprise then that the González leadership's interest in 1980s renewal was driven by international motives, besides domestic ones, perhaps to a greater extent than in the case of any other European party. Identifying Spain's modernisation with the breaking down of international barriers, the Socialist leadership saw Spanish participation in the European renewal debate as a way of raising the PSOE's profile abroad, and making the wealthier northern countries' socialist parties take their southern counterpart more seriously. Spain's socialists have strong nationalistic ambitions, their chief aspiration being for Spain to catch up with the stronger European economies during the next few decades.

González himself has regularly reminded his party of the importance of renewal,[8] and it may be that there is an element of personal ambition behind his desire for the PSOE to play an active role in European discussions. Since 1982 he has always played a direct role in the development of Spain's external relations and it has been suggested that one of his ambitions is to preside over the Socialist International, although he himself has tried to quash such speculation.

Domestic factors also help account for Spanish participation in the renewal process. Electoral considerations are in fact quite important. In spite of being a governing party, the PSOE has been able to contemplate what some parties would regard as the 'luxury' of programmatic renewal because of the extremely comfortable electoral lead it has enjoyed since 1982 over its nearest rival, the right-wing *Partido Popular* (formerly *Alianza Popular*). With a lead of almost 20 percentage points when renewal was first mooted in the mid-1980s, and communist rivals to the left taking years to recover from the PCE's electoral disaster of 1982, the PSOE had the opportunity to discuss its programme without being preoccupied with a need to outbid other parties.

TABLE 1
SHARE OF THE VOTE IN SPANISH GENERAL ELECTIONS (%)

|        | 1977  | 1979  | 1982  | 1986  | 1989  |
|--------|-------|-------|-------|-------|-------|
| PSOE   | 29.3  | 30.5  | 48.4  | 44.4  | 39.6  |
| AP/PP  | 8.3   | 6.0   | 26.2  | 26.1  | 25.8  |
| UCD    | 34.6  | 35.0  | 7.1   | –     | –     |
| CDS    | –     | –     | 2.9   | 9.3   | 7.9   |
| PCE/IU | 9.4   | 10.7  | 4.1   | 4.7   | 9.0   |
| CiU    | 2.8   | 2.7   | 2.7   | 5.0   | 5.0   |
| PNV    | 1.7   | 1.6   | 1.9   | 1.5   | 1.2   |
| Others | 13.9  | 13.5  | 6.7   | 9.0   | 11.5  |
| Total  | 100.0 | 100.0 | 100.0 | 100.0 | 100.0 |

Only towards the end of the Spanish renewal process were there unequivocal signs that the PSOE might lose its absolute majority in parliament, but from as early as 1986 there was growing party concern about the gradual descent of the Socialist vote from the pinnacle of 1982. The reduced vote in the 1986 general election was hardly enough to worry them, but subsequent elections and opinion polls suggested that the Socialists' control of parliament might soon become dependent upon co-operation with other parties, unless some initiative were taken

TABLE 2

NUMBER OF SEATS WON BY MAIN SPANISH PARTIES IN GENERAL ELECTIONS,
1977–89 (CONGRESS OF DEPUTIES)

|        | 1977 | 1979 | 1982 | 1986 | 1989 |
|--------|------|------|------|------|------|
| PSOE   | 118  | 120  | 202  | 184  | 175  |
| AP/PP  | 16   | 9    | 106  | 105  | 107  |
| UCD    | 164  | 168  | 12   | –    | –    |
| CDS    | –    | –    | 2    | 19   | 14   |
| PCE/IU | 20   | 23   | 4    | 7    | 17   |
| CiU    | 11   | 8    | 8    | 17   | 18   |
| PNV    | 8    | 7    | 8    | 6    | 5    |
| Others | 13   | 15   | 8    | 12   | 14   |
| Total  | 350  | 350  | 350  | 350  | 350  |

Key: PSOE: Spanish Socialist Workers' Party; AP: Popular Alliance, launched
PP: Popular Party 1989; UCD: Union of the Democratic Centre, dissolved
1983; CDS: Social and Democratic Centre, based on part of former UCD:
PCE: Communist Party of Spain, launched IU: United Left 1986; CiU:
Convergence and Unity (Catalan nationalist alliance); PNV: Basque
Nationalist Party (suffered split in 1986).

Sources: The data in both tables are based upon Anuario El País 1987 and
Anuario El País 1990.

to bring about a PSOE revival. One of the ambitions behind renewal
was to find policies and strategies that would make the party hegemonic
for the foreseeable future; in this sense Programa 2000 was an attempt
to consolidate the support of a majority of the Spanish electorate around
the PSOE.[9]

Equally, it was a product of the concern felt in broad sections of the
party about the neo-liberal drift of government policy, which some
Socialists felt was alienating the 'progressive' vote. In the economic
sphere González's government adopted tough monetarist policies
which, although they eventually produced impressive growth rates, also
led to the worst unemployment situation in Europe and frustrated hopes
of a reduction in social inequality. Meanwhile, Spanish foreign policy
also swung to the right, as signalled by the party U-turn over NATO.[10]
Among party intellectuals there were hopes that a process of programmatic renewal might redirect the government back to social democratic
norms, and restrain the drift into neo-liberalism and 'Atlanticism'.

The close relationship between the PSOE and the intelligentsia is extremely relevant to the renewal process. The universities had been centres of open anti-Francoism from 1956 onwards and although the Socialist Party organisationally had been notoriously weak on the campuses during the Franco era, radical academics had rushed to join the PSOE in the mid-late 1970s. Since then, university academics have played an important role in the development of party strategy and ideology. Various journals linked to the PSOE, such as *Leviatán*, *Zona Abierta* and *Sistema*, have allowed intellectuals to develop theoretical arguments, while in contrast the party press (*El Socialista*) has limited the input of ordinary party members to correspondence columns not noted for their heterodoxy. Since the mid-1970s a group of sociologists headed by José Félix Tezanos has played an influential role in interpreting public opinion and the changes in Spanish society, and has influenced PSOE responses to them. Equally, the role of economists and technocrats has grown since the party's accession to office in 1982. No fewer than 28 per cent of the party parliamentary group elected in that year were educators and the 17 ministers appointed by González had 25 university degrees between them, including six doctorates.[11]

The prominent presence of so many intellectuals helped maintain the party's ideological concerns during a decade that saw the PSOE in office transported a long way from conventional socialist policies by the country's critical economic condition in the early 1980s and the party's own determination to consolidate its hold on Spain's political centre. The intellectuals' presence has produced resistance to the pragmatic-technocratic drift that has occurred under the influential presence of neo-liberals in the cabinet, led by the successive finance ministers Miguel Boyer and Carlos Solchaga.

The role of the intellectuals would probably be less significant if González were as omnipotent within the PSOE as Andreas Papandreou has been within the Panhellenic Socialist Movement (PASOK) in Greece or Bettino Craxi in the (since renamed) Italian Socialist Party (PSI). During the 1980s, however, the Spanish party's internal power structure was characterised more by diarchy than by autocracy. Since the days of his early political activism in a Young Socialist group at Seville, González had formed a political partnership with fellow Andalusian Alfonso Guerra, who in the 1980s went on to serve simultaneously as deputy prime minister and as deputy leader of the PSOE. Even before 1982, González had been far less concerned with party organisation than Guerra, the head of the PSOE 'apparatus', but governmental responsibility made a power-sharing arrangement between the two men even more necessary. Guerra had always been involved more than González in organising election campaigns and managing party congresses, and in 1982–91 his power was greatly enhanced because the post of deputy prime minister enabled him to become a governmental 'filter', influencing the matters that were brought before González. This arrangement helped ensure a margin – albeit very limited – of internal party pluralism, even though formally González headed both the cabinet and party.

It is not merely a personal relationship that is at stake here. There has been sporadic political tension between the cabinet and the party executive since 1985, culminating in a serious rift in the early 1990s. The neo-liberal economic policies of the government, while not opposed in principle by the 'Guerristas' (Guerra and his protégés), have been constrained by *guerrista* resistance from within the party. This resistance has come from the electorally-minded party managers because unpopular economic policies have lost votes for the party and have alienated former labour supporters; and also because the technocrats have periodically gone onto the offensive, seeking to replace *guerristas* in key positions. In 1985 Miguel Boyer failed in a bid to become deputy prime minister and in 1990 his successor Carlos Solchaga tried, again unsuccessfully, to have liberal ministers elected onto the party executive.

As part of their efforts to frustrate the ambitions of the technocrats, the *guerristas* have recognised the advantage to be gained from mounting an ideological offensive against their rivals. In this sense, *Programa 2000* can be seen as a product of the party's factional struggles. Although considered 'populist' by many of their critics, the *guerristas* have had an interest in promoting ideological and programmatic discussion because they realise that what the technocrats stand for is not easily defensible in terms of socialist values. Moreover, given that programmatic renewal has been a European phenomenon, *Programa 2000* would be used by the *guerristas* to enlist international support for a renewal process which they themselves always controlled, and in this way to isolate their liberal ministerial rivals further.

The fact that the Spanish political system is more decentralised than the Portuguese or the Greek systems has also facilitated a modicum of debate in the PSOE. The existence of regional governments controlling substantial resources has led to the emergence of certain regional 'barons' in the Spanish party, who on a few rare occasions have acted in concert to impose their will on González and Guerra. Debate has been facilitated moreover by the existence of a strong, closely related but autonomous socialist labour confederation, the General Workers' Union (UGT). With substantially overlapping memberships and histories of close collaboration, the PSOE and UGT began the period of

Socialist government as close allies, but from 1985 they moved towards confrontation, chiefly due to the effects of government economic policies. Although few party members publicly declared any sympathy for the UGT (for fear of shortening their own political careers), there appear to have been greater numbers who *sotto voce* pleaded for the government to offer more to labour in the hope of reunifying the 'Socialist Family'.[12]

All this is not to suggest that the PSOE power structure is markedly polycentric: just that it is sufficiently so for there to be occasional internal disagreements and discussions. These existed in the 1980s over Spain's membership of NATO and over the deteriorating relationship between the party and the UGT, although they were muffled by the effects of strong party discipline and a traditional distaste for airing differences in public (a legacy from years of confronting authoritarian regimes).

Thus the PSOE in the mid-1980s had both some structural prerequisites for a renewal process and multiple motives to proceed to one. Above and beyond the broader desire of socialist parties for self-renewal in response to recent social developments, the peculiarly domestic motives in the Spanish case were: the *guerrista* factional motive; a widespread wish to reaffirm the party's social democratic credentials because of government deviations to the right; and the party leadership's ambition for both the PSOE and Spain to join the European big league.

THE INITIATIVE

The initiative for the 1980s renewal in the PSOE dates from September 1985 when, two years before the official debate was organised, Alfonso Guerra began to hold a series of annual conclaves involving some 35–50 socialist politicians and intellectuals in the attractive Valencian coastal town of Jávea. The participants, whose average age was below 40, included the man subsequently designated as coordinator of *Programa 2000*, Manuel Escudero, and the social scientists Tezanos and Elías Díaz, who subsequently edited Editorial Sistema's series of books based on these meetings.[13] Among the major intellectual concerns of the participants were how to manage the economic crisis of the period and move forward to some type of economic democracy; how to develop an alliance with the new social movements; and how to ensure the introduction of a welfare state in Spain.[14] The declared intention was to stimulate debate about the future of socialism, to show the need for the theoretical renewal of socialism in view of social changes that had made some traditional socialist conceptions anachronistic, and to meet the challenge posed by the impact of neo-conservative ideas.[15]

Around the same time, Escudero and others were influenced by the precedent set by the Socialist Party of Austria (SPÖ), which had drawn up a long-term programme, *Perspectiven-90*, designed to provide strategic guidance for the party in the 1990s. Their proposal quickly won the sponsorship of Alfonso Guerra.[16]

There is no reason to doubt the presence of either a genuine renewal motive or a desire for long-term strategic orientation within the Spanish party. However, these were undoubtedly accompanied by more factional motives. The raising of theoretical issues, which had programmatic implications, came just at the moment when tensions between the *guerristas* and the government technocrats were generating a power struggle within the cabinet, with González serving as arbiter. Meanwhile the UGT was beginning to show its disenchantment with government policy after two years of monetarist measures and industrial restructuring that had brought unemployment to peak at virtually three million.[17] Those who gathered in Jávea included some fairly independent-minded socialist academics, such as Ramón García Cotarelo (who later became marginalised from the renewal process) but the majority could be described as 'the young guard of Alfonso Guerra'.[18]

Almost entirely excluded were the handful of social democrats in the government, including the Education Minister and former university professor, José María Maravall, who had written extensively on party strategy and the sociology of Spanish Socialism, and was an ideological influence upon González. Just as striking was the absence of the party's weak left-wing current, *Izquierda Socialista*, and of the neo-liberal government figures. The outcome was a delicate balancing act: while direct criticism of the government was studiously avoided, the intellectuals who gathered at Jávea did present a theoretical critique of liberal economic ideas.[19] Thus no serious account of the motives behind *Programa 2000* could ignore the battle for power between different currents within the PSOE, especially the central conflict between *guerristas* and economic liberals.

THE PROCESS OF RENEWAL

Following the predominantly intellectual initiation of the debate in 1985, the party's official renewal process was authorised by the party executive in October 1986 and launched the following year. The commission entrusted with overseeing the process was exclusively *guerrista* in composition.[20] By now, however, the emphasis was upon involving the public, rather than private discussions among selected guests at an attractive holiday resort (although these gatherings continued to take place on an annual basis). The announced ambition was to involve no fewer than one million 'progressive' Spaniards, in addition to PSOE members, in a debate that would generate 10,000 proposals.[21]

However, intellectuals continued to play a key role in developing the debate since it was from their ranks that were drawn the 200 'collaborators' who drafted the duplicated materials upon which the debate was initially based: no fewer than 15 volumes containing 120 studies of social, economic and political topics, which were presented to González in December 1987.[22] The Jávea group predominated within the teams of economists, sociologists and political scientists that co-ordinated the work of the collaborators. The studies were designed to analyse aspects of contemporary Spanish reality so that the forthcoming party debate would have a massive amount of information upon which to base a discussion about future strategy. There were seven volumes on the economy, six on sociology and only two dealing with political problems (this bias reflecting Escudero's personal contacts, as an economist, and the underdevelopment of political science in Spain).[23]

After the sanctioning of the debate at the 31st Congress of the PSOE in January 1988, a series of four books was published,[24] synthesising the contents of the preceding duplicated volumes and isolating relevant topics for debate. Accompanying them were a whole host of pamphlets concentrating on specific policy areas, such as health, pensions, youth, the administration of justice, and so on. Debates were organised both within the party and beyond it. A network of 60 debating centres was established in major cities throughout the country and a total of 66 regional and provincial co-ordinators and 5,742 local, zonal and sectoral organisers of *Programa 2000* were appointed. In most provinces, 'groups of collaborators' – involving party and non-party members – were established, and special training courses were organised by the party for them. To promote discussion, 'Committees in Support of *Programa 2000*' were also set up to try and incorporate progressive elements at provincial level. Meanwhile the number of experts consulted grew to 800. By August 1988 no fewer than 10,600 debates had been held on *Programa 2000*, involving 593,500 participants: 42 per cent of them at meetings of PSOE branches and 58 per cent at public meetings or joint meetings, according to party figures.[25] These participants drafted almost 60,000 proposals which were used as a basis for the next phase: drafting a manifesto which would then be similarly debated widely prior to its revision and final discussion by a party conference or congress.

By the time that the first draft of the *Manifiesto* was presented to the public in January 1990, events in Central and Eastern Europe had brought the communist movement into crisis and thus raised new issues for those socialist parties, like the Spanish, that faced significant competition from a communist party. The debate on *Programa 2000* was quite well advanced by this time, and although the *Manifiesto* draft was supposedly to be modified during 1990 in response to debate, its ideas on how to respond to the crisis of communism were no doubt heavily influenced by the views of members of the *Programa 2000* Commission. They were in charge of preparing the initial draft and then, following further debate within and beyond the party, producing the second draft which was endorsed by the party executive in June 1990 and which then went to the 32nd PSOE Congress the following November. There, some 1,198 amendments were considered by two congress commissions, one dealing with ideological questions, the other with political strategy. Thereafter the ideological part of the text was approved by the congress on a 99.76 per cent vote (one abstention) while the strategic part received unanimous endorsement.[26]

THE EUROPEAN DIMENSION

Parallel to this process there were regular exchanges with other socialist parties. There were discussions on programmatic change with the Austrian, German, Dutch, British, French, Portuguese, Italian, Swedish and Norwegian parties, and the studies of international questions benefited from internal seminars involving economists from the USA, Italy, Portugal, France, Britain, Germany and Scandinavia.[27]

During the renewal exercise the PSOE maintained a high profile within the Socialist International. González personally presided over the commission that drafted the International's new *Declaration of Principles*, approved in June 1989 to replace the 1951 document. The Spaniards also took the lead in publishing the new journal supported by the International, *El Socialismo del Futuro*, which promised to involve prestigious political and academic figures and encourage debate between different currents of socialist thought. The Spanish edition of the journal (published by Editorial Sistema) appeared first, ahead of planned German, French, English, Italian, Portuguese and Russian editions. Its presentation in March 1990 enabled the PSOE leaders to assemble Acchille Occhetto, Michel Rocard, Claudio Martelli, Adam Schaff, Regis Debray and (Gorbachev adviser) Vadim Zagladin in Madrid, Oskar Lafontaine having come 10 months earlier for the announcement of the launch plans and to present Editorial Sistema's

Spanish edition of his book, *The Society of the Future*.[28]

It is not easy to determine the extent of external influence upon the Spanish debate. PSOE sources emphasise that their debate was essentially Spanish-oriented. Although the *concept* of the renewal exercise – to produce a 'programme' to guide the party for at least the next decade – came from Austria, the *content* of *Programa 2000* owed very little to the SPÖ: Neither was there a strong British influence. Programme coordinator Escudero was very well informed about Labour Party developments, having been in contact with the British party while studying for his doctorate in Economics at the London School of Economics; he was thus well aware of the differences between the two parties' situations (dissimilar relationships with trade unions and intellectuals, the existence of a communist rival in Spain, and so on).

Probably the main point of reference for the Spaniards was the German SPD. The PSOE certainly took a great interest in the SPD process, which ran a few months ahead of the Spanish one. Along with Holland, Austria and France, Germany was one of four countries cited by Guerra as a place supposedly experiencing a similar programmatic process, when the PSOE's draft Manifesto was presented in January 1990.[29] Guerra and Lafontaine were leading figures in the editorial team of *El Socialismo del Futuro* and even participated in a joint PSOE-SPD meeting at Barcelona in September 1990 to debate socio-economic programmes for the 1990s, shortly after the SPD's new programme had been approved at the Münster congress. On that occasion, both parties defended the idea of socialist party autonomy *vis-à-vis* trade unions in elaborating socio-economic policy in order to acquire broader popular support even if this meant clashes with the unions.[30] Both parties had been strongly criticised by trade unionists, who themselves had joined forces internationally to criticise the direction of party policy and to campaign jointly over the Social Charter.

However, one should be wary of making too much of the Spanish-German relationship: *Programa 2000* certainly echoed the SPD's concerns about adapting economic growth to the needs of environmental protection, but this was less of a preoccupation in Spain. There, the expression of ecological concern served the *guerristas* as useful ammunition in their battle against the neo-liberals, with their emphasis upon growth and competitiveness, but both sectors of the PSOE are committed to closing the developmental gap in Europe and have argued against the poorer countries having to meet the same environmental standards as the wealthier ones. Moreover, it is arguable that by the 1980s, reversing the political juxtaposition of the early 1970s, the PSOE stood to the right of the SPD.

It is also the case that the SPD and PSOE have adopted rather different responses to Acchille Occhetto's calls for a new European Left. While the SPD had been engaged in a constructive dialogue with the Italian Communist Party (PCI) for several years (notwithstanding the feelings of Craxi's Socialists), the PSOE at first denounced Occhetto's unitary calls as a manoeuvre designed to besiege the Italian Socialist Party (PSI), which the Spaniards defended by sending a high-level delegation to its congress in May 1989. While the German and some other European socialist parties recognised the PCI as part of the European democratic left even before Occhetto became its leader, the Spanish and Italian socialists argued that the reunification of the left could happen only if the communist parties were to repent their sins and heresies and return to their mother parties as prodigals.[31]

Later, once the abandonment of the communist tradition by Occhetto seemed more definite, he was presented by the Spanish Socialists as the star of the European left summit in Madrid in March 1990, but in circumstances indicating that the PSOE line had not changed. Spanish Communist Party leader Julio Anguita was not invited to the presentation of the new international journal, *El Socialismo del Futuro*, while pro-PSOE former PCE leaders such as Santiago Carrillo and Enrique Curiel were among the guests.[32] Curiel and almost 200 other pro-Occhetto former communists joined the PSOE in October 1990, on the eve of the latter's 32nd Congress. Carrillo's 800-strong Spanish Workers' Party (PTE) dissolved itself into the PSOE the following February.

### THE SIGNIFICANCE OF *PROGRAMA 2000*

The document produced at the end of the PSOE renewal exercise was a manifesto rather than a programme.[33] The emphasis was thus upon general principles rather than specific commitments, although a few policy recommendations were introduced during the 32nd Congress. The most important shift announced in the Manifesto was the PSOE abandoning its self-definition as some kind of workers' party, although it retained the name of the Spanish Socialist Workers' Party. Signalling the party's overwhelming electoralism, democratic socialism was presented as a project capable of attracting a majority of the citizenry, and as an autonomous project, independent of any social class, sector or movement. And to underline the shift, a reform of the party statutes made it no longer 'obligatory' for PSOE members to join the UGT and stipulated that, if they did so, they had to defend the party line therein (that is, even if party policy clashed with UGT policy).

As an exercise in programmatic renewal, *Programa 2000* must be considered a disappointment. For the most part the *Manifesto* restated traditional democratic socialist values and made only very vague references to new concerns (the environment, left unity). Virtually none of the concrete proposals were new.[34] The quality of the product suffered from the ulterior motives of the *guerristas* in initiating the process: to the extent that it had factional purposes and was under *guerrista* auspices, *Programa 2000* was unlikely to produce a fruitful debate. From start to finish the party's left and liberal elements played only peripheral roles.

The process none the less graphically illustrates the limited degree of democracy and pluralism within the PSOE, and the party's internal tensions at this time. The 'debate' in Spain was managed so successfully by the *guerristas* that hardly any sounds of discord were heard. If debate involves arguments and controversies, then there was scarcely any debate in Spain, in a party governed in the 1980s by Guerra's law: 'If anyone makes a move, they will not appear in the photo'. Even in the words of programme co-ordinator, Manuel Escudero, the 'debate' was characterised by 'enrichment rather than controversy'.[35] Despite the large number of people involved, the nature of the process always left the initiative with its initiators: any individual or group was free to submit proposals to the commission but no votes were taken on the documents at any public meeting or branch meeting of the party, and a case for federalism presented by the Catalan Socialists was simply ignored.

Only in the final stages did some internal criticism emerge. Culture Minister Jorge Semprún pointed to the Manifesto's lack of analysis of the market economy, claimed that the new programme was out of date before it was even approved, and averred that programmatic renewal was impossible without prior 'renewal' of the 'Leninist-type' party apparatus. The *guerrista* response – which flew in the face of the proselytising character of *Programa 2000* – was to remind people that the ex-Communist Semprún was not a member of the PSOE.[36] Criticism also came from the PSOE's left-wing current, *Izquierda Socialista*. Its leading figure, Antonio García Santesmases, found the 'new internationalism' theme of the Manifesto evocative of the more idealistic PSOE of the 1970s, but questioned whether it was not just rhetoric of the kind that had not prevented the PSOE from supporting NATO in the 1980s. He was opposed to the party directing its appeal at the whole of society, at the expense of links with unions and new social movements: 'A socialism without trade unions leads to electoralism, inter-classism and de-ideologization, and a governmental socialism without the sustenance of the social left will never transform the values of eco-pacifism into reality.'[37]

At the culminating 32nd Congress, the modifications made to the draft *Manifiesto* were mainly refinements, embellishments and stylistic improvements. The few truly political amendments tended to make the document more conservative. Removed from the draft document were specific commitments to co-operatives and to job security (including a proposal to convert temporary jobs into permanent ones). Both texts referred to the 'possibility' of creating company investment funds but the final version stressed that this should be by agreement with management; it omitted a reference to union participation in the proposed funds' administration, although 'worker participation' was mentioned. Brought into the final text were recognition of the need to study the inadequacies of the current abortion legislation, support for a reduction in the length of military service, more extensive discussion of environmental problems, and some new paragraphs on the problems of the countryside (where the PSOE vote has risen in recent years).

The congress confirmed the weakness of the party's dissident minorities. The executive report received unanimous support and the Federal Committee report 93.69 per cent, the remaining abstentions indicating the maximum voting strength of the left. All the resolutions, including those relating to *Programa 2000*, received at least 99 per cent of the votes. Rather than try proposing a global alternative to the Manifesto, the left concentrated just on an amendment urging a more definite commitment to investment funds, but this was rejected overwhelmingly by the congress. One of the keys to such unity was that two-thirds of the delegates were public office holders, dependent on the party leadership for their careers. González's opening speech was in no way apologetic about this situation: indeed, he urged the party to work to ensure that the remaining delegates also became office holders during the 1990s.[38]

Thus the renewal exercise did not involve a great debate within the party. This was bound to cast doubt upon the declared intention to 'open the party to society' and to involve progressive sectors of the public in the debate. Although the political resolution of the 32nd congress declared the PSOE to be a 'plural party',[39] neither this nor the ambition to become a common home for the Spanish left were facilitated by the largely monochrome nature of the congress and the left's complete exclusion from the party's representative bodies. Stage management of the congress reached the extreme of excluding all television cameras other than those of the PSOE's own film crew, in order to control the images of the congress presented to the public.[40]

In terms of its aim of involving new sectors of society with the party,

*Programa 2000* may be considered only a partial success. It did not fulfil the original objective of involving one million people in addition to party members. The final total of 950,000 people having participated in 14,900 debates, half internal, half external, falls significantly short of this target.[41] Moreover, these are cumulative totals that ignore the fact that the public was involved in two stages of the process, both in examining the discussion documents and the draft Manifesto. Given that the party membership at the time of the 32nd congress was 262,835,[42] it is likely that the real number of non-party participants was no more than a quarter of a million. Some of these people may have been put off by the lack of controversy, and some participants pulled out when their proposals were ignored. None the less, this still represents a significant number of people to have been drawn into the orbit of the PSOE.

Equally, while most groupings of the left, including the Communist-led *Izquierda Unida*, found nothing attractive in *Programa 2000*, it did play a part in bringing Curiel's 'Italians' into the PSOE; their experience will be observed with great interest by the Catalan Communists, traditionally the most pro-PCI sector of Spanish Communism. Although Curiel and his colleagues did not play an organised role in the renewal process, the reiteration of some traditional democratic socialist ideas by the PSOE (support for the welfare state, references to equality and solidarity) helped reassure these ex-communists that the PSOE was resistant to the neo-liberalism associated with certain government ministers and party technocrats. They also considered that the *Manifiesto* was more 'internationalist' than the liberals would have liked.[43]

Intrinsically the product of the renewal exercise was disappointing enough but circumstances towards the end of the process also conspired to minimise its programmatic effect. The attempt to produce a document of long-term strategic significance was overtaken by events that left the PSOE much more concerned with the immediate future. The latter half of 1989 saw a decline in the Spanish economy, a major haemorrhage of votes for the PSOE in industrial working-class areas (following the general strike in December 1988), and the collapse of communist regimes in Eastern Europe. The first two of these events greatly exacerbated internal conflict between neo-liberal ministers and *guerristas* in the PSOE, with the former pressing for unpopular economic measures designed to prepare the economy for stiffer competition in 1993, and the latter favouring concessions to the unions in order to counteract the fall in working-class support. This conflict made it necessary to hold the 32nd Congress early, which deprived *Programa 2000* of a conference exclusively devoted to programmatic debate, and it ensured that the congress would be dominated by a power struggle rather than discussion of the *Manifiesto*. The crucial issue was whether Finance Minister Solchaga would be successful in getting some liberal ministers onto an expanded party executive: a move thwarted by the *guerristas*.

Since that congress, the balance of power in the PSOE has shifted somewhat in the direction of the liberals. Guerra's resignation from the government in January 1991 was followed by a reshuffle in which the *guerristas* ended up with only secondary portfolios while Solchaga emerged as a super-minister with authority over all ministries concerned with the economy. Three main factors led González to dispense with Guerra's services (after previously insisting that he would resign himself if Guerra did): growing public pressure for Guerra's resignation because of the central involvement of his brother Juan in a major corruption scandal; an ever more pressing need to make the economy more competitive as the single European market drew nearer; and the paralysing effect of liberal-*guerrista* rivalry on the work of the government during 1990.[44] However, the *guerristas* remained in control of the party executive and the Socialist Parliamentary Group and were thus a formidable obstacle to the goverment's economic plans at the start of the new decade. This may explain why González began once more to issue calls for party renewal, as if the recent manifesto were a dead letter.[45]

Thus *Programa 2000*, about which very little has been heard since the party's 32nd Congress, appears to have been stillborn: if its inception owed partly to party factionalism, the outcome of that conflict seems to have denied it any marked influence upon socialist policy-making.

The crisis of communism helps explain why the end product was so vague and non-committal. González has argued that socialists must be flexible if they, rather than the right, are to reap the benefits from this crisis. 'Flexibility has been the key to the response of democratic socialism' to events in the Soviet Union, he maintained, at the presentation of the draft manifesto.[46] Equally, flexibility has been defended by González in his capacity as prime minister, rejecting party constraints upon government decision-making. He has made it clear that *Programa 2000* is not the programme of his government and he placed the decisions of the 32nd Congress in perspective when he told delegates that he presided over the government of Spain, not the government of the party: 'Government is in Moncloa, not in Ferraz' (the party headquarters).[47]

Whether *Programa 2000* will have any significant influence upon the government is thus doubtful. Its main immediate effects were to strengthen *guerrista* control over the party (but crucially, not over the government) and to establish a modest network of sympathisers around the PSOE, which may serve as a basis for future gradual growth. It was always less important programmatically than strategically. The only new departure, already heralded in practice by Socialist leadership behaviour was to assert the autonomy of the PSOE project and the ambition to base this on an electoral majority, rather than anchor it to predetermined social sectors such as the labour movement. Yet this will make programmatic flexibility even more important in the future. So too will the attrition of the PSOE vote, which may force the Socialists to reach an agreement with another party if they wish to govern beyond 1993. Ironically, the purported programmatic renewal in Spain in the late 1980s resulted in a downgrading of the party programme, at least as a guide to the behaviour of socialists in government.

## NOTES

The author wishes to thank the Research and Innovations Sub-Committee of the University of Warwick for funding a research visit to Madrid in September 1990, and Benny Pollack for helpful comments on the initial draft.

1. Paul Heywood, *Marxism and the Failure of Organised Socialism in Spain (1879–1936)* (Oxford: OUP, 1990); Richard Gillespie, *The Spanish Socialist Party* (Oxford: Clarendon Press, 1989), Ch. 1; *Estudios de Historia Social* (Madrid, Instituto de Estudios de Sanidad y Seguridad Social), No. 8–9 (1979).
2. R. Gillespie and T. Gallagher, 'Democracy and Authority in the Socialist Parties of Southern Europe', in T. Gallagher and A.M. Williams (eds.), *Southern European Socialism* (Manchester: Manchester UP, 1989).
3. David Walker, 'Towards a Predominant Party System? Spain since 1977', Strathclyde Papers on Government and Politics, No. 65 (1989); cf. R. Gillespie, 'Regime Consolidation in Spain: Party, State, and Society', in Geoffrey Pridham (ed.), *Securing Democracy: Political Parties and Democratic Consolidation in Southern Europe* (London: Routledge, 1990), pp. 137–9.
4. For evidence of this, see, e.g., Felipe González, speech at 31st Congress of PSOE, 22–24 Jan. 1988, *El Socialista* (Madrid), 446 (1988).
5. Carlos and José Martínez Cobo, *La segunda renovación* (Barcelona: Plaza & Janés, 1991); Gillespie (note 1), Ch. 4.
6. Gillespie (note 1), Ch. 4; E. Nash, 'The Spanish Socialist Party since Franco: From Clandestinity to Government, 1976–82', in D.S. Bell (ed.), *Democratic Politics in Spain* (London: Pinter, 1983).
7. J.J. Linz, *El sistema de partidos en España* (Madrid: Narcea, 1979), p. 89.
8. See, e.g., his public pronouncements reported in *El Socialista* 446 (31 Jan. 1988), 486 (30 Sept. 1989) and 494 (31 Jan. 1990). His support for renovation is also in evidence in his introduction to the Spanish edition of Peter Glotz, *Manifiesto por una nueva Europa* (Madrid: Editorial Pablo Iglesias and Siglo XXI, 1987).
9. *El Socialista* 514 (30 Nov. 1990), p. 13.
10. Donald Share, *Dilemmas of Social Democracy: The Spanish Socialist Workers Party in the 1980s* (Westport, CT: Greenwood, 1989), Chs.4–6; R. Gillespie, 'Spanish Socialism in the 1980s', in Gallagher and Williams (eds.), (note 2); Gillespie, 'Spain's Referendum on NATO', *West European Politics* 9/4 (Oct. 1986), pp. 238–44.
11. PSOE, *Hacia el cambio . . . 100 días de gobierno* (Madrid: PSOE, 1983), *passim*.
12. R. Gillespie, 'The Break-up of the "Socialist Family": Party-Union Relations in Spain, 1982–89', *West European Politics* 13/1 (Jan. 1990), pp. 47–62.
13. For the revised Jávea discussion papers, see A. Guerra *et al.*, *El futuro del socialismo* (Madrid: Editorial Sistema, 1986), *Nuevos horizontes teóricos para el socialismo*

(Sistema, 1987) and *El nuevo compromiso europeo* (Sistema, 1987).

14. Personal interview with Manuel Escudero, federal co-ordinator of *Programa 2000*, Madrid, 26 Sept. 1990.
15. Ibid.
16. Ibid.
17. Gillespie, 'Break-up of the "Socialist Family" ' (note 12).
18. *El Independiente* (Madrid), 4 Nov. 1988.
19. *El País* (Madrid), int'l ed., 12 Jan. 1987.
20. The membership of the commission was Alfonso Guerra (president), José María Benegas, Francisco Fernández Marugán, Salvador Clotas, José Félix Tezanos, Roberto Dorado and Manuel Escudero.
21. *El Socialista*, 429 (15 May 1987); PSOE, *Programa 2000* (pamphlet), 1987, p. 6.
22. *El Socialista*, 441 (31 Dec. 1987).
23. Details of how the PSOE debate was organised are to be found in PSOE, *Programa 2000* (note 21). The 15 volumes of studies can be consulted at the Fundación Pablo Iglesias in Madrid.
24. PSOE, Comisión del Programa 2000, *Aspectos y problemas de la vida política española; La sociedad española en transformación: Escenarios para el año 2000; Evolución y crisis de la ideología de izquierdas*; and *La economía española a debate* (Madrid: Editorial Pablo Iglesias 1988; 2nd ed. co-published with Siglo XXI, 1988).
25. *El Socialista* 483/4 (1–31 Aug. 1989) and 503 (16 June 1990).
26. Ibid., 513 (15 Nov. 1990); *El País*, int'l ed., 5 Nov. 1990.
27. *El Socialista* 510 (30 Sept. 1990).
28. Ibid., 478 (31 May 1989) and 498 (31 March 1990). The first issue of *El Socialismo del Futuro* (1990) contained articles by Gorbachev, Brandt, Guerra, Lafontaine, Adam Schaff, Fernando Claudín, Ernest Mandel, Giorgio Napolitano, José F. Tezanos, Luciano Pellicani, Ulf Himmelstrand and Andrzej Werblan. Publication was to be on a biannual basis with No. 2 appearing in Madrid in Nov. 1990 and carrying papers from the Jávea meeting of 1989.
29. *El Socialista* 494 (31 Jan. 1990).
30. Reported in *El País* int'l ed., 12 Sept. 1990.
31. *El Independiente*, 12 May 1989.
32. *El País*, int'l ed., 26 March 1990.
33. For the complete text, see *El Socialista* 514 (30 Nov. 1990).
34. For a fuller discussion of *El Manifiesto del Programa 2000*, see R. Gillespie, *Socialist Programmatic Renewal in Spain*, Univ. of Warwick, Working Paper No. 104 (April 1992), pp. 16–20.
35. Personal interview with Escudero, 26 Sept. 1990.
36. *El País*, int'l ed., 23 July 1990, 30 July 1990, 22 Oct. 1990.
37. Antonio García Santesmases, 'El mosquito y el elefante', *Leviatán* (Madrid), 39 (1990), p. 127.
38. *El Socialista* 513 (15 Nov. 1990). The *Manifiesto del Programa 2000* was later published as a book with introductions by Willy Brandt, Felipe González and Alfonso Guerra (Madrid: Editorial Sistema, 1991). In his, González describes his government as having carried out the greatest process of economic liberalisation that our country has known'. See the review in *El Socialista* 525 (15 May 1991).
39. Ibid.
40. Ignacio Sotelo, 'Morir de éxito', *El País*, int'l ed., 26 Nov. 1990.
41. *El Socialista* 510 (30 Sept. 1990). This issue also gives details of the number of copies of each *Programa 2000* publication that were produced.
42. Ibid., 513 (15 Nov. 1990).
43. Personal interview with Enrique Curiel, Madrid, 27 Sept. 1990.
44. *El País*, int'l ed., 17 Dec. 1990, 7 Jan. 1991.
45. Ibid., 1 July 1991.
46. *El Socialista*, 494 (31 Jan. 1990).
47. Ibid., 513 (15 Nov. 1990); *El Independiente*, 17 Feb. 1989.

# Reconstructing Dutch Social Democracy

## STEVEN B. WOLINETZ

*Programmatic and organisational reviews are an effort to distance the Dutch Labour Party (PvdA) from styles and postures assumed in the 1970s. Current efforts were stimulated by the economic situation, the failure of the polarisation strategy and exclusion from power. Reports generated after the 1986 elections resulted in changes in strategy and the style and content of the 1989 election manifesto. A report published in 1991 urged changes in party organisation and the ways in which programmatic issues were considered. A central thrust has been to re-establish the PvdA as a moderate but influential force.*

Like many of its counterparts, the Dutch Labour Party (PvdA)[1] found itself compelled to re-examine its policies in the 1980s. However, programmatic review has differed from experiences elsewhere. At issue were not only previous positions but also strategy, organisation and internal political culture. During an initial phase from 1986 to 1989, the PvdA generated a series of reports that resulted in changes in both strategy and tactics and the tone and content of the party's election manifesto.[2] However, the process did not end there. In 1991 and 1992 the Dutch party found itself considering a further report on organisation and programmes.

The PvdA's preoccupation with organisational questions recalls an earlier period of renewal. In the late 1960s and early 1970s the PvdA underwent a series of changes which altered its internal politics and external posture. Power shifted to younger activists who zealously scrutinised the actions of leaders, and the party assumed a harder line *vis-à-vis* prospective coalition partners. By the mid-1980s party members were increasingly doubtful about such practices. Programmatic and organisational reviews were attempts to come to terms not only with the intellectual problem of what social democrats could accomplish in the 1990s but also the postures of the 1970s and early 1980s.

### BACKGROUND AND CONTEXT

Changes in the strategy, style and posture of the PvdA in the late 1960s and early 1970s form a backdrop for programmatic and organisational reviews in the 1980s. Before 1967 the PvdA had been a regular, if not always content, participant in coalition politics. Reorientation was a facet of broader changes in the party system. Reacting to declining support and the pressures of New Left, a faction which appeared in 1967, and to the opportunities presented by a changing party system on the other, the PvdA recast itself as a more radical and aggressive political force.[3]

At the insistence of New Left, party rules were modified to give greater influence to members. 'Organised mistrust' of leaders became a regular feature of PvdA internal life. Congresses became participatory events in which members of the caucus and party executive had no greater voice than ordinary delegates. The new ethos shifted power to those who could speak well and had more time to attend meetings – typically younger, better-educated members of the middle classes – and encouraged an influx of new members.[4]

External postures changed as well. The PvdA characterised itself as a 'party in action' and adopted the polarisation strategy. Emphasising differences between itself and other parties served multiple purposes: maximising electoral strength by forcing voters who wanted progressive policies to opt for the PvdA or one of its allies;[5] increasing PvdA influence in coalition formations; dividing the Protestant and Catholic parties and preventing the formation of a single interconfessional party; building a more adversarial party system. Before elections the PvdA specified the conditions under which it would enter cabinets in order to gain greater leverage afterwards. Initially this meant no coalitions with the Catholic Party, but in 1971 and 1972 this was restated as a demand that parties should declare with whom and on what terms they were willing to govern. Later variants demanded fixed distributions of portfolios or excluded certain parties.[6]

The programmatic and ideological influence of New Left was less direct. Rather than imposing a new synthesis, New Left and others who entered in their aftermath made themselves felt by opening up the party to a broader range of perspectives. Previous habits of systematic analysis were submerged. Instead, the views expressed in party programmes became more diverse and heterodox, and changes occurred in the ways in which positions were held and used.[7] Rather than serving as guides to action in a multi-party system, party programmes functioned as statements of activists' commitments and devices through which leaders and coalition partners might be controlled.[8] This took on a new dimension when the PvdA's statement of principles was rewritten in 1977: in order to assess how far and for what reasons compromises had been made, election manifestos were to be drafted using the same headings employed in the statement of principles.[9]

Changes in positions resulted not from a direct reversal of previous stances but rather from a slow accretion of demands. In foreign policy, the PvdA gave greater emphasis to north-south relations, expressed doubts about NATO, and later opposed deployment of cruise missiles. In domestic policy, existing commitments were broadened to include the democratisation of economic and social institutions, environmental concerns, and women's issues. However, less attention was devoted to the translation of goals into well-integrated programmes. Instead, PvdA manifestos became more detailed. Party gatherings were taken up with minute discussions of programmes and the ways in which they should be changed. Proposed amendments to the 1977 programme occupied a thick A4 size booklet, 430 double column pages in length; the programme itself ran to 94 pages. In 1986 a total of 4,125 amendments were submitted.[10] Declaratory statements beginning 'Er Komt' (There will be) left little room for analysis or explanation.

The new moods spilled over into a revised statement of principles. The 1946 and 1959 formulations committed the PvdA to a 'just order for labour'. Private enterprise was acceptable so long as it served the public interest.[11] In contrast, the 1977 version combined elements of feminism and anti-capitalism and committed socialists to a new domestic and international economic order. The aim of democratic socialism was not to promote reforms in a capitalist society, but rather to produce a democratic and socialist society that would be different from existing capitalist and state socialist societies.[12]

This new ethos altered the character of the PvdA. In the 1950s and early 1960s the PvdA had been known for the quality and expertise of its representatives. The PvdA was pragmatic and realistic about what could be achieved. In the 1970s the PvdA espoused a variant of socialism that was different not so much in content, but rather in style and posture, and it lacked obvious priorities. If the socialism of the 1950s and 1960s was known for its realism and sense of limits, the socialism of the 1970s was a socialism of all things possible.

THE 1980S

Reorientation enabled the PvdA to rejuvenate itself and recover from the electoral decline of the 1960s (see Table 1). Nevertheless, by the 1980s the PvdA had to come to terms with a different set of problems: rising unemployment and economic stagnation; the failure of the polarisation strategy; and the coming together of a centre-right policy coalition committed to austerity and market-led recovery.

PvdA policies in the 1970s had been predicated on the assumption that the economy could sustain an expanded public sector. However, as early as 1975 a PvdA-led cabinet was forced to limit the annual growth of the public sector to one per cent of national income. Industrial employment declined in the 1970s. By 1981–82 the Dutch were faced with stagnant growth, mounting deficits and an unemployment rate approaching 12 per cent.[13]

PvdA difficulties were compounded by the failure of the polarisation strategy. In 1972–73 the PvdA and its allies were able to divide the confessional parties and secure the formation of the left-of-centre den Uyl cabinet. However, in part because of PvdA actions, the Protestant and Catholic parties came together in the Christian Democratic Appeal (CDA). Christian Democratic support stabilised at 29–35 per cent of the popular vote, allowing the CDA to resume the pivotal position that the three confessional parties had previously enjoyed. As in the pre-1967 party system, the PvdA's ability to govern depended on the predilections of the confessionals. Overbidding by the PvdA in 1977 resulted in the formation of a Christian Democratic-Liberal cabinet. Four years later the lack of a centre-right majority permitted the PvdA to return to government. However, disagreements on job creation led to a breakup in 1982, new elections and the formation of a Christian Democratic-Liberal cabinet under CDA parliamentary leader Ruud Lubbers. Although its vote in elections between 1972 and 1986 ranged between 27.3 and 33.8 per cent, the PvdA was able to govern for only five years between the adoption of the polarisation strategy in 1969 and its replacement in 1989.

The exclusion of the PvdA meant that it fell to centre-right governments to cope with the economic crisis. In contrast to the previous centre-right governments, the first and second Lubbers cabinets implemented austerity measures. The indexation of public sector salaries and benefits to private sector wages was suspended in 1982 and public sector salaries were cut by three per cent in 1983. Annual budgets were trimmed to reduce deficits.

The PvdA responded more quickly to the economic situation than to its political position. The PvdA argued for reductions in working hours and the creation of part-time jobs as solutions to structural unemployment. By 1986 the party had developed detailed plans for job sharing and job creation.[14] Nevertheless, the PvdA found it difficult to abandon previous strategies and tactics. Radical visions continued to be articulated by some members of the party executive, including the party chairman, Max van den Berg. Although the polarisation strategy was

TABLE 1

PERCENTAGE OF THE VOTE RECEIVED BY THE MAJOR PARTIES, 1946–89

| | PvdA | D'66 | KVP | ARP | CHU | VVD[a] |
|------|------|------|------|------|------|------|
| 1946 | 28.3 | | 30.8 | 12.9 | 7.8 | 6.4 |
| 1948 | 25.6 | | 31.0 | 13.2 | 9.2 | 7.9 |
| 1952 | 29.0 | | 28.7 | 11.3 | 8.9 | 8.8 |
| 1956 | 32.7 | | 31.7 | 9.9 | 8.4 | 8.8 |
| 1959 | 30.4 | | 31.6 | 9.4 | 8.1 | 12.2 |
| 1963 | 28.0 | | 31.9 | 8.7 | 8.6 | 10.3 |
| 1967 | 23.6 | 4.5 | 26.5 | 9.9 | 8.1 | 10.7 |
| 1971 | 24.6 | 6.8 | 21.8 | 8.6 | 6.3 | 10.3 |
| 1972 | 27.3 | 4.2 | 17.7 | 8.8 | 4.8 | 14.4 |
| | | | CDA[b] | | | |
| 1977 | 33.8 | 5.4 | 31.9 | | | 17.9 |
| 1981 | 28.3 | 11.1 | 30.8 | | | 17.3 |
| 1982 | 30.4 | 4.3 | 29.4 | | | 23.1 |
| 1986 | 33.3 | 6.1 | 34.6 | | | 17.4 |
| 1989 | 31.9 | 7.9 | 35.3 | | | 14.6 |

a. In 1946, the Party of Freedom
b. Formed by the merger of the KVP, ARP, and CHU

*Source*: H. Daalder and C. Schuyt (eds.) *Compendium voor Politiek en Samenleving* (Houten: Bohn Stafleu Van Loghum, 1991), pp. A1300–27.

formally abandoned in 1982 (in the sense that the PvdA no longer advanced strict criteria for its participation in cabinets), the PvdA seized the cruise missile issue as a device to rally support and divide the Christian Democrats.[15]

The 1986 elections were a turning point. The PvdA made its defence of the welfare state and opposition to deployment of cruise missiles central features of its campaign and urged voters to deprive the Christian Democrats and Liberals of their majority. The PvdA won 33.3 per cent of the popular vote and an additional five seats but was unable to prevent Christian Democrats and Liberals from forming a second Lubbers cabinet. Defeat amid victory – ten seats had been predicted earlier – encouraged rethinking. Questions had been raised about the wisdom of current strategy and tactics throughout the 1970s and early 1980s. The sceptics now gained the upper hand. Although there was a tendency to attribute the outcome to factors specific to the 1986 campaign, separate commissions were established to review the operation of the party organisation, programmes, and strategy and tactics.[16]

## THE INITIAL PHASE: 1986-89

Programmatic and organisational review has been an extended process. One can distinguish an earlier phase from 1986 to 1989, in which problems were defined, alternatives explored and some changes made and a later but still incomplete phase in which the PvdA returned to programmatic and organisational issues.

The first phase was taken up with the reports prepared after the 1986 elections. The commission on party organisation (the Middel commission) reported in October 1987. *Politiek à la Carte in Plaats van Politiek as Dagschotel* (Politics à la Carte instead of Politics as a Main Dish) was a short document, critical of the party's internal culture and ethos. The party was overly preoccupied with the definition of programmes and the control of elected representatives and had failed to build contacts outside the party. Advisory channels were stagnant. Links between local, regional and national organs were confused, hindering democratic control. Neither national nor regional party organs provided services to local sections. Rules and procedures were excessively complicated and the party was dominated by a *vergadercultuur* (meeting culture) which discouraged participation. The Middel commission recommended reducing the number of meetings, providing more services for party sections and re-examining the tasks of regional organisations and the party council.[17]

The Commission on Programmatic Renewal (the Pronk Commission) issued its report in November 1988. *Schuivende Panelen* (Sliding Panels) was a book-length working paper intended to focus the programmatic debate. The report reconsidered social democratic positions in the light of social, economic and political changes. In the introductory chapter, themes developed in previous reports are examined and the goal of 'guaranteeing a high standard of living in its broadest sense', which was central to the 1963 report by the party's research bureau, *Om de Kwaliteit van het Bestaan* (On the Quality of Existence), is reasserted. However, it is recognised that the ways in which these and other goals can be pursued have been altered by the internationalisation of the economy and culture, technological change, threats to the environment, demographic changes and growing individualism.[18]

Successive chapters stress the need to balance conflicting goals and develop policies that have some chance of being implemented. The idea of a new international economic order is rejected in favour of balanced reductions in forces and a gradual transfer of competences to international organisations. In the chapter on cultural policy, the emphasis has shifted from imposing an egalitarian or solidaristic culture to ensuring equality of opportunity and individual choice. The chapter on social welfare insists on a link between employment and work rather than a right to income. The latter, it is argued, would reinforce divisions between active and non-active portions of the population.[19]

The chapter on political order acknowledges elements of neo-conservative and new left critiques of the state: the more the state becomes involved in society, the more it becomes entangled with it and remote from those whom it governs. Entanglement occurs because the state becomes surrounded by the interests which it seeks to regulate and is unable to move without their consent. The solution is to limit the tasks assigned to the state so that the state can act more effectively when it is engaged and to decentralise tasks to lower levels more amenable to popular control.[20]

The chapter on the economy examines the limits of previous strategies and argues for increased emphasis on markets and planning. In the past, socialists relied on five basic tools, socialisation, the collectivisation of demand, redistribution, planning and regulation, but none of these can be used in its original form. Socialisation is rejected out of hand and demand management is ineffective in open economies. Nor is it possible to rely on economic growth to achieve a broader distribution of wealth or to restrict growth to protect the environment. Instead, measures to promote environmentally-desirable growth are needed; the state should collectivise demand for a cleaner environment and improved infrastructure. Government should be involved in areas where market demand is weak, but intervention is to be with rather than against the market. More planning does not mean targeting segments of the economy but rather planning for environmental and social needs.[21]

The report also proposes a shift in competences to international organisations and the involvement of organised interests in policy-processes:

> The possibility of the Dutch government carrying out an independent economic policy is not only limited by the internationalisation of the economy, but also by the increased complexity of economic interrelationships and by the increasingly strong position of market partners: business, banks and other financial institutions, employees organisations, public sector interest groups and the like. If the government wants to steer, regulate, order or plan, that

cannot be done without these organisations, over their heads, but only with their consent.[22]

The Pronk report concludes with a plea for a new style of thinking. Simple answers are inadequate for complex questions, and finding solutions is not only a matter of taking positions but also acquiring power. The options raised:

> have the character of a durable balance. In political terms that inevitably translates into a compromise, albeit one which cannot be permitted to block further progress. Not only is this more ambitious and effective than bearing witness or acting on one's own, but it also demands more creativity. It is a matter of creatively combining ambitious aims and an effective use of small margins.[23]

The third report, *Bewogen Beweging: Sociaal-democratie als program en methode* (Moved Movement: Social Democracy as Programme and Method) dealt with strategy and tactics. Prepared by a committee that included party leader Wim Kok, *Moved Movement* incorporated both the criticisms of *Politics à la carte* (the Middel report) and the social analyses of *Sliding Panels* (the Pronk report) into a plea for a more conciliatory and extroverted strategy and more open party organisation. The report is critical of the ways in which programmatic commitments have been turned into non-negotiable demands. The polarisation strategy has kept the PvdA from governing by eliminating prospective partners and making it easier for others to exclude the PvdA, the document maintains. Non-negotiable demands have also made the position of the PvdA within cabinets untenable. The PvdA has narrowed its options by failing to encourage progressive elements in other parties. Social democracy is a method in which ideas are tested against practice, but opposition provides little opportunity to do so. The PvdA must recast itself as a governing party willing to make compromises and more open to social trends and developments.[24]

INTERIM OUTCOMES

Together, the three documents provided the PvdA with a basis for revamping the programme and organisation. *Sliding Panels* was debated in party sections and publications in spring 1988. Surprisingly, in view of PvdA 1970s thinking, its conclusions elicited little opposition. Pim Fortuyn and Siep Stuurman's *Socialisten in no nonsense tijd* (Socialists in

No-Nonsense Time) offered a different point of view, but its publication paralleled rather than followed the Pronk report.[25] Even if silence could be taken to mean acceptance, translating the three reports into tangible changes was another matter. Both the Middel report and *Moved Movement* urged changes in PvdA organisation and practices, but neither contained specific recommendations on how these were to be achieved. In their absence, the task of bringing about change fell to the party executive, which did little to promote organisational change. *Sliding Panels* had been intended to focus debate rather than supply answers. Conclusions from an continuing discussion were to be used as a basis for the 1990 election manifesto. However, this process was cut short by the party executive's decisions to summarise the outcome of discussions in a report (which finally appeared in January 1989)[26] and by the fall of the Lubbers government in a few months later, precipitating early elections in September. This left little time to discuss the election manifesto.

Under the circumstances, the extent of change depended very much on the predilections of the party leader and those around him. Wim Kok, who had succeeded Joop den Uyl after the 1986 elections, pressed for changes in some areas but not in others. Thus, the polarisation strategy was definitively abandoned, a more conciliatory posture was assumed in the election campaign, and efforts were made to demonstrate that the PvdA could match the fiscal rectitude of the Liberals and the Christian Democrats. Efforts were also made during the 1989 campaign to reach out to a broader range of groups and learn from them.

The 1989 manifesto, *Kiezen voor Kwaliteit* (Vote for Quality), provides a measure of the extent of change. *Vote for Quality* is more conciliatory than its predecessors. Instead of advocating a complete change of direction, it stresses the correction of imbalances and building on economic recovery. Centre-right cabinets have focused on the operation of markets but failed to make improvements in infrastructure or the delivery of services. Government should promote economic expansion but ensure that its benefits are more widely shared. Deepening cleavages need to be bridged by renewed solidarity, not only between those who work and recipients of benefits but also present and future generations. Reflecting *Sliding Panels*, there are repeated calls for balance, durable change and greater consensus. There is also explicit recognition of the limits of government action and the need to reduce deficits.

In addition, the format is different: the 1989 manifesto is a cross between the detailed election programmes of the past and the focus on major themes which some had desired. Major sections begin with broader thematic analyses but tail off into lists of demands. However, these are fewer in number than in previous manifestos.[27]

Because of the circumstances in which it was drafted, the 1989 manifesto did not reflect the internal balance of power in a party engaged in debate but rather implicit compromises struck by a party leader and others anxious not to stir controversy. Changes in positions, and more particularly, in style and posture enabled the PvdA to return to government in a centre-left coalition under CDA leader Ruud Lubbers. However, programmatic and organisational renewal remained incomplete. Little had been done about the organisational problems signalled in the Middel report and *Moved Movement* or the process through which programmes were formulated. Both were the subject of a later stage of programmatic and organisational review.

THE SECOND PHASE: RETURN TO THE BROADER PROJECT

Had the PvdA's return to government been wholly successful questions of programmatic and organisational renewal might have been forgotten. However, the PvdA had joined a cabinet committed both to 'social renewal' (meaning social reform) and further reduction of the deficit. PvdA leader Wim Kok assumed the finance portfolio. The need to maintain budget discipline raised doubts about whether PvdA influence was sufficiently visible in the cabinet. Sagging support – particularly the anticipated setbacks in the 1990 municipal elections – set the stage for a second phase of the discussion. At the behest of party chairman, Marianne Sint, a further commission was entrusted with proposing concrete means by which the changes proposed in earlier reports could be implemented. Chaired by J.A. van Kemenade, Minister of Education in the den Uyl cabinet and Mayor of the city of Eindhoven, the commission covered the same terrain as the Middel commission but probed much deeper. Not only organisational but also programmatic issues were considered.

The van Kemenade commission reported in July 1991. Like the Middel commission, it criticised the introverted character of the PvdA, the high thresholds for participation which the party demanded, and the functioning of the extra-parliamentary organisation. *Een Partij om te Kiezen* (A Party to Vote For) considers the internal life and organisation of the PvdA in the light of changes in Dutch society and politics. Dutch social democracy had originated as a mass movement but it was no longer possible to sustain a mass party in an individualistic society. Previous loyalties and identifications had become blurred. Recasting the PvdA as a more participatory party in the 1970s had resulted not in a party more open to society but one more isolated from it. Complicated decision-making procedures and long meetings resulted in high thresholds for participation and domination by in-groups. The PvdA indulged in extended discussions of election programmes but programmatic discussion tended to be ritualised and repetitive. Recruitment procedures were stagnant: rather than serving as a link between state and society, elected representatives were drawn from the same narrow stratum of active members.[28]

Changes in operation and internal norms were needed. The report recommended extensive changes in party structure (reorganisation around governmental units, the abolition of the party council, drastic reductions in the size of the party congress), more open recruitment procedures (e.g., wider searches for candidates), and a continuing process of programmatic discussion. The quadrennial redrafting of election manifestos was to be replaced by annual congresses which would debate specific themes on the basis of reports by the party's research bureau; these would be incorporated into shorter, more thematically focused election programmes.[29]

The van Kemenade commission also commented on the changing content of social democratic ideology. Social democracy began as a movement opposed to the state, but soon concerned itself with using state power to bring about change. The PvdA is closely identified with the welfare state but this is increasingly problematic, the commission felt. The state is being asked to cut back and continue functioning at the same time, and the PvdA is forced into a defensive posture, which weakens its capacity to mobilise. As the state has assumed more tasks, it has become more fragmented and bureaucratic. The current problem is to maintain control over an internally divided and sometimes intrusive state. Doing so requires detachment from the state and an integrated view of how it can be controlled.[30]

The van Kemenade report asks the PvdA to reconsider both whom it represents and the core elements of social democratic thinking. The original target group, the report argues, was the working class and later organised labour. However, the identity and solidarity of the working class have become blurred and the PvdA instead characterises itself as the representative of the weak and those left behind by the economic system. This reverses the previous identification with those who work and fails to recognise that most PvdA supporters benefit from the existing economic order. Earlier commitments to nationalisation have been replaced by acceptance of the market as a mechanism for increasing wealth, and by state intervention and social insurance to ensure fairer distribution of wealth and opportunities. Nevertheless, the myth of socialisation haunts the party and sets an unrealistic standard against which policies are measured. The core element of social democracy has been neither socialisation nor the defence of any particular group but rather ensuring effective citizenship. If the PvdA wishes to play an influential role in Dutch politics, it must find new ways to give content to that notion.[31]

The van Kemenade report draws explicit connections between organisation and procedure and party programmes, proposes specific remedies, and indicates directions that the PvdA should follow in revising programmes and ultimately the party's statement of principles. The intent is to modify the ways in which programmatic issues are considered (broad thematic debates instead of morselised argument on details), diversify the kinds of candidates recruited, and alter the operating style of the party. Its recommendations were to be debated at the March 1992 congress. Even if adopted, they were not likely to produce immediate results. Instead, the aim was to set processes in motion that would end in a reconstruction of Dutch social democracy.

ANALYSIS AND PROSPECTS

The idea of open-ended processes of programmatic and organisational review differs considerably from previous conceptions in the PvdA or its predecessor, the SDAP. Prior to the 1970s major restatements of party programmes had been guided by party leaders, working closely with intellectuals who justified and explained positions. Change in the 1970s reflected the pressures of New Left and others who entered the party in its wake; revision of the party's statement of principles took place with little assistance from party leader den Uyl, who disowned the result.[32]

The current process is different yet again. Party intellectuals have played a major role in defining alternatives and suggesting directions, but the leadership has for the most part remained in the background. Rather than leaders imposing directions, academic arguments are used to give credence to proposed changes, not only in programmes but also in the ways in which they are formulated. Reasserting a pragmatic and realistic mode of analysis has been a central concern.

The concern with process, organisation, and ultimately internal ethos and political culture, represents an effort to come to terms with previous processes of renewal and change. A central goal has been re-establishing the PvdA as a moderate force, able to influence the direction of policy. Doing so has involved introspection and analysis. Lengthy reports have been mooted, analysing social, economic and political trends, the evolution of social democracy, and the changing role of parties in society. Internal practices have been targets of extended criticism. This protracted process has generated neither sharp debate and reaction, nor for that matter much action. Instead, the PvdA resembles patients who are instructed by their physician to change their life style, acknowledge the diagnosis, but go on living as before.

The absence of debate may seem surprising in view of the prescription and the earlier transformation of the PvdA. However, the PvdA had lost its radical edge. Party members were older. Former radicals had been pushed aside or faded into the woodwork. Others had changed their views or recognised the limitations of previous tactics. What remained were the practices and reflexes of the previous decade and after long periods in opposition, a desire to govern.

In addition, divisive positions had been avoided. Following the first round of reports, the party leadership opted for positions different in style and content but not necessarily controversial. Whether this will continue to be so is another matter. The release of the van Kemenade report coincided with a cabinet decision to reduce sickness benefits and long-term disability payments. Endorsed by PvdA ministers, this decision sparked far greater controversy and internal haemorrhaging than any of the reports discussed here. Although a special party congress endorsed the ministers' position, party members found the PvdA's support for cuts difficult to accept. Numerous resignations followed. The raw wounds that were opened suggest that change in the PvdA's defence of the welfare state will be controversial.

Where then is the process of programmatic and organisational renewal going? In the absence of systematic debate in which one can assess the strength of opposing positions it is difficult to say. Thus far, the process has been guided by party intellectuals with a definite point of view, but party leaders have remained on the sidelines. Whether this will continue to be the case is questionable. The PvdA vote declined to 24.8 per cent in the 1990 municipal elections and 20.4 per cent in 1991 provincial elections and for a time the PvdA ranked fourth in opinion polls behind both the Liberals and Democrats '66.[33] The need to reverse such trends may force the PvdA to confront issues that might otherwise be avoided.

*Postscript*

At its congress in March 1992 the PvdA adopted many of the organisational changes that were recommended in the Kemenade report, including abolishing the party council and restructing the party congress. Whether these will result in programmatic changes and the desired rejuvenation of the party remains to be seen.

## NOTES

1. The formal name of the Dutch social democratic party is *Partij van de Arbeid* or Labour Party. However, its adherents are commonly referred to as socialists. The Labour Party succeeded the pre-war Social Democratic Workers Party (SDAP) in 1946. The terms socialist and social democratic are often used interchangeably in the Netherlands.
2. Like many Dutch parties, the PvdA makes a distinction between its election programme (*Verkiezingsprogamma*), revised at every election, and its statement of principles (*Beginselprogramma*). We will refer to the former as the election manifesto and the latter as the statement of principles.
3. Steven B. Wolinetz, 'The Dutch Labour Party: A Social Democratic Party in Transition' in W. Paterson and A. Thomas (eds.), *Social Democratic Parties in Western Europe* (London: Croom Helm, 1977), pp. 342–59. See also Wolinetz, 'The Netherlands: Continuity and Change in a Fragmented Party System' in Wolinetz (ed.), *Parties and Party Systems in Liberal Democracies* (London: Routledge, 1988), pp. 141–55 and Bart Tromp, 'Party Strategies and System Change in The Netherlands', *West European Politics* 12/4 (Oct. 1989), pp. 82–97.
4. Wolinetz, 'Dutch Labour Party', pp. 359–60. On the background of party members see among others Bert Middel and Wijbrant H. van Schuur, 'Dutch Party Delegates', *Acta Politica* XVI/16 (1981), pp. 241–63.
5. In 1971 and 1972 the PvdA formed an electoral alliance with Democrats '66 (D'66) and the Radical Political Party (PPR).
6. Tromp (note 3), pp. 92–4. Philip van Praag, Jr., *Strategie en Illusie: Elf jaar intern debate in de PvdA (1966–1977)*, diss., Univ. of Amsterdam (Amsterdam: Het Spinhuis, 1991), pp. 347–68.
7. New Left had no clearcut doctrine or ideology and was primarily concerned with gaining influence. Earlier successes encouraged further turnover and internal diversification. See van Praag, pp. 375–84.
8. Paul Kalma and Marnix Krop, 'Het program als fetisj: Twintig jaar oppositiecultuur in de Partij van de Arbeid', *Socialisme en Democratie* 43/9 (Sept. 1986), pp. 271–3.
9. Bart Tromp, 'Beginselprogramma: noodzaak en onmogelijkheid', *ibid.*, 47/4 (April 1990), p. 105.
10. *Beschrijvingsbrief voor het buitengewoon kongress te houden op 27, 28, en 29 januari 1977* (Amsterdam: PvdA, 1977). *Voorwaarts: Het verkiezingsprogramma van de Partij van de Arbeid voor de Tweede Kamerverkiezingen op 25 mei 1977* (Amsterdam: Partij van de Arbeid, 1977). M.L. Zielonka-Goei, *Uitzicht op de Toekomst: De totstandkoming van verkiezingsprogrammas voor de Tweede Kamerverkiezingen van 1986*, diss., Univ. of Leiden (Delft: Euborn Uitgeverij, 1987), p. 50.
11. *Beginselprogram 1959* van de Partij van de Arbeid, sections I. 1c; IV. 28, 29, contained in *Kompas* (Amsterdam: Partij van de Arbeid, 1959), pp. 7, 13.
12. *Platform of Principles* (Amsterdam: Partij van de Arbeid, 1977), section IV. 1, p. 29. English trans. by J. Rudge.
13. OECD, *OECD Economic Surveys 1986/1987: Netherlands* (Paris: OECD, 1987), p. 12.
14. See J.A.M. van Kemenade, J.J.M. Ritzen and M.A.M. Woltgens, *Om een Werkbare toekomst: Aanzetten tot een middellange termijn beleid, gericht op volledige werkgelegenheid en economisch herstel* (Rapport Tweede Kamer Fractie PvdA, 1986); *Werk Maken: Technologische en Sociale Vernieuwing van de Economische Structuur* (Amsterdam: Partij van de Arbeid, 1986), and *Werk Delen: De Noodzaak van een Verdere Verdeling van Arbeid* (Amsterdam: Partij van de Arbeid, 1986).
15. Tromp, 'Party Strategies' (note 3), pp. 93–4.
16. See the PvdA's election post-mortem, 'Evaluatie Verkiezingen 1986' (Partij van de Arbeid internal report, 1986), which was in fact moderately critical of the strategy used.

17. *Politiek à la Carte in Plaats van Politiek as Dagschotel* (mimeo: Partij van de Arbeid, 1987), pp. 4–17.
18. Commissie Programmatische Vernieuwingen, *Schuivende Panelen: Continuiteit en vernieuwing in de sociaal-democrati* (Amsterdam: Partij van de Arbeid, 1987), pp. 20–21, 24–57.
19. Ibid., pp. 107–11, 127–29ff, 161–71.
20. Ibid., pp. 155–60.
21. Ibid., pp. 70–74, 77–80, 93–98.
22. Ibid., pp. 102–3.
23. Ibid., p. 191.
24. Partij van de Arbeid, *Bewogen Beweging: Sociaal-democratie als program en methode* (Amsterdam: Partij van de Arbeid, 1988), pp. 65–68, 70–71, 87–90ff.
25. Pim Fortuyn and Siep Stuurman (eds.), *Socialisten in no nonsense tijd* (Nijmegen: SUN, 1987).
26. Partij van de Arbeid, *Om de Kwaliteit van de Toekomst* (Amsterdam: Partij van de Arbeid, 1989).
27. Partij van de Arbeid, *Kiezen voor Kwaliteit: PvdA Verkiezingsprogamma* (Amsterdam: Partij van de Arbeid, 1989), pp. 1–4ff.
28. Partij van de Arbeid, *Een Partij Om te Kiezen* (Amsterdam: Partij van de Arbeid, 1991), Pt. II, pp. 26–31.
29. Ibid., Pt. I, pp. 6–10.
30. Ibid., Pt. II, pp. 12–16.
31. Ibid., Pt. II, pp. 17–19.
32. Tromp, 'Beginselprogramma', p. 105.
33. *Keesings Historisch Archief*, Vol. 60 (March 1990), p. 120; ibid., Vol. 61 (March 1991), p. 147.

# Towards Renewal? The British Labour Party's Policy Review

## ERIC SHAW

*This contribution explores the process of programmatic renewal in the British Labour Party from 1987 to 1991, the so-called Policy Review. It considers the mechanics of the review, the key programmatic changes that occurred and the main factors shaping the process. It concludes that a substantial overhaul of policy took place, but queries whether this constituted 'programmatic renewal'. It briefly considers Labour's future programmatic orientation in the wake of a fourth successive election defeat.*

A year ago – indeed an hour after the polling booths closed on 9 April 1992 – the Labour Party could contemplate the task of putting into effect the programme to whose formulation it had devoted immense effort since 1987. At the last moment, the cup was dashed from its lips and more long years in the wilderness now beckon. Whether the programme so assiduously constructed in the preceding years will be revised is a question to which we will return in the conclusion.

The wheel had turned full circle – for the effort at programmatic renewal (the Policy Review) had been borne out of the bitter ashes of defeat. In 1983 a strife-torn party that was ineptly led had suffered a stunning débâcle. Four years later the smooth and much-acclaimed professionalism of Labour's campaign had not spared it another crushing defeat. Nothing short of a thorough-going and sweeping reappraisal of its programme was required, party leaders concluded, if it were to become electable again: hence the Policy Review.

This study will, first, examine the mechanics of the Policy Review, then explore the nature of programmatic change and the factors that shaped its course, and then finally briefly consider Labour's options for the future in the wake of a fourth, devastating, repulse at the polls.

### THE MECHANICS OF THE POLICY REVIEW

The Policy Review was set in motion in autumn 1987 and was extremely ambitious in scope. Seven Policy Review Groups (henceforth PRGs) were established with very broad remits covering all aspects of policy.

The procedure used built upon the practice of joint National Executive Committee (NEC)-Shadow Cabinet policy-making first instituted in 1983. Each PRG was headed by two co-convenors, one from the NEC, the other from the Shadow Cabinet. The groups consisted of seven to nine members, drawn from the two sponsoring bodies and topped up with senior trade unionists – a format designed to lock in co-operation from the three main institutional units constituting the party. The work of the various PRGs was co-ordinated by the Campaign Management Team composed of senior party officials and politicians. In general, the relationship between frontbenchers and their aides on the one hand, and the NEC and Walworth Road (party headquarters) on the other was much more amicable than in earlier years.

The PRGs relied heavily on assistance from outside experts drawn mainly from the academic world and, to a lesser degree, from the unions. These experts fell into two categories: a small inner circle of advisers who were fully immersed in the work of the PRGs and a much more numerous outer circle. The members of this outer circle partici-pated in a more *ad hoc* fashion in the Policy Review process, being commissioned to write papers, attend seminars on specific topics or join study groups. The newly established (in 1988) Institute of Public Policy Research (a pro-Labour think tank) played an important role in funnel-ling ideas to the Policy Review. (One of its senior researchers, Patricia Hewitt, a former senior Kinnock aide, was particularly influential). Party officials also exerted a degree of influence including Head Office researchers (most notably Geoff Bish, the party's Director of Policy), frontbench political advisers and senior members of the leader's office. PRGs were also urged to learn from the experience of sister parties in Europe,[1] although in practice much depended on the interests and contacts of individual members.

For a mixture of internal party and electoral reasons, Labour was keen 'to ensure that the women's perspective (was) fully covered.'[2] A Women's Monitoring Group (containing all the women members of the PRGs) was established (and later upgraded after opinion research in 1989 indicated that Labour was failing to attract women supporters) and was authorised to check that women's needs were taken fully into account by all PRGs.[3]

A deliberate effort was made to adjust policy to bring it more into line with prevailing public attitudes. Digests of quantitative data were pro-duced by the Party's Political Intelligence Officer and most PRGs received presentations from the Shadow Communications Agency which specialises in qualitative research. Communications professionals within the Shadow Agency also advised on public responses to the presentation and – in effect – the content of policy. Peter Mandelson, the party's influential Director of Campaigns and Communications (until 1990) ensured that their findings reached the highest levels. Although the agency's precise influence is a matter of some dispute and difficult to compute since its advice tended to point in the same direction as the leadership wished to move, it was undoubtably considerable.

Another mechanism was employed to narrow the gap between the party and public opinion, the 'Labour Listens' project. Initially, it was accorded a significance almost equal to that of the Policy Review itself – Neil Kinnock, the party leader, dubbed it 'the biggest consultation exercise with the British public any political party has ever undertaken'.[4] But the party never really decided whether it was primarily a public relations ploy or a serious consultative exercise. As a result it fell between two stools and was an embarrassing flop. Specially organised public meetings were poorly attended and produced little of value. By the end of the first phase of the review 'Labour Listens' was allowed, quietly and unobtrusively, to wither away.

Attempts were also made to stimulate membership involvement, but these were hardly more successful. Traditionally policy development has been the preserve of a narrow enclosed world of Shadow Cabinet and NEC members, Head Office staff, trade union leaders and outside advisers. Tom Sawyer, a senior National Union of Public Employees (NUPE) official and leading NEC member and the prime mover behind the Policy Review, was deeply committed to encouraging far more rank and file involvement. Thus early in the second phase of the review an elaborate political education pack was dispatched to all constituencies and branches. In addition, the NEC proposed to hold regional forums to which Constituency Labour Parties (CLPs) would be invited to send delegates to debate aspects of the Policy Review. However, the forums never took place – due to lack of interest – and the level of response to the political education pack was disappointing. To compound the problem, there was no proper mechanism for feeding constituency submissions into the Policy Review process. As a result they had a negligible effect on policy.

Of course, constituencies have a constitutional right to participate in policy-making through submitting Conference resolutions. In practice this too was largely irrelevant, for a variety of reasons. CLPs cast only about 10 per cent of the total vote; no procedure was available to enable Conference to amend Policy Review reports; and resolutions at odds with the Policy Report were for the most part simply ignored – most notably calls at both the 1989 and 1990 Conferences demanding major cuts in defence spending.[5] As a result, Sawyer's hope that the Policy

Review would institute a more participative approach to policy-making was never realised. The key actors were – as in the past – the leader and his frontbench colleagues, the larger unions and the NEC. But it would be quite wrong to conclude that it was a closed process whose ends were more or less predetermined. The leadership managed the review with a fairly loose rein, only intervening forcefully over a few particularly sensitive matters (trade union law, nuclear weapons).

Four Policy Review reports were published between 1988 and 1991. The object of the first, *Social Justice and Economic Efficiency*, was to produce a statement of values, goals and major policy themes. It was the least influential and soon forgotten. The detailed elaboration of policy was left to the second phase; its report, by far the bulkiest, was entitled *Meet the Challenge, Make the Change*. Submitted to the 1989 Conference it announced substantial programmatic innovations. The original function of the third phase was to finalise any outstanding policy issues and then concentrate on the promotion of the new programme. But the rather surprising ease with which *Meet the Challenge, Make the Change* was navigated through Conference convinced the leadership that, on some issues, it had been unduly circumspect. Presented to the 1990 Conference, *Looking to the Future* signalled a further significant shift to the right. A fourth, initially unintended, report, *Opportunity Britain*, was delivered to the 1991 Conference. Its main purposes were to keep Labour in the public eye and to ensure that the Conference's agenda was set by the leadership, but there were a few significant clarifications of policy. All four reports were endorsed overwhelmingly by Conference.

## THE CONTOURS OF PROGRAMMATIC CHANGE

The end product of the Policy Review was a far-reaching change in Labour's programme and ideology. But to assess its significance and measure the distance travelled, we require a benchmark to act as a point of comparison. Most commentators took as their benchmark a highly statist model of socialism, that is, one defined in terms of a commitment to state ownership and economic planning.[6] But this was quite misleading. It is true that in the years 1979 to 1983 the party embraced a radical programme of extended public ownership, economic planning and industrial democracy. But this period – the high tide of the left – was an aberration and not typical of either the party's operative programmes (as embodied in election manifestos) or its conduct in office.

To assess the process of programmatic change we need to represent more accurately what Labour has actually stood for and what it sought to achieve in office. This can be supplied by what we shall call the traditional social democratic model, a body of values, objectives and policy orientations to which Labour has adhered since at least the late 1950s. It was composed of the following key features:

1. Socialism was defined primarily in terms of values. The most prominent, or at least most distinctive, of these was equality which Tony Crosland, the leading postwar social democratic theorist described as 'the most characteristic feature of socialist thought today'.[7] This was combined with an equally firm commitment to social justice and social welfare.

2. The equation of socialism with public ownership was rejected, but the model did envisage a substantial public sector comprised largely of the utilities and of industries deemed to be 'failing the nation'.

3. Whilst the model accepted the basic infrastructure of the capitalist economy, it favoured a significant measure of state intervention to cajole the market into behaving in socially desirable ways and to promote balanced economic growth.

4. Full employment and sustained economic growth were adopted as the foremost objectives of economic policy and the means to achieve them was primarily Keynesian demand-management. Indeed Keynesianism was seen as the main solution to the oscillations of the capitalist economy, rendering socialist supply-side measures of secondary importance.

5. However the major instrument to accomplish socialist objectives was the welfare state. Whilst production was to be left mainly in private hands, the model anticipated a socialisation of consumption in which the economic surplus of the private sector would be recycled to meet social needs. Further, the model involved a 'top-down' approach to social change, in which the definition and meeting of social needs were placed mainly in the hands of bureaucratically organised welfare organisations.

6. In response to growing inflationary pressures from the late 1960s onwards, a further element was added to the model: the development of 'social contract'-style corporatism linking the state, employers and the unions. The core of this arrangement was a bargain between the government and the unions in which wage restraint was traded in exchange for policy concessions and granting the Trades Union Congress (TUC) institutionalised rights of access to key policy-making centres.

This model constituted Labour's dominant policy paradigm. It provided the driving force behind successive Labour election manifestos and – more haltingly – behind Labour's conduct in government. The hold of this paradigm was temporarily undermined in the early 1980s when, as we have noted, a more radical programme was adopted. The story of the Policy Review is at one level the return to 'normalcy'; less obvious is whether it offered a *renewal* of the model.

### Socialist Values and the Policy Review

Unlike in the Gaitskellite period of the 1950s, the authors of the Policy Review did not set out consciously to redefine Labour's 'socialism'. Since the members of the Policy Review groups were drawn from both the right and soft left and were given considerable latitude in interpreting their remit, it is not surprising that, in its initial phase, a wide range of views was represented. Simplifying a little, we can distinguish between two main schools of thinking: these we will label the neo-revisionist and the ethical socialist.

The neo-revisionist position was essentially an attempt to adapt Crosland to the realities of the 1990s. Faced with an ideologically far more assertive Conservatism, there was general agreement within Labour's ranks that it must demonstrate that it, too, was a party of freedom. Condemning the Tory conception as abstract and meaningless, it argued that real freedom entailed full access to such life-enhancing resources as a decent education, a good quality health service, a job and an adequate income. So much was common ground within the party. But the neo-revisionists wished to go further – to redefine the party's ideology *primarily* in terms of the pursuit of individual freedom. 'Being part of a collective', Kinnock suggested in July 1987, 'is not as strong as it used to be. Our initial approach has got to be from the party to the individual.' The message ought to be: 'socialism looks after the individual'.[8] This was essentially the neo-revisionist message. The party's official doctrinal statement, *Democratic Socialist Aims and Values* (largely written by Roy Hattersley), opened with the ringing declaration that 'The true purpose of democratic socialism and, therefore, the true aim of the Labour Party, is the creation of a genuinely free society in which the fundamental objective of government is the protection and extension of individual liberty'.[9]

But there was another ideological strand (and one with deep roots in the party's history) competing for attention in the Policy Review, the ethical socialist strand. This was represented by the soft left, which included leading figures within the Policy Review process such as David Blunkett, Bryan Gould and Michael Meacher. Socialism, it asserted, was not to be equated with the expansion of state ownership and control. Nor was it simply a matter of redistribution and individual freedom, however desirable these were in themselves. It was also about the way people relate to one another and hence the creation of social and economic arrangements that institutionalise and strengthen ties of mutual and reciprocal obligation, solidarity and fellow feeling. From this perspective, collective forms of organisation were seen as having an intrinsic value, as means by which solidarity and fraternity could be expressed.

Although this strand surfaced in some sections of the Policy Review (particularly those produced by the social policy PRG co-convened by Blunkett), it was largely overshadowed by neo-revisionism.[10] The ideological significance of the Policy Review, in short, was twofold: it sought to disengage socialism from the expansion of state power, to champion a distinctively social democratic individualism. But it also represented a move away from an equally important tradition, the association of socialism with community and fellowship. Beer commented a generation ago that revisionism had 'attacked socialist ideology at its heart – the doctrine of fellowship'.[11] The Policy Review resumed the assault.

### Public Ownership

In another respect, the Policy Review completed the revisionist mission – the discarding of public ownership as a significant object of party policy. As recently as 1986 the party had pledged a future Labour government to 'an ambitious programme to move towards wider social ownership'.[12] This concept referred not to state ownership but to the enfranchisement of workers through establishing industrial democracy, and reflected the view held by soft leftists like Blunkett, Gould and Meacher that the essence of socialism was the diffusion of economic power. In its earlier stages, the Policy Review continued to toy with ideas of social ownership[13] but these soon lost favour. This was partly because the form of industrial democracy that the People at Work group – and, in particular its co-convener Michael Meacher – espoused (the works council) aroused strong trade union objections. More fundamental, however, was mounting resistance from the leadership: schemes for the democratisation of industry only caused difficulties as the party moved, gradually but ineluctably, towards an accommodation with the business establishment.

With the transfer of both Gould and Meacher from economic portfolios – and their replacement by the more pragmatically minded Gordon Brown and Tony Blair – *any* serious challenge to the status quo vanished from Labour's agenda. Pledges to return to the public domain privatised industries and utilities became progressively more sparing and proposals to extend public control to virgin territory more or less disappeared:

Labour's 1992 election manifesto only contained a single guarded reference to restoring public control to the National Grid.[14]

In an earlier clash over public ownership, Nye Bevan had defined the debate as being 'between those who want the mainsprings of economic power transferred to the community and those who believe that private enterprise should still remain supreme but that its worst characteristics should be modified by liberal ideas of justice and equality'.[15] With the Policy Review, Labour opted clearly and unambiguously for the latter approach. The existing pattern of ownership ceased to be seriously questioned: in Kinnock's words, 'the question is what an industry does, not who owns it. Ownership is a matter for the ideologists.'[16]

### The State and the Market

The social democratic model envisaged a state-regulated market. But how extensive was this regulation to be? Discussion of the role of the state in economic life has been clouded by a failure to clarify both the *purposes* and the *form* of state intervention. State intervention may be either system-transcending or system-affirming. By system-transcending we mean policies intended ultimately to effect fundamental changes in the operation of the existing market economy. By system-affirming we mean policies geared to tackling market imperfections in order to accomplish broadly agreed goals, such as boosting productivity and investment. The Policy Review unhesitatingly chose the latter. 'In very many areas of the economy', *Meet the Challenge, Make the Change* declared, 'the market and competition are essential in meeting the demands of the consumer, promoting efficiency and stimulating innovation, and often the best means of securing all the myriad, incremental changes which are needed to take the economy forward.[17]

But the market was not perfect. It neglected general needs such as education and training, research and development and an adequate infrastructure; it was pervaded by short-term thinking and behaviour; and it could not procure balanced economic growth, protect the environment or promote social justice. 'The difference between ourselves and the Conservatives', *Looking to the Future* averred, 'is not that they accept the market and we do not, but that we recognise the limits of the market and they do not. The market can be a good servant, but is often a bad master.'[18]

This left open the precise form of state involvement. To clarify the type of choices the party made, it may be useful to distinguish between three types of state intervention: *strategic, ad hoc* and *functional*.

By strategic we mean organised and concerted intervention which seeks to influence resource-allocation decisions through regulating or directing activity in the market (e.g., French-style *dirigiste* planning, Japanese MITI-type sectoral industrial strategy). In theory, Labour has for years been committed to this type of intervention. In practice, as the record of Labour governments in the 1960s and 1970s illustrates, the pattern of industrial intervention was primarily *ad hoc* in character, designed for limited and specific objectives.[19]

In the earlier stages of the Policy Review, influential voices – most notably Bryan Gould, then co-convener of the main economic PRG – pressed for a *strategic* form of industrial intervention. Their voice was sufficiently loud to be registered in *Meet the Challenge, Make the Change*. It proposed a Medium Term Industrial Strategy, to be administered by a strengthened Department of Trade and Industry (roughly modelled on the Japanese MITI) and two new institutions, British Technology Enterprise and the British Investment Bank.

The intention was to break the stranglehold of the City of London financial institutions, which Gould held mainly responsible for the short-termism so damaging to British competitiveness. (He also regarded it as an undemocratic encumbrance whose prerogatives a Labour Party serious about dispersing power must curb). But others within the leadership were dubious about Gould's inteventionism – reflected in the ambiguous note often sounded by *Meet the Challenge, Make the Change* – and it was their views that eventually prevailed. In October 1989 Gould was replaced as industry spokesman by the centrist Gordon Brown. Brown, the increasingly influential Shadow Chancellor John Smith, and John Eatwell, Kinnock's personal economic adviser, secured the adoption of a more conciliatory stance towards the City which entailed disavowing Labour's more interventionist ideas. Thus earlier plans for an enhanced state role in the investment process were largely dropped and in the party's manifesto the various interventionist agencies (the National Investment Bank, British Technology Enterprise and Regional Development Agencies) were assigned relatively modest functions.[20]

This drift away from interventionism reflected the by now widespread lack of confidence within Labour's senior echelons in the state's capacity to prod or cajole industry into increasing manufacturing investment, still less to provide that investment itself. Rather the state should concentrate on those tasks which the market was either unable or unwilling to discharge, that is, it should pursue a policy of *functional intervention*. On the supply-side, this meant tackling inadequacies in training, R&D and regional development, and discouraging industrially damaging takeovers. In the macro-economic sphere it meant established an economic environment sufficiently stable to restore business confidence and, hence, raise the level of investment. The axis of such intervention was to be *partnership* with the private sector. Labour's 1992 election manifesto summed up the party's approach: 'A government which business can do business with.'[21]

## Full Employment

Aside from high welfare spending, the policy plank with which social democratic parties have been most closely identified is full employment. The right to work has been seen as a fundamental social right, the availability of a job as the prerequisite of any advance towards a fairer, freer and more equal society. Keynesian strategy had converted the aspiration to full employment into a feasible policy objective and enabled Labour to reconcile the goals of higher welfare spending and rising living standards with economic growth and job security. Under the Policy Review, Labour has abandoned this strategy on the grounds that it was no longer viable. In John Smith's words, it was no longer possible to manage demand in such a way as 'to sustain pre-ordained rates of growth or economic activity'.[22] Full employment could no longer be restored by Keynesian means. As a result, Labour came to define its object as the promotion of policies 'to achieve *the fullest level of employment possible*'.[23]

This represents a crucial programmatic shift, and one which did not fully receive the attention it merited. Two main considerations seem to have been responsible. First, the recent experience of western social democratic governments – particularly the British in the 1970s and the French in the early 1980s – seemed to indicate that Keynesianism did not work any longer. Second, in an increasingly interdependent world economy, with its deregulated currency and capital flows and liberalised trading arrangements, nationally-oriented Keynesian strategies appeared obsolete. In place of the traditional Keynesian aims of full employment and growth, Labour adopted as the main aim of its economic policy the creation of a stable economic environment. A vital means to achieve this was seen as exchange rate stability which, in turn, entailed membership of the European Exchange Rate Mechanism (ERM) at the existing parity. This presented Labour with a policy dilemma: how to reduce unemployment when the exchange rate was clearly pitched too high and markets were being lost? It was a dilemma which, for a while at least, it was spared having to face.

## The Welfare State

The welfare state lies at the very centre of the social democratic model. It seeks to socialise consumption by ensuring that basic human needs are met and access to vital resources such as health and education is provided by the conscious will of the community rather than left to market forces. It is the essential means to realise the socialist goals of freedom, equality and solidarity.

David Blunkett, the co-convener of the PRG dealing with welfare policies (Consumers and the Community) and most other members of the group were mindful that although the public services remained popular there was considerable dissatisfaction with their remoteness, inefficiency and lack of responsiveness. They understood that excluding the consumers of welfare from any collective involvement in their planning and delivery promoted an alienation from 'bureaucracy' which the Tories had skilfully exploited. They also recognised that Labour's reputation had suffered from its image as a party which cared more about those who delivered public services than for those for whom they were delivered. The Consumers and the Community group responded to these criticisms by offering a range of measures to encourage the more efficient delivery of services and greater accountability to the consumers. For example, within the health service Labour proposed an NHS Quality Commission to monitor value for money, performance agreements between the Department of Health and health authorities setting down performance targets (e.g., reduction of waiting lists) and service agreements between health authorities and providers specifying quality of services.[24]

All this reflected a broad consensus within the party. A rather more difficult matter was the question of the funding of the welfare state. Labour was not convinced (rightly as it transpired) by quantitative opinion surveys that time and again showed that most voters were willing to pay more in taxes in return for better public services. Its own qualitative opinion research showed that it still suffered from its image as a high tax party.[25] Labour strove assiduously to shed this image. To this end it steadily tightened its fiscal stance and confined itself to only a few cast-iron pledges: an increase in pensions and child benefits, and a (relatively modest) cash injection for the NHS. These were to be funded by higher taxation of the richest ten per cent or so of tax-payers by introducing a new 50 per cent tax rate for those earning over £40,000 a year and by lifting the ceiling on National Insurance Contributions. These tax proposals were designed to allay fears of higher tax imposts by ensuring that 80 per cent of the population would benefit (though most only marginally) from reduced taxation under a Labour government.

In fact, this 'fiscal prudence' placed Labour in a dilemma. The main thrust of its attacks on the government was the latter's neglect and underfunding of the public services: the implication was that Labour would remedy this. But, as we have seen, its own firm commitments were modest, and it countered inevitable Tory criticism by promising that it would finance further improvement of the public services only from the increments of economic growth. The Conservatives and their allies in the tabloid press ruthlessly exploited Labour's vulnerability here and – ironically – were able to persuade many voters that, after all, it was the high tax party.

## Trade Unions, Employers and the State

The last Labour government had crumbled by May 1979 largely because of the outburst of industrial militancy after years of pay restraint. How to cope with the inter-related problems of pay and inflation, and the role of the unions in society has dogged the party ever since. The key role occupied by the unions in the party has meant that on this issue the leadership's ability to reshape policy has been more constrained than on most others.

Elements within the party (and not solely on the right) continued to favour a revamped social contract-type approach but this did not convince the leadership for three main reasons. First, there were doubts about the feasibility of an incomes policy given the increasing fragmentation of the wage-bargaining process; second, the majority of unions remained strongly opposed to any incomes policy; third, the leadership was fearful of the electoral costs of proposing to return the unions to the high councils of government.

Finding an alternative proved difficult and in the first two stages of the Policy Review the issue of inflation was largely ducked. Eventually, the party adopted a two-pronged approach. The first was membership of the EC's ERM. Under a fixed rate regime companies would no longer have the option of a competitive devaluation if they conceded high pay claims. The result would be a loss of markets and hence rising unemployment. In other words Labour hoped that the ERM's disciplining effect would deter inflationary wage claims.

Second, Labour anticipated that in practice union leaders would have been so relieved to see their party returned to power that they would have been amenable over pay. The plan was to involve them in the process of economic decision-making via the device of the National Economic Assessment. But the details were nebulous. The NEA was initially envisaged, in the early 1980s, as a corporatist-style, tripartite system of policy-formation. Fear that it might be accused of seeking to revive union power led the party to downgrade it and by the 1990s it had been reduced to a looser consultation exercise. It is unclear how and whether it could have worked, or indeed what it was supposed to do.

Whether there was any realistic alternative to a revival of corporatism for a government serious about ending mass unemployment was a question that in the end Labour never had to tackle.

## A European Party

So far we have considered how traditional social democratic priorities were modified to meet changing circumstances. To what extent has the model itself been extended to encompass new concerns? Two points are worthy of note here: Labour's Europeanisation and its (partial) 'greening'.

For years enthusiasm for European integration has been a hallmark of European social democracy (outside Scandinavia). This was never shared by the Labour Party: indeed, its 1983 general election manifesto actually called for British withdrawal from the Community. This commitment was soon dropped but Labour remained cool towards the EC. Europeanisation only really began with the Policy Review – a process reflected and symbolised by changing attitudes towards the ERM: outright opposition was replaced by cautious neutrality which in turn gave way to positive enthusiasm. By the conclusion of the review, the party had totally reversed its traditional stance. During the Maastricht negotiations of December 1991, Labour was bewailing Conservative tardiness over European economic and political integration. It was a historic reversal of roles. Labour had discarded the chrysalis of years of hostility to the EC and emerged as a pro-European party – perhaps the single most dramatic change in its programme. Why did this happen?

One reason is certainly electoral. Party strategists saw mileage in exploiting the deepening Tory rift over Europe. Presenting Labour as the European party also helped in their efforts to project it as modern and running with the tide, whilst support for the ERM was intended to convince the City of Labour's fiscal rectitude. But these pragmatic considerations were matched by the growth, throughout the labour movement, of a genuinely more benign attitude towards the Community. The unveiling of the Social Charter played a notable part here, especially within the unions. The unions also began to appreciate their consultative status in EC institutions – at least some compensation for their exclusion from the corridors of power in Whitehall. The growing immersion of both the unions and the party in European bodies (such as the Confederation of EC Socialist Parties and the European Trade Union Confederation) also helped wean them from parochial attitudes, a process accelerated by the spread of bilateral contacts (e.g., joint Labour Party-SPD working groups). But perhaps most important of all, by the end of the 1980s, the bulk of Labour's economic policymakers were convinced that participation in a steadily more integrated EC was vital to deliver the stable economic environment that was seen as the prerequisite of sustained economic growth.[26]

## The Greening of Labour?

There has been for several years extensive debate about the rise of a new 'post-materialist' agenda of politics. The staple fare of traditional social democratic politics – jobs, wages, living standards and welfare benefits – are now ( it has been argued) being superseded by post-materialist concerns, above all environmental matters. How responsive has Labour been to these new concerns?

Because Britain's economic performance has consistently lagged behind that of other north European countries, 'materialist issues' have continued to dominate political debate whilst the close ties between Labour and the unions has meant that economic and industrial questions have always been to the forefront of its programme. Throughout the 1970s and 1980s, however, there was a steady rise of interest in environmental issues. The first real breakthrough came in 1986 when – partly in the wake of the Chernobyl nuclear accident – Labour published its first major statement on the environment. At the same time, the unions were growing more sympathetic to green-tinged polices reflecting the rise in importance of white collar and public sector unions at the expense of manufacturing ones, assiduous lobbying by environmental pressure groups and attitude shifts in the public at large.[27] Then the totally unexpected success of the Greens in the June 1989 European elections converted the environment (temporarily) into a high saliency issue.

In autumn 1989 Labour's chief environment spokesman, Jack Cunningham, was replaced by the more sympathetic Bryan Gould. Shortly after, the party produced its most comprehensive and far-reaching policy document on the environment, *An Earthly Chance*, whose main points were incorporated into the final Policy Review report, *Opportunity Britain*. These included a new legally enforceable right to a clean environment, the creation of a tough new Environmental Protection Executive and pledges to press for a European Environment Charter and majority voting on the Council of Ministers on environmental issues.[28]

Labour's greater receptivity to environmental matters is real enough but it does not amount to a conversion to the 'post-materialist agenda'. As long as 'bread and butter' issues continue to hold sway as the voters' main concerns, modifications in party policy will fall far short of the greening of British social democracy.

*Determinants of Programmatic Change*

The Policy Review, one right-wing Labour MP commented, 'represents potentially the biggest shift in the Party's stance and direction for thirty years.'[29] The interesting question is not solely that this occurred, but that it occurred with such modest resistance. We can distinguish here between two sets of factors, the electoral and the internal political.

*Electoral Factors.* On three occasions Labour had been repudiated by the electorate and many within the upper reaches of the party concluded that a fundamental reappraisal of its doctrine and programme was indispensable. No significant development of policy was considered without the most careful attention to likely public responses. In most cases the message supplied by opinion research was clear: the voters were worried that a Labour government would lead to higher taxation, a resurgence of trade union power, and inflation. They wanted reassurance that Labour was safe, 'moderate' and not in thrall either to the left or the unions. It was not difficult to dub the more radical policies favoured by some in the Policy Review process – a more interventionist industrial policy, higher and more redistributive taxes – as vote-losers.

The electoral imperative operated at another level too. Labour was now a far more disciplined party, aware of the destructive effects of highly-publicised internal disagreements. All participants in the Policy Review were under great pressure not to disturb the amity within the party or to harm the new image of moderation which seemed to be reaping a harvest of voters. This imparted a bias towards blandness which was reinforced by the compulsions of Labour's electoral strategy. This could be summed up as: the Tories are digging their own grave, the tide is flowing towards us. Keep calm and disciplined, and, above all, avoid anything that might agitate or unsettle the public mind. Thatcherism represented extremism, confrontation, even (in one Kinnock speech) 'social engineering'. To this Labour sought to counterpose an image of moderation, competence and common sense. From this strategic perspective – to which Labour continued to cleave after Mrs Thatcher's departure from the scene in November 1990 – those who urged more daring policies could easily be pilloried as disturbers of the peace.

Labour, the leadership in effect urged, could only anticipate electoral success to the extent that it adapted to those aspects of the Thatcher revolution that ran with the popular grain. The adjustment of the party's stance on privatisation, the market and labour law were the most notable examples of this. Nor was this simply a matter of accommodating mass opinion. To regain an image of economic competence, the party sought to impress the 'opinion leaders' (that is economic commentators in the media and business) of the realism and sobriety of its policies. This entailed expunging any policies (e.g., a significant rise in public spending, an interventionist industrial policy) that offended orthodox opinion.

*Internal Party Factors.* A range of internal party factors also facilitated programmatic change. The first was a shift in the internal pattern of alignments. In the mid-1980s the soft left had occupied a strategic position within the party. It ensured the leadership a handsome majority in all key arenas in the struggle against the hard left and was thereby able to secure important policy positions, in particular on defence and social ownership. But by the end of the 1980s the hard left was a spent force, the soft left was losing much of its cohesion whilst the right had fully recovered its composure. At the same time, a new breed of pragmatists was emerging. They included rising political stars, such as Gordon Brown, Tony Blair and Margaret Beckett – highly articulate, polished performers with a ready grasp of their portfolios, unencumbered by much ideological baggage and animated by a single-minded determination to secure electoral victory. By 1989 an alliance of the traditional right and the pragmatic centre formed the dominant axis within the party and the soft left found its capacity to shape the course of policy development slowly draining away.

The second change was an intensification in the support which the unions were prepared to offer to the leadership. They did of course still expect to be fully consulted and, on matters touching their vital interests, for the leadership to show flexibility.[30] But they willingly accepted the overall responsibility of the political leadership to set the main lines of policy and top union leaders did their best – in the interests of electoral victory – to refrain from making politically embarrassing demands.[31]

A third change was the growing prominence of the Shadow Cabinet in the formulation of policy.[32] While many of the 'social' portfolios continued to be held by soft leftists, after the October 1989 reshuffle most key economic posts were occupied by Shadow Cabinet members holding positions further to the right. The leader himself – whose role tended to expand in the course of the review – increasingly came to throw his considerable weight behind the ascendant centre-right block.

Fourth, internal membership constraints also progressively loosened. In the early stages of the Policy Review, the leadership, wary of vexing the rank and file by too sudden a reversal of policy, had proceeded gingerly. While ordinary members exercised little direct influence, fear of reigniting the destructive civil war of the early 1980s compelled some respect for their most treasured convictions. But evidence began to mount of a profound change of mood in the party. One by one, hard left members lost their places in the election of the constituency section of the NEC, as in successive conferences Kinnock won standing ovations. The hard left was clearly losing its grip on constituency activists and the old rallying cries that had aroused passions in the past now failed to stir the soul of the party.

This was not because revisionism had swept Labour's ranks – indeed recent research shows that the average member remains solidly to the left of centre.[33] The willingness to stomach programmatic innovations for which there was little real enthusiasm was due to another, and crucially important factor: the desperate yearning for electoral victory which swept aside many doubts and reservations. It constituted, as one shrewd and experienced commentator noted, a 'profound, genuine and largely spontaneous change of mood in the grassroots'.[34]

Finally, a spirit of sombre realism now pervaded the party. In the early 1980s many were convinced that, given sufficient resolution, a Labour government genuinely committed to a programme of radical social change could overcome all entrenched obstacles. By the end of the decade, it was evident to most that the internationalisation of the economy, with its mighty waves of capital and currency swirling across national frontiers, had seriously eroded national economic sovereignty. Brash defiance was replaced by fear of the punishment that could be wreaked upon too adventurous a government. In John Smith's words: we lived in an interdependent and highly unstable world 'where capital movements in Tokyo, New York and London can subvert the economic policies of nation states'.[35] In consequence, Labour – apprehensive that a run on the pound or a flight of capital might scupper its election prospects – strove hard to reassure financial opinion of its soundness and reliability, although to little avail, as it transpired.

CONCLUSION: WHITHER LABOUR?

With the Policy Review, Labour equipped itself with a set of solid and practical policies – though it was less successful in furnishing a clear sense of purpose or a vision of the future. Since its prime purpose was to render Labour more electable, the obvious question is where does the party go from here?

The first point to make is that the Policy Review never marked as radical a departure in Labour's thinking as many commentators seemed to believe; rather it signified a resumption of its traditional role as a party of social integration striving to reconcile the interests of capital and labour and to restore a national consensus. Yet it would be wrong to conclude that the Policy Review was simply the final triumph of the revisionist prospectus. All leading actors in the exercise understood that conditions had changed and that the traditional social democratic model needed to be amended in some fundamental respects. Where they differed was how. And they continue to do so.

In a sense, there were always two Policy Reviews: as already identified at various stages of the analysis, there were two currents of thought, championed respectively by the right and the soft left. The first triumphed and those on the soft left who felt uneasy about the drift of policy stifled their doubts in their interests of party unity. After Labour's defeat, the debate has resumed. to undestand how this debate is likely to proceed, we must place it in a dual context, one electoral, the other economic.

*The Electorial Context.* An unprecedented fourth successive drubbing at the polls is bound to have prefound repercussions within the Party, but the precise nature of those repercussions will be influenced by the lessons Labour reads from its defeat. For some commentators the lesson is simple: the voters have repudiated even a mild collectivist programme and the traditional social democratic project has now reached its terminal stage. The way forward lies through a more unqualified acceptance of the free market and the now ascendant ethos of individualism.

In so far as this is correct a further, and fundamental, reappraisal, of Labour's programme would be essential if it were to have any proposal of returning to power. But *did* the voter reject collectivism? While it is clear that, despite all its efforts, Labour failed to reasure millions of its potential supporter that it would not impose heftier taxation, the evidence suggests that this was less a matter of the voters rejecting Labour's tax and spending policies than having a highly distorted view of what those policies were.[36] Though an analysis of Labour's defeat is beyond the scope of this essay, it is no means evident that either its policies or its values lay at the root of its failure.

*The Economic Context:* Some commentators have also claimed that the election sounded the death-knell of any challenge to free market economies. If Tory claims that Britain is on the brink of economic prosperity prove correct, then indeed Labour will be under great pressure to adapt to the new economic consensus (as have its sister parties in Spain and, to a large degree, France) and hence abandon much of taditional social democracy. But this is unlikely: it is more realistic to anticipate that under present policies Britain, in the words of the Cambridge economist Wynne Godley, 'will remain trapped in recession indefinitely' as the economy stagnates and unemployment rises inexorably.[37].

If the objective conditions for a revival of support for social collectvism and economic interventionism remain, then a renewed social democratic challenge is still a viable option. What form could it take? Adventitiously, the leadership race following Kinnock's resignation turned into a contest between men who represented the two impulses within the Policy Review, the soft left Bryan Gould and the right-wing John Smith. However, Smith's victory in the contest owed less to the brand of politics he espoused (indeed his campaign manager was the leading soft leftist, Robin Cook) than the belief that he was the man most capable of leading Labour to victory in 1996 or 1997. So Labour's future ideological path remains uncertain. It may be useful here to sketch out the two main alternatives.

The first in effect will be to continue the dominant logic of the Policy Review, stripped perhaps of some of its more electorally contentious items. We shall dub this the social liberal option. Its strengths are that (with Smith in the saddle) it will enable Labour to project an image of moderation, practicality and competence. Its weaknesses (as we have noted) are that it is by no means clear how it can reconcile such goals as higher growth, full employment and an expanding welfare state with its fiscal and monetary stance. In short, the social liberal logic appears to point towards the dilution of the traditional social democratic model as it adjusts to constrained circumstances rather than towards any renewal of that model.

This takes us to the second alternative, which we can call the left social democratic. This remains more firmly committed to traditional social democratic goals, and more critical of the emergent policy consensus which impedes progress towards them. Thus Gould, in his bid for the leadership, resuscitated his critique of the City and his case for a more interventionist industrial strategy, and ventilated the reservations he had always felt about Labour's relapse into financial orthodoxy.

But to what extent does this alternative offer the possibility of a *renewal* of the social democratic model? It is too early to say, though some of the ideas sidelined or discarded during the Policy Review (e.g., schemes for work councils, collective share-holding, social ownership) and some that were retained (e.g., steps towards empowering the consumer of public services and providing for more flexibility and choice) provide some of the ingredients of such a model. But if, as seems likely, empowerment is its central theme, it will have to accept that any course that challenges the great constellations of business power is a risky one. Further – and partly for this reason – it will also have to confront the fact that a purely national social democratic programme may no longer be a feasible option and will therefore have to give priority to constructing (in alliance with Labour's sister parties) a *Euro*-social democratic strategy.

In effect, the choice for Labour is whether it accommodates to the existing distribution of power and wealth, hence effectively abandoning a distinctive social democratic project, or questions it. For many commentators, the former is the only realistic alternative. But – as a glance across the Channel would tell them – no more than its alternative is this self-evidently a winning strategy.

NOTES

1. 'The Policy Review Process and International Experience', *NEC Home Policy Committee*, PD(1) 1226, Jan. 1988.
2. *NEC Home Policy Committee* minutes, 13 March 1990.
3. 'Women's Perspective in Policy and Campaigning Documents', note from G. Bish (Labour Party Director of Policy) to Policy Review Group members, 12 March 1990.
4. *Guardian*, 29 Oct. 1987.
5. These were carried by the two-thirds majority which constitutionally qualified them for inclusion in Labour's programme.
6. See, e.g., P. Kellner in *The Independent*, 11 April 1989.
7. A. Crosland, *The Future of Socialism* (London: Cape, 1956), p. 113.
8. C. Hughes and P. Wintour, *Labour Rebuilt* (London: Fourth Estate, 1990), pp. 38–9.
9. Labour Party NEC, *Democratic Socialist Aims and Values* (London: Labour Party, 1988), p. 3.
10. See R. Plant, 'Citizenship, Liberty and Markets: Ideological Renewal in the Labour Party', paper presented to Political Studies Assoc. conference, 1989.
11. S. H. Beer, *Modern British Politics* (London: Faber, 1969), p. 238.
12. Labour Party NEC, *Social Ownership* (London: Labour Party, 1988), p. 2.
13. See, e.g., *Meet the Challenge, Make the Change* (London: Labour Party, 1989), p. 15.
14. Labour Party, *It's Time to get Britain Working Again* (London: Labour Party, 1992), p. 13.
15. Quoted in W. H. Greenleaf, *The British Political Tradition*, Vol. 2 (*The Ideological Inheritance*) (London: Routledge, 1983), p. 470.
16. *Observer*, 7 Sept. 1989.
17. *Meet the Challenge, Make the Change*, p. 10.
18. Labour Party NEC, *Looking to the Future* (London: Labour Party, 1990), p. 6.
19. B. Jones and M. Keating, *Labour and the British State* (Oxford: Clarendon Press, 1985), pp. 87, 91–4.
20. *It's Time to get Britain Working Again*, p. 13.
21. Ibid, p. 11.
22. Transcript of speech, 16 April 1990.
23. *Opportunity Britain*, p. 8. Emphasis in the original.
24. Ibid, pp. 13–19.
25. Hughes and Wintour (note 8), pp. 137–9.
26. S. Tindale, 'How Labour went European', *Tribune*, 13 Sept. 1991.
27. N. Carter 'The Labour Party and Environment Policy', paper presented to Political Studies Association conference, 1991.
28. *Opportunity Britain*, pp. 21–2.
29. G. Radice, *Independent*, 23 May 1989.
30. Here a pivotal role was played by the 'Contact Group' of senior frontbenchers, trade unionists and party and TUC officials.
31. See Lewis Minkin's definitive study, *The Contentious Alliance: Trade Unions and the Labour Party* (Edinburgh: Edinburgh UP, 1991), especially pp. 468–9, 478.
32. To such a degree that it provoked some rumblings on the by now generally compliant NEC. *NEC Home Policy Committee* minutes, 13 March 1990.
33. P. Seyd, P. Whiteley and D. Broughton, 'Labour's Reorganisation Down at the

Grassroots', paper presented to PSA specialist group conference on 'Elections, Parties and Public Opinion', 1990.

34. Ian Aitken, *Guardian*, 1 Oct. 1990.
35. *Tribune*, 7 July 1990.
36. In particular, many voters appeared to have swallowed the (false) Tory claim that *average* income-earners would pay substantially more under Labour's tax plans.
37. *New Statesman and Society*, 30 March 1992.

# Trade Unions and the Politics of Social Democratic Renewal

## ANDREW J. TAYLOR

*One of the characteristic features of social democratic parties is their close political relationship with trade unions. For most of the twentieth century social democratic parties and trade unions cooperated in a common reform programme which embraced public spending, Keynesian economic management and tripartite politics. This traditional policy and political relationship came under increasing strain in the 1970s and 1980s with the rise of the new right and as new issues emerged which did not fit neatly into traditional labour movement politics. Social democracy entered a period of electoral decline and the party-union relationship came under increased strain as party and union interests diverged. Unions had, none the less, a direct interest in the success of programmatic renewal, which was intended to increase the parties' electability. For the most part they acquiesced in a process that was likely to reduce their influence over the parties. This suggests that the party-union relationship will endure but will take on a more distant and flexible form.*

In the 1980s social democracy was portrayed as, if not in its grave, then verging on terminal decline. Electoral difficulties, recession and structural economic change were eroding those groups of workers that had formed social democracy's organisational and electoral bedrock. However, social democracy is not doomed and, as in the 1950s, its parties responeded with programmatic renewal.[1] Social democracy's decline was blamed partly on these parties' close links with the unions, and yet the party-union relationship is a defining characteristics of social democratic parties. History, however, has created a complex organisational and doctrinal legacy, and the party-union relationship can be seen as an example of 'hardened power' complicating renewal.[2] Reconciling 'old' and 'new' social democracy risks the further erosion of what remains its largest single source of organisational and electoral support: the labour movement.[3] (See Appendix tables for details).

The structure of social democratic parties implies considerable union power. The party-union relationship developed from the unions' industrial and parties' electoral weaknesses; by co-operating the latter became governing parties. Social democratic parties argue that socialism can be built not by the uprising of a class but by integrating a wide range of socio-economic groups into an electoral conglomerate extending beyond the organised working class. As social democratic parties seek to reform society by winning a parliamentary majority, they are motivated by electoral and political considerations wider than those of the unions. Unions acquiesce because social democratic governments are most likely to be favourably disposed to their interests. The supra-class electoral strategy has expanded the parties' room for manoeuvre in dealing with union demands that are felt to be inimical to the party, government or movement's interests.[4]

Programmatic renewal was a response to the collapse of the 'classic model' of social democracy (strong, reliable working-class electoral support, collectivism, and a Keynesian welfare state with varying degrees of corporatism), which provided a policy matrix in which unions played a key role. The 'new model' accepted the reality of partisan dealignment (but not realignment), the market, individualism and the fact that 'traditional' working-class politics and organisations were in relative decline. The rationale for the link remains valid but the political environment of the 1980s pointed to a looser, more flexible party-union relationship.[5]

Social democratic politics are produced by the interaction of the 'political' and 'industrial' wings in pursuit of differing but overlapping objectives. Union political activity is neither inevitably socialist in style nor aspiration, while electioneering means a social democratic party cannot afford to be perceived as a union party. The party-union relationship varies according to the party's stage of development. In the early years of electoral take-off, unions are dominant; less so when the party has achieved office and secured an electoral constituency extending beyond the unions and working class.[6] Unless the party wins office, union goals will not be realised and this encourages the supremacy of the party's conception of which policies win votes. Although the party-union relationship is not static, social democratic politics early on tended to reflect the union culture and issues dominant at their founding: the doctrines, ethos and structures of male, blue-collar manufacturing unions. Programmatic renewal sought to retain union loyalty whilst adapting to new issues and changes in social structure which threaten the unions' traditional place within social democracy. In all the cases considered in this essay, unions have considerable influence inside the party (only in the British case are unions formally affiliated to the party) and unions could have defended the status quo thereby limiting the prospects for renewal. However, the unions proved reluctant to assert themselves in the renewal process.

## TRADE UNIONS AND THE REDEFINITION OF SOCIAL DEMOCRACY

In Sweden the Social Democratic Party's (SAP) 1982 election victory with *The Third Way* (neither Keynesianism nor Monetarism) coincided with a severe political-economic crisis and resulted in instability in government-union-party relations. The 1985 and 1988 elections indicated social democracy's exhaustion and culminated in the loss of the 1991 election.[7] This placed the Swedish Trade Union Confederation (LO) in a difficult and complex position: economic success depended on the LO's ability to secure support for austerity while portraying social democratic government as the best defence of an increasingly restive membership.

In this period the SAP attempted to pre-empt the non-socialist agenda by espousing tax reform, postponing the nuclear power phase-out, and applying to join the European Community (EC). The LO saw the tax reform as a major concession to market liberalism whilst the EC had been traditionally regarded as a 'capitalist club' and membership contrary to Swedish neutrality. Two other changes struck at traditional LO interests: full employment was replaced by low inflation as the prime objective of macro-economic policy, while attempts were made to control public spending and limit the welfare state.[8]

Despite the opening to market liberalism, the SAP continued to lose support as economic difficulties became allied with a widespread hostility to Social Democratic hegemony. The LO was seen by some Social Democrats as an obstacle to renewal while the LO became increasingly vocal in opposing SAP economic policies.[9] The LO argued for the continued viability of the Swedish model but acknowledged that its relationship with the SAP would become more difficult, requiring improved liaison and cooperation between the LO and SAP. The LO's dilemma was how to maintain the traditional relationship and preserve its legitimacy in the eyes of union members.[10]

On 15 February 1991 the government was defeated in the Riksdag on an austerity package which, among other things, sought a freeze on wages and a ban on strikes. The Prime Minister resigned, but then reformed his administration and presented a revised package to the Riksdag which effectively rejected his finance minister's policy prompting his resignation. The LO accepted austerity in order to defend the welfare state and economic competitiveness, but union members (particularly in the public sector) were less convinced. Some Social

Democrats meanwhile felt that *The Third Way* was undermined by the LO, whose influence in the party secured the dilution of essential policy changes, contributing to electoral defeat in 1991.

Though the LO cannot be blamed for electoral defeat, it is the case that the party-union alliance, an important element in social democratic hegemony since 1932, is increasingly problematic for both participants. After 1982 union leaders felt compelled to share responsibility for policies which antagonised their members, whereas the SAP leadership recognised that their dependence on the unions was disliked by non-traditional SAP voters. Since the 1950s, when the relative decline of the traditional working-class became apparent, the SAP has been targeting white-collar/middle-class voters and these groups have become increasingly unreceptive to traditional social democracy. The structural fragmentation of the working class is accompanied by political fragmentation, so eroding the 'naturalness' of the SAP-LO connection. Economic crisis, the export of capital, the opening to the EC and the internationalisation of the economy have reinforced domestic political forces hostile to traditional Swedish politics. The result has been that, while the LO remains influential within the SAP, these changes have challenged and reduced the unions' influence in the wider political economy.[11]

The LO/SAP relationship, though politically close, is structurally indirect and is weakening appreciably.[12] Though there remain powerful forces supporting its preservation, the most likely outcome is a more 'pluralistic' party-union relationship which, in turn, has implications for programmatic renewal. The LO leadership wish their close relationship with the SAP to continue but it is significant that in recent years the LO has been developing its own programmes. These developments, together with membership discontent, pressure from the international economy, white collar and public sector discontent, the fragmentation of blue-collar solidarity and the SAP's adaptation, point to a looser party-union relationship.

The German Social Democratic Party (SPD) is no stranger to programmatic renewal. Since the 1950s the SPD and the unions have recognised that they must attract large numbers of voters outside the traditional party culture, but a powerful traditional worker milieu persists and it inhibited renewal.[13] This was complicated by the shift in the left-right continuum in the party: the 'old' left based on the unionised industrial working-class is seen now as being on the 'right', whereas the 'new' left of white collar public/private sector workers has been attracted to Green policies.[14] The rise of the Greens was a by-product of the Brandt-Schmidt years, whereas the defection of blue-collar voters to the Christian Democrat Union (CDU) was blamed by many in the unions on the SPD abandoning its traditional constituency.[15] The SPD's 1987 defeat in Hesse was crucial. Defeat was blamed on the defection of blue-collar voters disenchanted by the flirtation with the Greens to the Christian Democrats, and in the SPD heartland of Hamburg the party was paralysed by conflict between the 'new' and 'old' SPD.

At the 1989 Münster congress Oskar Lafontaine (SPD Prime Minister in the Saarland) challenged SPD orthodoxy, arguing that jobs would be created if the employed worked less and accepted a cut in earnings. He agreed with the Metalworkers (IG Metall), for example, that the working week was too long, but alienated IG Metall by calling for pay cuts and suggesting that the unions were partly responsible for unemployment. This 'stab in the back' was denounced by the leaders of IG Metall and the Public Sector and Transport Workers (OTV) as mimicking CDU/CSU policies. Lafontaine was warned that he was jeopardising the party-union link and the Chemical Workers (IG Chemie), an extremely moderate union, accused him of careerism. However, he enjoyed the support of some party grandees and many SPD members welcomed the speech for opening up debate. Lafontaine was challenging traditional SPD politics which had failed to exploit the unpopularity of the Kohl government, but blue-collar workers and the unions were antagonised, claiming that his policies would increase the space available to the right, to the SPD's detriment.

The SPD has considerable problems managing the unions but its electoral strategy depends, in part, on union support.[16] 'Lafontaine-ism' was blocked at the 1989 congress but the 1990 election programme emphasised gender and environmental issues, despite union disquiet at the direction of SPD policy. A bloodbath was avoided and traditionalists were persuaded to accept some of Lafontaine's arguments. The unions backtracked on their demand for a shorter working week with no loss of pay, but blocked calls for greater labour flexibility.

The movement's reaction to German reunification was ambiguous and its implications for renewal are considerable as the SPD and Trade Union Confederation (DGB) are now faced with the task of reconciling the post-industrial economy of the West with the collapsing heavy industry of the East. Unions and party welcomed unification but expressed concern about its economic and social implications for western Germany. Reunification brought an influx of members into the DGB but in the elections the SPD took control of only one of the five eastern *Länder*. The economic restructuring of the East will have to be financed by the DGB's members and SPD voters in the West, thus creating the potential for a major geographical-consumption cleavage in labour movement politics. This raises the possibility of traditional class politics in the East and social partnership politics in the West.[17]

In Norway the unions' response in 1984 to the Labour Party's (DNA) difficulties and the centre-right's rise was to offer wage restraint in return for protecting welfarism and full employment. This was followed by *The Freedom Campaign*, the movement's response to the conservative challenge and the Progress Party's populist appeal. However, social democracy's traditional electoral base was being eroded due to declining youth support, a shrinking blue-collar class, and weakening traditional class loyalties.

The Norwegian Trade Union Confederation (LO) and individual unions had a key role in *The Freedom Campaign* despite the Labour Party's (DNA) fears that this would lead to damaging criticism.[18] Not to be involved was equally dangerous, so the problem was not whether to support Labour but how. LO policy (endorsed by the party) envisaged an improved communications strategy to ensure that the union voice was not swamped in an increasingly pluralistic party policy process, while the political education programme would raise social democracy's profile. The labour press with 37 newspapers (20 per cent of total circulation) was reorganised to improve its campaigning. Opening the party's policy process to non-party groups, its changing membership and *The Freedom Campaign*, both sides recognised, meant a diminution of the unions' traditional position but not an inevitable loss of influence.

By 1989 the *The Freedom Campaign* had produced rhetoric and organisational cooperation but little renewal and there was a perception that the LO's traditions made it difficult for it to adapt. The labour movement's joint campaign was agreed at the Drammen Conference (October 1988) and in April 1989 the LO General Council urged union members to work for a Labour victory. The pre-election party congress approved a programme that corresponded well with LO priorities (jobs, fair distribution and environmental protection) and a second conference (May 1989) stressed the importance to the unions of a majority Labour government. The LO had a very active role in the 1989 election but the result was disappointing: Labour produced its worst performance since 1945 although there was no change in the left-right balance in the Storting. Programmatic renewal had not gone far enough. Futher modifications to the traditional social democratic project, to which the unions remain firmly wedded, would result in a decline in union influence.[19]

*The Freedom Campaign* stressed the changing ecology of Norwegian social democracy which meant that Labour had to be demonstrably more than a union party. Party-union conflict was predicted to increase and relations with non-LO organisations multiplied as Labour broadened its base in an electorate concerned with issues and values other than class loyalty. The LO's own programme identified a need to win skilled groups, the growing service sector and the increasing numbers of women entering the labour market. Unions would have to stress 'quality of life' issues, pay closer attention to individual needs, and place greater emphasis on grassroots work. Hostility to renewal was muted by loyalty to the 1986 minority Labour government. None the less, there were rumblings from unions about the downgrading of their influence, complaints which received the retort that the movement was greater than the sum of its parts. Debate in the unions on programmatic renewal concentrated on specifics rather than general principles although the Municipal Workers Union criticised threats to public spending. Nevertheless, the unions recognised the party's primacy.

The LO acknowledged the need for a 'realistic and credible programme' and that change would be painful, but it recognised that unless it participated, the initiative would be surrendered to unsympathetic elements. The unions accepted that the movement's priorities might not coincide with theirs' but claimed that renewal did not require the abandonment of traditional values (freedom, equality and solidarity), just their redefinition and re-presentation in terms of current problems instead of past struggles. The LO co-operated with a wide range of social movements to avoid being branded a sectional interest, and individual unions surrendered sectional objectives in the interests of the movement.[20]

The right's surge in Danish politics compelled the unions to pursue a mobilisational-partisan line. The Danish Trade Union Confederation (LO) declared that 'Due to the confused political situation it has been necessary for the [unions] to take clear stands. The free market . . . cannot solve our economic problems'. In 1988 the LO concluded, 'The extent to which wage-earners interests are safeguarded . . . is completely dependent on . . . achieving greater political influence'.[21] Resisting the right's offensive against the social democratic state encouraged the LO to promote not only closer party-union cooperation but also a 'popular front' of progressive forces.[22] In the 1988 election the LO mobilised on behalf of social democrats inside and outside the workplace. The government's adherence to free market solutions, a downgrading of co-operation with the LO, and spending cuts were interpreted as intended to undermine public confidence in social democracy and blame the unions for Denmark's economic difficulties.[23] The 1989 LO annual meeting gave its support for the party policy statement, *Gang i 90'erne*.[24] Policy was left to the party so long as basic LO interests were accommodated, and the LO concentrated on voter mobilisation and controlling the left, a role limited by the presence of powerful new left groups in the public sector unions. Emphasis was placed on the unions' political education system (the FIU) and an enhanced media strategy to promulgate democratic socialist values.[25]

In the December 1990 elections the Social Democrats made significant gains, but mainly at the expense of the Socialist People's Party, so the left-right balance in the Folketing was not affected and a minority Conservative government remained in office. The government's refusal to work with the Social Democrats or modify its policies was bitterly condemned by the LO. At its 1991 Congress the LO reaffirmed its strong support for the party and noted that after 20 years of decline, 60 per cent of the LO's membership had voted for the party in the December elections. This justified both the nature and direction of programmatic renewal and the LO's policy of supporting the party to 'halt the right-wing demolition of the welfare society'.[26]

The British Labour Party's Policy Review was an extended critique of the established policy-making process and, by extension, was critical of the most important element: the trade unions.[27] The relationship between the affiliated unions and the Labour Party is unique. Nowhere in Western Europe do unions have such a visible role in the party, especially in the executive and policy-making structures. Despite this, the unions have seldom asserted themselves; indeed the chief characteristic of their involvement has been reticence. Despite their bloc votes they have never sought to impose a leadership, bureaucratic style or programme on the party; rather their influence has served to close off policy options. Unions recognise that the electoral vitality of the Labour Party depends on engaging and retaining the enthusiasm of the constituency activist, and overt use of union power might damage this commitment. They also recognise that Labour's image as a 'trade union' party is electorally unattractive.[28]

The unions regard themselves as the fulcrum of the Labour Party. This is not an easy role as the affiliated unions are not politically monolithic and their bloc vote arouses antagonism. The merging of constituency and union discontent over the Wilson years saw the unions drawn into constitutional reform. After 1979 they supported constitutional reform, but after 1983 they shifted their weight to enhancing Labour's electoral popularity. The desire of all parts of the Labour Party for a new beginning created a consensus on the need for renewal.

The Policy Review launched at the 1987 conference was to rethink all aspects of Labour's appeal after three consecutive election defeats. Party leaders intended the Policy Review to boost Labour's credibility by amending policies that had strong grassroots support; any hostile reaction would be checked by union bloc votes. Doubts about the 'real' purpose of the Policy Review emerged and some unions were, as in the past, anxious to 'close off' certain options. Union leaders, though concerned about the Review's direction, acquiesced in the marketisation of social democracy because of their desire to see another Labour government.

Suspicion of markets is inherent in trade unionism: its economic and political rationale (including party affiliation) is to cushion the effects of markets on their members. Market socialism came uncomfortably close to asking union leaders openly to endorse market sovereignty. As a result, the unions were pulled in two contradictory directions: welcoming the Policy Review but suspicious of its direction. Unions were anxious not to be stampeded into a process whose outcome they might not be able to control but for which they would be held responsible.[29]

Both the leadership's failure to secure union acceptance of One Person, One Vote (OPOV) and the challenge to the deputy leader in 1988 underlined the need for party caution in the Policy Review, but the prominence given by the media to the unions' role strengthened the desire to 'do something' about the bloc vote. As the Review progressed, reform of the bloc vote acquired greater importance as it symbolised Labour's weaknesses (the lack of a mass base and financial dependence on the unions); yet a secure bloc vote was tremendously valuable to the leadership. The 1988 conference empowered the National Executive Committee (NEC) to explore the use of membership ballots, and a motion calling for reform of the bloc vote was referred to the executive. The October 1988 National Executive Committee meeting began the overhaul of internal party democracy. Though careful not to question conference sovereignty it concluded that democracy should be based on OPOV. The NEC's Conference Procedures Committee's report, *The Future of Labour Party Conference, Policy Making and Representational Structure*, was approved by the 1989 conference.

The committee's final proposals, *Making Policy For the 1990s*, recommended basing policy-making on individual members (via OPOV) and reducing the weight of the union bloc vote from 90 to 70 per cent, and ultimately to 50 per cent. A 170-member national policy council would be elected biennially from all sections of the party which, via seven policy commissions (the model being the Policy Review), would establish 'rolling' programmatic change and recommend policies to a conference to which the unions and constituencies had lost the right to directly propose policy changes. This is the most radical change in the party's power structure since the 1918 constitution. It draws on Swedish and

German models of party policy-making, its objective being to improve party manageability and promote electability.

Reform is based on the thesis that those who attend union and party branch meetings, thereby controlling their organisation's decision-making process, are unrepresentative of the membership and electorate. The unions accept the bloc vote's reduction but are less sure about the policy council: since union representatives will be in a minority, union influence is bound to decline. These proposals were accepted by the 1990 party conference, to come into effect after the 1992 election. By 1993 Labour's policy process will be comparable to those of other social democratic parties.

The programmatic review also envisaged changes in the union-Labour government relationship, a change that can be described as 'no more Social Contracts'. *Social Justice and Economic Efficiency* (1988), the report of the People at Work group, called for creating a constructive relationship between employers and unions to take account of changes in economic structures as well as the legacy of Thatcherism. Drawing on the 1986 *People at Work* report, it proposed a new framework of positive employment rights and noted the constructive role played by German and Swedish unions in economic management. Under the *Charter for Employment* (1986) there was to be no wholesale repeal of post-1979 union legislation, but employees and trade unionists would be guaranteed equal rights with employers. *Meet The Challenge, Make The Change* (1989) identified inflation as the chief threat but rejected incomes policy and social contracts, stressing instead supply-side measures to ease production bottlenecks, and the notion that investment and growth must precede consumption, a formulation traditionally disliked by the public sector unions.

The unions were appeased by a commitment to a national minimum wage, although this annoyed private sector unions (notably in engineering) which feared its impact on differentials. Economic manageability and consensus would be promoted by a Department of Trade that enjoyed close links with both sides of industry. *Looking To The Future* (1990) envisaged a 'national economic assessment' to create a consensus on competing economic claims.[30]

Labour's economic policy is deeply influenced by German models of social partnership. This policy received a boost with the introduction of the EC's Social Charter to which both Labour and the Trades Union Congress (TUC) are committed. As a result of the Policy Review and Labour's defeat in 1992, the party-union relationship will change dramatically despite the failure to create a mass base. Attempts by unions to unseat MPs, public opinion's dislike of the party-union link, and the efforts of some union leaders to determine the outcome of the subsequent party leadership election means that a reduction in union influence is inevitable. Neither party nor union leaders wish to be drawn into the vortex of social contract exchange politics. Both know they could never satisfy the other's aspirations.

## UNIONS, PROGRAMMATIC RENEWAL AND POST-MATERIALIST VALUES

Programmatic renewal also coincided with the rise of new issues, notably environmentalism and gender, which challenged established union political, policy interests and values.

### Environmental Issues

Unions recognised the electoral and political importance of being seen to be green but expressed concern at the impact of green policies on their members' employment prospects and living standards, a point not lost on the political parties. Green policies, however, might cost the electoral support of those who feared for their jobs allowing their opponents to portray social democracy as 'anti-prosperity'. On the other hand, green influences were strong amongst the party activists and in some countries office seemed attainable only in alliance with Greens. Public sector unions were in a particularly difficult position. Programmatic renewal's argument that public service provision now depended on wealth creation rather than redistribution clashed with the membership's strong commitment not only to public services but also to post-materialist values.

Environmental issues were non-controversial in Labour's Policy Review. Although seen by all as important, there was an implicit consensus that there were other issues of more direct importance for electability. Despite their improved performance in the June 1989 European elections, the Greens posed no substantial electoral threat and the salience of green issues declined thereafter. There was none the less a political incentive to integrate green issues into programmatic renewal if they did not threaten the primacy of economic growth as the prime policy objective.[31] A major source of controversy was nuclear power. This was especially so in the TUC where the pro- and anti-nuclear power unions divided broadly along left-right lines.[32] This split was patched over and was not transmitted into the party's Policy Review which remained committed to a non-nuclear energy policy. Pressure was further reduced by the government's moratorium on the construction of new nuclear power stations until 1994. Labour's energy spokesman called for a coal-based energy policy but emphasised that this did not mean a Swedish-style nuclear phase-out and that it would be accompanied by government aid for the installation of clean burning technology in coal-fired power stations.[33]

In Sweden the LO expressed disquiet over the economic consequences of green politics, with particular concern focusing on the dilemmas of Swedish energy policy.[34] The 1980 referendum and subsequent legislation required the phasing out of Sweden's nuclear power stations by 2010. The SAP's attempt to ride the green wave conflicted with a developing alliance between the LO and business, who were worried about competitiveness and unemployment. A committee chaired and appointed by the Prime Minister plus three leading Social Democrats attempted to formulate a consensus on energy policy and in the January 1990 cabinet reshuffle the energy and environment portfolios were split. The energy portfolio was given to a confidante of the prime minister who was also an LO vice-president who had called for 'circumspection' on the nuclear issue; the environment minister was a longstanding opponent of nuclear power. Both were members of the prime minister's working party. Although the government proceeded with several costly environmental policies the nuclear phase-out became symbolic of the SAP's commitment (or lack of it) to green issues. The SAP's postponement of the phase-out did not produce a severe political crisis as other issues dominated the 1991 election, but the phase-out controversy further strained the party-union relationship.[35]

The SAP managed with some success to integrate green politics but was reluctant to add to its difficulties with the LO by adopting an environmental policy that jeopardised relations at a time of economic crisis. The 1990 Programme sought to reconcile green issues with traditional social democratic concerns and included opposition to nuclear power. The SAP's February 1991 environmental programme, which aimed at solving the problem of industrial pollution by 2010, was cautiously welcomed by Swedish employers but not the Greens. Significantly, the drafting committee included LO representatives who insisted that the maintenance of full employment be accorded equal status with environmentalism. In the energy field the SAP's image as 'the concrete party' and growing economic problems posed a difficult strategic problem for which there was no clearly apparent solution. As Sweden is Europe's most energy-intensive society, it was impossible to achieve a popular or consensual solution to the dilemma caused by the nuclear phase-out, which has since been shelved.

In Norway the Labour Party's environmentalism caused problems with the LO.[36] A 1977 party proposal to ban the development of a major hydro-electric project on environmental grounds provoked a fierce debate within the DNA which opted for a compromise, leaving the final decision to a Labour government. Individual members of the LO played a major role in the group that blocked the proposal for an outright ban. Labour's 1985 election programme stressed 'traditional' social democratic goals (growth, full employment and so on), but there was a marked shift in the *Freedom Campaign*, and subsequently, towards environmental issues. This caused disquiet in the LO, the LO general secretary warning Labour that environmentalism should not be pursued at the expense of employment. In response, the party's youth movement criticised the 'old men' in the LO for their lack of enthusiasm for green politics. The sensitivity of environmentalism in the LO-DNA relationship is shown by the fact that these questions are handled at meetings where no written record is kept, especially in the Co-operation Committee which handles LO-DNA relations. The resulting consensus is then fed into the deliberations of the Central Committee and the committees preparing the DNA's election programmes. Within the LO, the key division on environmental issues is between unions in the energy-intensive manufacturing sector and the public sector unions who tend to favour conservation over growth.

In Germany the SPD's flirtation with 'Red-Green' policies and politics antagonised some major DGB unions, especially the Chemical Workers.[37] The political salience of the nuclear issue pulled many union members (particularly in the public sector) in the opposite direction, but in general the DGB unions remained sceptical of the SPD's attraction to green politics, arguing that 'Due regard [must] be taken of environmental measures' potential effects on employment'.[38] The flirtation with the Greens was seen as symptomatic of the baleful influence of white-collar/ middle class activists out of touch with core SPD blue-collar supporters, whilst the experience of local coalitions indicated that Greens were unpredictable and unreliable allies.

The Kohl government's nuclear power moratorium and the electoral ebbing of the Greens eased internal tensions but environmental issues remained a potentially deeply divisive issue given the cost of unification. The unions argued that Germany could not easily afford both and they opposed precipitate environmental policies, except in the East, although the DGB reflected East German trade unionists' concern that an environmental clampdown when coupled with the economic strains of unification would lead to explosive social unrest. The 1990 SPD election programme did emphasise environmental issues but considerable doubt remains as to whether an SPD government anxious for a co-operative relationship with the unions would feel able to redeem its green pledges.

Environmental issues caused relatively few problems in Denmark and and Danish Social Democrats have approved extensive environmental programmes with the agreement of the LO.[39] In Denmark environmentalism never became a major domestic issue given the consensus surrounding a non-nuclear/renewable energy policy and extensive recycling programmes. Unions and party have agreed upon environmental policies and programmes that are conditional on readjustment costs being borne by society as a whole and not solely by working people. There remains, however, considerable doubt as to the feasibility of this. The Danish *Energy 2000* programme, for example, has been criticised for grossly underestimating the cost of its linked energy and environmental policy. Spiralling costs might make it difficult to maintain Denmark's environmental consensus, leading unions to call for relaxed controls to ease the transition.

*Gender Issues*

Labour movements have long established structures for women, and the enhancement of women's rights is a central objective of trade unionism and social democracy.[40] However, low levels of unionisation and the suspicions of male-dominated unions of women workers as a threat to male status and differentials traditionally have limited women's influence in the labour movement. As a result of the growth of the women's movement and employment, the structures, policies and attitudes of both party and union were challenged as women asserted their separate interests in the labour movement.

These changes were, in part, a recognition not only of wider social change but also of electoral and labour force change.[41] The structures of the workforce and employment changed in the recession, with skilled, unionised males being replaced by semi-skilled, part-time, often nonunion, women workers. Recruiting women was, for many unions, part of their survival strategy but they recognised that attracting women required changes in their policies and procedures. The public sector being the largest source of female employment, public sector unions such as the National Union of Public Employees in the UK, OTV in Germany, and the Danish General Worker's Union have done much to attract women, although the same developments are beginning to appear in traditionally male-dominated manufacturing unions.[42]

The importance of women as voters and party activists underpinned the pressure for similar organisational and programmatic changes within social democratic parties. In the 1980s the traditional aspiration for economic equality merged with the development of a specifically women's policy agenda, coupled with positive discrimination to boost women's representation within the labour movement. Labour movements have long recognised the importance of gender and gender issues although the effectiveness of their response has varied. Interestingly, despite a historical commitment to equality in the Scandinavian labour movements, the Danish Social Democrats have instituted a 40 per cent quota for women and the SAP is discussing the feasibility and desirability of a quota system.

There is within West European social democracy and trade unionism a general tendency towards organisational and policy change favourable to women. Consequently, there was relatively little overt conflict over gender issues in programmatic renewal except where it affected the distribution of power and influence. There is a considerable overlap of union and party policy and general agreement on what ought to be done. As with green issues, however, gender politics require considerable and therefore costly public policy changes. The public provision of, for example, child-care facilities for women who wish to return to the workforce are expensive. Meanwhile the desire for more flexible working practices to enable women to combine family and career excited the suspicion of male trade unionists who feared that flexibility would worsen their pay and working conditions.

The SPD's approach to gender issues has become something of a model. By the 1960s, postwar social change had created a new generation of women with high expectations. The SPD initially benefited electorally but began to lose women's votes in the 1970s.[43] Faced with the Green upsurge and its overt attempt to transform women's role in society, the SPD rethought its attitudes. The increasing visibility and assertiveness of women within the SPD led to a much higher profile for womens' issues in the SPD's programmes and for constitutional change to establish a quota system whereby women were to hold a minimum of 40 per cent of all party posts by 1998. Quotas were regarded with suspicion by more traditional labourist elements in the SPD as yet another threat to their position, but it is important to remember that most DGB unions in the 1970s and 1980s gave high priority to recruiting women, and women union leaders are increasingly influential in the SPD elite. Furthermore, the demand for quotas crystallised the perception that the DGB/SPD were forfeiting their claim to be the leading progressive political force in society, leading many male trade unionists and party members to reconsider movement customs and attitudes.

The SPD's approach was followed explicitly by the British Labour Party. A 1989 conference resolution formed the basis for a consultation process that produced a report, adopted by the 1990 conference.[44] This established a quota system and set the ultimate goal of 40 per cent of all posts being occupied by women by the mid-to-late 1990s. This quota system was in addition to enhancing the existing system of women's committees, and parallel changes were to be encouraged in the selection of parliamentary candidates. Hostility to the quota system was muted and enjoyed the support of major unions that had, in both the Policy Review and their own organisations, placed increased emphasis on the role and special needs of women.

The resolution of gender issues in the Norwegian Labour movement was eased by the dominance of Gro Harlem Brundtland as party leader and prime minister. Women hold about half of the key positions in the party, and women's issues (notably the related questions of employment opportunities and child-care provision) figured prominently in the Labour Party's programme and election appeal. In 1983 Labour changed its rules to ensure that 40 per cent of the candidates were women, with the objective that 40 per cent of its MPs would eventually be women. Aided by Norway's party list electoral system the percentage is currently about 30 per cent. There have been, however, some complaints about the low priority given to 'traditional' workers compared to women and white collar groups.

Institutional change in the labour movement lags behind the changes in women's consciousness and policy: certainly attitudinal change cannot be decreed by institutional change, but without such change new policies are likely to have little impact. Gender issues and politics represent a symbolic and direct challenge to the old dominant culture of the labour movement. Essentially, this has been a male-manual worker culture which, although eroded by industrial restructuring and social change, still predominates. The new culture fuelled calls for affirmative action on behalf of women, accompanied by programmatic change, and it represented a challenge to the established distribution of power. Gender politics symbolised the shift from 'old' to 'new' social democracy and some unions feared that this would reduce their influence. It is equally clear, however, that if unions and parties are to recover voters and recruit new occupational groups, they must take gender issues seriously and modify their structures, procedures and policies accordingly.

## TRADE UNIONS AND PROGRAMMATIC RENEWAL: CONCLUSIONS

During the 1980s the traditional social democratic project – full employment, public spending and tripartite politics – was eroded by mass unemployment, industrial restructuring and the rise of the new right. Confronted by electoral difficulties, social democratic parties reassessed their policies and structures, adopting 'market' socialism and jettisoning traditional aspects of social democracy. This led to a questioning of the trades unions' relationship with the parties and naturally aroused suspicion inside the former. However, unions support social democratic parties to achieve specific and general goals that are unrealisable if the party is unelectable. The unions expected that programmatic renewal would create an electable and responsive party, but recognised that renewal would undermine their influence. The politics of programmatic renewal were concerned with finding a new intra-movement and inter-organisational consensus.

Unions, on the whole, were reactive and defensive for four reasons. First overt and vigorous use of union influence would cost support from electorates who perceived social democracy to be union-dominated. Second, unions subscribe to a democratic ethos that constrains the overt assertion of their power against other segments of the movement. Third, unions are conscious that not all their members support social democracy; hence partisanship might cost members. Fourth, the primacy of the electoral process gives the party control over the definition of social democracy. None of the parties has deployed a restrictive definition of social democracy.

Unions, however, could not and would not meekly acquiesce in jettisoning matters of vital interest. Social democracy's emphasis on employment and production issues proved capable of embracing organised labour but post-materialist values posed more of a threat as these were more hostile to the unions' traditional interests. Although they have few sanctions (assertion might reduce party electability, withdrawal would deny them a party-political vehicle), parties cannot afford to over-antagonise a major source of support. The history and structure of the party-union relationship shows that, despite misgivings, the unions cannot bloc programmatic renewal. This is for two reasons:

## Pragmatism

In all the cases considered here the unions traditionally have accepted a vague definition of social democracy. The flexibility of Clause 4 in the Labour Party parallels that of the programmatic parties whose statements are designed to last for decades. In Germany the Bad Godesberg consensus is under challenge and with it the interests of the unions, in Norway the LO has recognised that *The Programme for Action* did not go far enough and further renewal is unavoidable. Danish unions confronted by a fragmented party system and electoral decline accepted the requirement of a rethink. In Britain the unions have accepted a Policy Review that has slaughtered many sacred union cows, and stomachs a reduced place in the party policy process. In Sweden the situation was slightly different as the unions' problem was not to help the party regain, but rather retain, power. Confronted with the SAP's rethinking of traditional policies in the face of economic difficulties, the LO concluded that its own organisational interests, those of its members, and of society required that it support social democracy.

*Electoralism*

Both the unions and social democracy are committed to liberal democratic parliamentarianism. Society can only be reformed, and union members' interests defended, by a social democratic party being elected to government. This means that the party cannot rely solely on union or working-class votes and it requires that the unions defer to the party's electoral strategy. Unions and parties co-operate to achieve separate yet overlapping goals, but this exchange is not symmetrical. Socio-economic change and electoral decline, coupled with often unhappy experiences in government, compelled social democratic parties in the 1980s to reconsider their programmes and image. The unions were a cause and target of programmatic renewal, but nowhere was union suspicion of programmatic renewal pushed to the point where the relationship was jeopardised.

What emerges so strongly from the politics of programmatic renewal is the unions' *relative* powerlessness and quiescence. Unions are sufficiently powerful to place obstacles in the way of renewal. They did not do so for the simple reason that they had no political option other than social democracy. Long-term change in the political ecology of social democracy required a reformulation of policy and strategy in the interests of electability. Programmatic renewal will inevitably reduce union influence but renewal does not require the breaking of the party-union link: rather, its evolution into a looser and more flexible form.

NOTES

1. G. Esping-Andersen, *Politics Against Markets* (Princeton, NJ: Princeton UP, 1985) stresses adaptability, while A. Przeworski, *Capitalism and Social Democracy* (Cambridge: CUP, 1985) emphaises decline. For a survey of social democracy in the 1970s and 1980s, see G. and L. Radice, *Socialists in the Recession* (London: Macmillan, 1986). My own study examines Norway, Sweden, Denmark, West Germany and the United Kingdom.
2. K. Heidar, 'Party Power: Approaches in a Field of Unfilled Classics', *Scandinavian Political Studies* 7/1 (Spring 1984), p. 13, and A.J. Taylor, *Trade Unions and Politics: A Comparative Introduction* (London: Macmillan, 1989), pp. 47–9.
3. W. Korpi, *The Democratic Class Struggle* (London: RKP, 1983), p. 9.
4. D.R. Cameron, 'Social Democracy, Corporatism, Labour Quiescence, and the Representation of Economic Interest in Advanced Capitalist Society', in J.H.

Goldthorpe (ed.), *Order and Conflict in Contemporary Capitalism. Studies in the Political Economy of Western Nations* (Oxford: Clarendon Press, 1984), pp. 143–78.

5.  D. Hine, 'Leaders and Followers: Democracy and Manageability in the Social Democratic Parties of Western Europe', in W.E. Paterson and A.H. Thomas (eds.), *The Future of Social Democracy: Problems and Prospects of Social Democratic Parties in Western Europe* (Oxford: Clarendon Press, 1986), pp. 262–5.

6.  F. Castles, *The Social Democratic Image of Society* (London: RKP, 1978), and A. Przeworski and J. Sprague, *Paper Stones: A History of Electoral Socialism* (Chicago: Chicago UP, 1986).

7.  L. Mioset, 'Nordic Economic Policies in the 1970s and 1980s', *International Organisation* 41/3 (1987), pp. 403–56, and D. Sainsbury, 'Scandinavian Party Politics Re-examined: Social Democracy in Decline', *West European Politics* 7/4 (Oct. 1984), pp. 67–102.

8.  H. Bergström, 'Social Democracy in Crisis', *Current Sweden* No.381 (May 1991), pp. 3–8, and R. Taylor, 'The Economic Policies of Sweden's Political Parties', ibid., No.383 (June 1991), pp. 3–5.

9.  H. Bergström, 'Social Democrats Still Going Strong – Incorporating The Green Wave', ibid., No.367 (Oct. 1988).

10. Speech by Stig Malm (LO President), *LO Congress 1986 (Documentation)* (Stockholm: LO, 23 Sept. 1986), p. 11.

11. For recent developments, see, D. Sainsbury, 'Swedish Social Democracy in Transition', *West European Politics* 14/1 (Jan. 1991), pp. 31–57.

12. *The Unions and the Party* (Stockholm: LO, 1985), pp. 8–9, and *The Swedish Trade Union Confederation* (Stockholm: LO, 1981), p. 8. See also, *Programme of the Swedish Social Democratic Party* (adopted by 1975 congress), pp. 7–11.

13. E. Kolinsky, *Parties, Opposition and Society in West Germany* (London: Croom Helm, 1984), pp. 81–7.

14. A.S. Markovits, *The Politics of West German Trade Unions* (Cambridge: CUP, 1986), pp. 80–3. *DGB Basic Programme* (4th Extraordinary Congress, March 1981) sets out the DGB's agenda for the 1980s. See also A.S. Markovits and C.S.Allen, 'The Trade Unions', in G. Smith, W.E. Paterson and P.H. Merkl (eds.), *Developments in West German Politics* (London: Macmillan, 1989), pp. 289–307.

15. R.J. Dalton, 'The West German Party System Between Two Ages', in idem *et al.* (eds.), *Electoral Change in Advanced Industrial Democracies* (Princeton, NJ: Princeton UP, 1984), pp. 104–33.

16. K. Von Beyme, 'The Changing Relationship between Trade Unions and the Social Democratic Party in West Germany', *Government and Opposition* 13 (1978), pp. 388–415; G. Brauthal, 'The Social Democratic Party', in H.G. Peter-Wallach and G.K. Romoser (eds.), *West German Politics in the Mid Eighties* (NY: Praeger, 1983), pp. 81–111, and S. Padgett, 'The West German Social Democrats in Opposition', *West European Politics* 10/3 (July 1987), pp. 333–56.

17. G. Timmins, 'Organised Labour Unification: The Social Dimension', in J. Osmond (ed.), *German Reunification: A Guide and Commentary* (London: Longman, 1992).

18. *LO Programme of Action 1985–89* (Oslo; LO 1985), p. 15. For the background to current politics see W.M. Lafferty and O. Knutsen, 'Leftist and Rightist Ideology in a Social Democratic State. An Analysis of Norway in the Midst of the Conservative Resurgence', *British Journal of Political Science* 14/3 (Autumn 1984), pp. 369–85.

19. *LO Inform International*, 24 Oct. 1988, p. 4, *LO General Council Statement*, 1 April 1989, and *LO Inform International*, 4 June 1989, p. 4.

20. *LO Inform International*, 2 Feb. 1987, pp. 4–5.

21. Thomas Nielsen (LO President), quoted in *Danish Labour News*, Jan. 1980, p. 1, and *Danish Labour News*, 2 May 1988, p. 4.

22. O Borre, 'The Danish General Election of 1987', *Electoral Studies* 7/2 (April 1988), pp. 15–18. See also E.S. Einhorn, 'Danish Politics in the 1980s: The Habit of Muddling Through', *Current History* No.81 (1982) and E. Olsen, 'The Dilemma of the Social Democratic Labor Parties', *Daedalus* (Summer1984), a comparative study of

Denmark, Sweden and Norway.
23. *Danish Labour News*, 4 Nov. 1988, pp. 1–10.
24. Ibid., 4 Dec. 1989, pp. 9–10.
25. Ibid., 1 March 1989, pp. 8–12. *FiU Handbook* (Copenhagen: LO, July 1988), p. 7, LO Action Plan: Media Strategy of the Trade Union Movement 1990–93, in *Danish Labour News*, 4 Dec. 1989, pp. 11–13.
26. LO 32nd Ordinary Congress Nov. 1991, Political Statement, in *Danish Labour News*, No. 1 (Jan. 1992), p. 27. The Social Democrat's new journal launched in Sept. 1990 took as its first headline, 'Yes to the Market Economy'.
27. This analysis is based on Andrew J. Taylor, *Trade Unions and the Labour Party* (London: Croom Helm, 1987), pp. 199–234 and pp. 242–81, and idem, unpublished paper, 'When Dinosaurs Ruled the Earth. The Trade Unions and the Labour Party's Policy Review' (PSA Conference, Univ. of Warwick, 1989).
28. N. Millward, 'The State of the Unions', in R. Jowell *et al.* (eds.), *British Social Attitudes. The 7th Report* (Aldershot: Gower/SCPR, 1990), pp. 27–50.
29. This section is based on a detailed analysis of trade union journals from the period after the 1987 general election.
30. *The National Economic Assessment and the Role of Coordinated Pay Bargaining* (London: Campaign for Work Briefing Paper, Aug. 1991) examines how this might be realised and draws on German experience.
31. *Looking to the Future: A Dynamic Economy. A Decent Society Strong in Europe* (London: The Labour Party, 1990), pp. 19–23.
32. See, e.g., TUC, *Nuclear Energy: Work To Be Done* (London: TUC, 1986) and *Nuclear Power and Energy Policy* (London: TUC, 1988).
33. F. Dobson MP and K. Barron MP, *Cleaner Coal: A Strategy for the 90s and the 21st Century* (PLP Energy Team Briefing Paper, 1991).
34. D. Sainsbury, 'The 1988 Swedish Election: The Breakthrough of the Greens', *West European Politics* 12/2 (April 1983), pp. 140–2, and M. Bennulf and S. Holmberg, 'The Green Breakthrough in Sweden', *Scandinavian Political Studies* 13/2 (Summer 1990), pp. 165–84. See also D. John, 'Changes in the Political Culture – Challenges to the Trade Union Movement: The Debate on Nuclear Energy in Swedish and German Trade Unions', in J. R. Gibbins (ed.), *Contemporary Political Culture Politics in a Postmodern Age*, Sage Modern Politics Series, Vol. 23 (London: Sage/ECPR 1989), pp. 144–71.
35. A. Burke, 'Learning to Live Without Nuclear Power', *Current Sweden*, No. 372 (March 1990).
36. I am grateful to Knut Heidar for providing the information on which this paragraph is based.
37. E. Papadakis, *The Green Movement in West Germany* (London: Croom Helm, 1984), W. Hülsberg, *The German Greens: A Social and Political Profile* (London: Verso, 1988), and W. Paterson, 'Environmental Politics', in G. Smith, W. E. Paterson and P. H. Merkl (eds.), *Developments in West German Politics* (London: Macmillan, 1989), pp. 267–88.
38. DGB, *The German Trade Union Movement*, p. 166, and Jahn, 'Changes in the Political Culture', (note 34).
39. The LO's 1991 congress, however, gave little prominence to environmental issues *outside* the workplace. See 'Solidarity and Innovation', *Danish Labour News*, No. 1 (Jan. 1992).
40. See European Trade Union Institute, *Women's Representation in Trade Unions* (Brussels: European Trade Union Inst., 1983), and A. H. Cook, V. R. Lorwin, and A. K. Daniels, *Women and Trade Unions in Eleven Industrialised Countries* (Philadelphia: Temple UP, 1984).
41. On average, women constitute about 43 per cent of the workforce in Denmark 45.8 per cent, West Germany 39.4 per cent, Norway 44.6 per cent, Sweden 47.9 per cent, and the UK 41.4 per cent. ILO, *Year Book of Labour Statistics 1989–1990* (Geneva: ILO, 1990).
42. The largest source of women's employment remains those occupations most closely associated with womens' traditional domestic roles as follows:

|  | Percentage Total Workforce | Largest Female Occupation | Percentage Employed in Largest Group |
|---|---|---|---|
| Denmark | 45.8 | Community, Personal | 23.4 |
| W. Germany | 39.4 | Health Services. | 13.4 |
| Norway | 44.6 | ibid. | 21.2 |
| Sweden | 47.9 | ibid. | 26.6 |
| UK | 41.4 | ibid. | 16.2 |

Source: ILO, Year Book of Labour statistics 1989–1990 (Geneva: ILO, 1990).

43. E. Kolinsky, Women in West Germany – Life, Work and Politics (Oxford: Berg, 1989), for detail.
44. Representation of Women in the Labour Party, Report of the Consultative Process (London: Labour Party, 1990), and Selection of Parlimentary Candidates, Report of the NEC Consultation (London: Labour Party, 1990).

APPENDIX TABLE A

THE SOCIAL DEMOCRATIC/LABOUR PARTY PERCENTAGE SHARE OF THE
VOTE, 1976–1992

| Year | Sweden | Norway | Denmark | UK | FRG |
|------|--------|--------|---------|------|--------|
| 1976 | 42.7 | | | | 42.6 |
| 1977 | | 42.4 | 37.0 | | |
| 1978 | | | | | |
| 1979 | 43.2 | | 38.3 | 38.0 | |
| 1980 | | | | | 42.9 |
| 1981 | | 37.1 | 32.9 | | |
| 1982 | 45.6 | | | | |
| 1983 | | | | 27.6 | 38.2 |
| 1984 | | | 31.6 | | |
| 1985 | 45.1 | 40.8 | | | |
| 1986 | | | | | |
| 1987 | | | 29.3 | 30.8 | 37.0 |
| 1988 | 43.2 | | 29.9 | | |
| 1989 | | 34.3 | | | |
| 1990 | | | 37.4 | | 33.5[1] |
| 1991 | 38.2 | | | | |
| 1992 | | | | 35.9 | |

*Note* 1. All-German Election. The SPD polled 35.7 percent of the vote in the Federal
Republic and West Berlin.

*Source: Keesing's Contemporary Archives.*

## APPENDIX TABLE B
### CHANGING OCCUPATIONAL STRUCTURE 1960–1989 (PERCENTAGE OF CIVILIAN WORKFORCE)

| INDUSTRY | *1960* | 1989 | Difference |
|---|---|---|---|
| Federal Republic | 47.0 | 39.8 | -7.2 |
| United Kingdom | 47.7 | 29.4 | -18.3 |
| Denmark | 36.9 | 27.4 | -9.5 |
| Norway | 35.6 | 25.3 | -10.3 |
| Sweden | 40.3 | 29.4 | -10.9 |
| *Average* | *41.5* | *30.3* | *-11.2* |
| MANUFACTURING | | | |
| Federal Republic | 34.3 | 31.6 | -2.7 |
| United Kingdom | 38.4 | 23.0 | -15.4 |
| Denmark | 25.1 | 20.8 | -4.3 |
| Norway | 25.6 | 15.2 | -10.4 |
| Sweden | 31.5 | 21.9 | -9.6 |
| *Average* | *31.0* | *22.5* | *-8.5* |
| SERVICE INDUSTRIES | | | |
| Federal Republic | 39.1 | 56.5 | +17.4 |
| United Kingdom | 47.6 | 68.4 | +20.8 |
| Denmark | 44.8 | 66.9 | +22.1 |
| Norway | 42.9 | 68.1 | +25.2 |
| Sweden | 44.0 | 67.0 | +23.0 |
| *Average* | *44.0* | *65.3* | *+21.7* |
| GOVERNMENT EMPLOYMENT | | | |
| Federal Republic | 8.0 | 15.5 | +7.5 |
| United Kingdom | 14.8 | 19.9 | +5.1 |
| Denmark | 15.2[1] | 29.8 | +14.6 |
| Norway | 15.4[1] | 26.9 | +11.5 |
| Sweden | 12.8 | 31.6 | +19.0 |
| *Average* | *13.3* | *24.8* | *+11.5* |

*Note* 1. Data for 1966

*Source*: *OECD Abstract of Historical Statistics 1960–1989* (Paris: OECD, 1991), Tables 2.10, 2.11, 2.12, and 2.13. (pp.40–8).

# Programmatic Renewal, and Much More: From the PCI to the PDS

## GIANFRANCO PASQUINO

*The Italian Communist Party has undergone a major, complex, and painful transformation. It has changed its name to the Democratic Party of the Left, along with its emblem, and its organisation. Having abandoned democratic centralism, the PDS has quickly become a party of factions. It has also attempted to create a shadow government, with mixed results. The PDS is today a party of women and men, though with reduced electoral attractiveness. As to programmatic renewal, the PDS has modified its programme to become more environmentalist and totally autonomous in its foreign policy. It has adopted a position highly favourable to the reform of Italian institutions and to the protection and promotion of citizens' rights. By so doing, it has lost some of its traditional electorate without acquiring a new one.*

The Italian Communist Party has always believed in programmes, in their formulation, their dissemination and their almost therapeutic quality. In the 1980s it twice created an Office for the Programme and entrusted it to important political personalities: the former Secretary-General of the Italian General Labour Confederation (CGIL), Luciano Lama, and the man responsible for economic affairs, Alfredo Reichlin – without tangible results. The PCI has paid a lot of attention to its Italian competitors' programmes. It has tried to enforce the programmatic accountability of successive Italian governments and to evaluate their performance by reference to their programmatic declarations. It has explained and justified its alliance strategy and policies on the basis of programmatic convergences and similarity of goals.

More recently, it has attempted to shape alliances and coalitions based on programmatic affinity more than on political contiguity. Indeed, the PCI has devoted much of its best energies to the drafting, discussion and publicising of its electoral and political programme, without much success. Even less so in recent times when it has become clear that the 'parliamentary road to power', the strategy chosen by Palmiro Togliatti for Italian Communism, had inevitably transformed itself into the electoral road to parliament (and some parliamentary influence), leading nowhere else.

Increasingly, but especially in the 1980s, communist bargaining in Parliament – which in some cases was not exactly based on programmatic assumptions and reliability – has been less successful and less profitable than at any time in the past. Finally, it became clear that, especially after the crumbling of the Berlin Wall, something else, something more, something better than just the drafting of yet another programme was needed to renovate the party and to improve its performance. Hence the decision suddenly announced on 12 November 1989 by the Secretary-General Achille Occhetto, in a Sunday morning speech to a group of Resistance veterans at Bologna, to change the name, emblem and structure of the PCI, and, needless to say, to draft a brand new programme.

What seemed to be a relatively easy and simple process – the secretary enjoyed a rather ample majority – resulted in a long, complex, acrimonious debate, a clash of personalities, bitter confrontations and reciprocal accusations of 'selling out' the revered patrimony of the PCI. To make a long story short, after Occhetto's initial declaration the party went through a couple of stormy Central Committee meetings and then convened, and duly held, a national congress at Bologna in early March 1990. The congress revealed that the secretary had the support of almost 70 per cent of the delegates, while the so-called *fronte del no*, those opposing the change, obtained the remaining 30 per cent, but it was internally divided. The congress was fought almost totally around the issue of the changes in the name and emblem of the party. Not much time was left nor utilised for discussing programmatic renewal. Even the discussions of party name and emblem were adjourned to another congress which would define the new political identity of the party and shape its programmatic profile.

In the meantime, in response to some of the Bologna congress decisions, a programmatic convention was held in Rome on 22–24 October 1990. Finally, when the energies of most party leaders and, more particularly, of the militants, had been drained and the enthusiasm of outside supporters all but extinguished, the last congress of the Italian Communist Party and, at the same time, the first congress of the newly-born Democratic Party of the Left (*Partito Democratico della Sinistra*, henceforth PDS) was convened in Rimini (29 January–2 February 1991).[1]

First, the Rimini congress ratified the decision to adopt a new name and emblem. The new symbol is an oak that does not replace completely the traditional hammer and sickle but grows out of them, both in order to suggest continuity rather than cutting of the roots and to prevent any attempt by internal and external opponents to utilise the old emblem. Second, the congress began to transform the structure and the programmes of the party. In order to understand not only the outcome, but also the process through which a programmatic renewal of the party was sought, and partially achieved, it is necessary to dwell on the structure of the party and its changes. The problems of the PCI were considered by external observers and party members alike to arise also from its structural rigidities, inadequacies and obsolescence.

RENEWAL OF THE PARTY ORGANISATION

Three issues were tackled under the heading of party organisation: democratic centralism, leadership and the shadow government. Frequently attacked by its external opponents and often criticised by some party members, democratic centralism had been abandoned in practice at least since Enrico Berlinguer's death in June 1984. A complex and not necessarily always authoritarian device, PCI democratic centralism was based on a shared ideology, on common, cherished goals, on accepted party discipline rarely to be enforced, on a degree of conformism, on a judicious process of co-optation, and on the expectation that a well-functioning bureaucracy would duly reward all its members. It had been largely successful both in relieving tensions within the party and in shaping a powerful organisation. Now that it has been officially abandoned, the former communists are encountering all the difficulties of a factionalised party.

Democratic centralism was challenged first in practice, in the wake of disappointing electoral results, particularly after election defeats in the late 1980s. It was questioned because it prevented the free flow of ideas and criticism from below; it operated as a silencer, and functioned in favor of continuity and against innovation. These consequences were particularly evident under the leadership of Alessandro Natta. His conservative management of the party was accompanied by the visible presence within the Executive and the Central Committees of three different factions: the centrists, or *berlingueriani*, the well-organised and disciplined *ingraiani* (from Pietro Ingrao, their quasi-charismatic leader) on the left, and the 'reformists' around Giorgio Napolitano on the right. The combination of a weak party secretary, chosen in order to avoid a devastating succession struggle in 1984, and the existence of organised factions without the possibility of majority voting, brought the party to a standstill. At that point, it became clear that democratic centralism had transformed itself into a major liability. In any case, few in the PCI desired its implementation any longer: it had been outgrown in the conscience of party members. The problem was that the alternative models of party organisation available in the Italian political market were not at all attractive.

Given their sharp and well-founded criticisms of the Socialist Party model – 'the party of the President', a model designed to produce and support the autocratic leadership of Bettino Craxi – and given their internal differentiation with no uncontested leader, the communists could hardly imitate such a model. Nor could they look to the Christian Democrats for inspiration. This party of factions had always been denounced by them – and indeed the incessant internal bickering that the Christian Democrats displayed to the public was not appealing, although in practice that peculiar constellation of factions has been very successful, precisely because of its many factions. The models of the other Western European communist parties were rejected outright, all being of the democratic centralist kind though with some significant variations.[2]

Some attention was given to the organisational models of certain European socialist parties, especially the French and Spanish Socialist Parties, the German Social Democrats, and the British Labour Party. For different reasons, the impossibility of creating a federated party such as the French one, the lack of a close relationship with a unified trade union movement such as the one attributed to the Labour Party, the exceptionality of a party such as the PSOE and, in any case, the perceived subordination of the party organisation to the party-in-the government,[3] these three models were discarded. More attention was devoted to the SPD organisation which seems to combine discipline and articulation of different internal positions while remaining a mass party. It is difficult to assess how much in practice was borrowed by the Italian Communists from the SPD experience, but democratic centralism was finally jettisoned.

As to the PDS organisation, two problems exist. The first one is the constant decline of old party members and the accompanying difficulty of recruiting new members, together with the increasing cost, in terms of time and energies of the militants, of recruitment drives. Occhetto's opponents attribute these difficulties to the secretary himself for having 'demoralised' the party and almost dissipated its healthy energies. Given a more than decennial trend of membership decline, this does not appear a convincing explanation. The other problem concerns the very structure of the party organisation and has two components: an internal one and an external one. As to the first, the PDS is trying to reorganise itself away from territorial structures, in particular, traditional and declining sections, towards thematic structures dealing with the environment, citizens' rights and day-to-day issues, in order to reach more individuals, to be more specialised, and to become more effective. Moreover, it is further reducing the number of party functionaries, introducing part-time employment within the apparatus, specialising its personnel, and decentralising somewhat the decision-making process.

Last but certainly not least, the party is moving towards becoming a party of both women and men. This means that many efforts are under way to achieve a balanced representation within the party leadership at all levels and in all elective assemblies. A very high quota, no less than 40 per cent, has been set for women's representation in all leadership and executive positions, reflecting the demands and the success of German social democratic women. One statutory clause requires a more or less equal gender representation. Some reorganisation of local units and the strengthening, at least on paper, of regional organisations were also inserted into the new statute. Rejected were the requests by some Committees for the Constituent, which had sprung up to support the political and programmatic renewal, to obtain forms of collective membership and to have the Secretary directly elected by the delegates to the Congress. Ironically enough, Occhetto was dramatically flunked by the members of the National Council, in both a technical and political 'incident', only to be elected at his second attempt.

All this said, the most burning question, that of organised factions, was not even confronted. The net result is that the PDS is still undergoing significant organisational difficulties. Externally, it is engaged in a bitter quarrel against the leaders and the more than 110,000 members of the splinter *Rifondazione Comunista* concerning the name, emblem, certain organisational headquarters (sections and federations where members of *Rifondazione* are in the majority), and funds. Internally, it is divided into three organised factions, or 'sensitivities', the euphemism PDS leaders are using to baptise them. More precisely, these are the groups around secretary Occhetto and vice-secretary Massimo D'Alema ('loyal, but not faithful to the secretary', as he himself has avowed), whose own political ambitions are undeniable; those around Ingrao and Tortorella; and the followers of Napolitano. The latter's 'Reformist Area' supports the secretary but, is often dissatisfied to such an extent that in some important federations, including that of Milan, there have been serious clashes followed by the exit of reformists.

Finally, the new party has succeeded in recruiting almost one million members, more than two-thirds of the 1990 PCI membership. If the same relationship between members and voters that existed for the PCI still pertains, that is, approximately 1 to 8–10, these data do not bode well for the PDS. One ought to add that membership in the new party lasts for three years. This means that the PDS has decided to deprive itself of the yearly recruitment drives that many considered to be potent instruments for mobilising existing members, activating some of them, reaching new potential members, and launching political campaigns. According to several critics inside and outside the PDS, this is the beginning of the demise of a mass party which may, however, persist in a few areas of traditional entrenchment, especially Emilia Romagna, and parts of Tuscany and Umbria.

Organisational difficulties and organisational solutions are always, and at the same time, the signal and the product of political and leadership problems.[4] Problems of this kind have plagued the PCI throughout the 1980s and were only muffled before Berlinguer's death. Both political and leadership problems had been postponed for too long under Berlinguer: they were bound to explode. The succession crisis began with the uncontested election of Natta in June 1984, the last accomplishment of democratic centralism in its conformist version, and a clear indication of the party leaders' inability to choose among competing political lines and candidates or to implement a generational turnover. It ended with the rather controversial election of Occhetto in July 1988. Almost a matter of necessity, since at the time Occhetto was already the vice-secretary and had been the co-ordinator of the Secretariat for several years, this election was anticipated by unprecedented criticism of Natta's party leadership (or lack thereof).

Occhetto's election did not mean much of a generational change, since he had been an important member of the leadership group for at least 20 years. To a certain extent, it intimated the beginning of the attempt to create a new leadership group. The legitimation of the new leadership group has proved to be very difficult. There is no Resistance mystique to be revived; no possibility of resorting to the blessing of the now extremely controversial figure of Togliatti; not even, for most of them, except Occhetto, the recognition of leadership qualities based on co-optation by Berlinguer. The handful of young men (and one woman), in their mid-30s to mid-40s, around the secretary do not appear to have impeccable credentials in the eyes of party members, militants, parliamentarians and rival leaders.

The change of the cherished name and emblem of the Italian Communist Party became an ordeal for Occhetto and his collaborators. So much so that, after many months of bitter and unproductive confrontation, the exasperated secretary denounced the existence of a group of oligarchs within the party. He was referring to old-timers such as Ingrao, Tortorella, Cossutta and former secretary Natta. In return, he was accused of behaving in a 'Caesaristic' way. Communist party debates have recently become very heated. Unprecedented, however, were two elements: first, that the secretary felt obliged to accuse his opponents in such a blatant way; second, that they should retort with such a strong accusation against a party secretary whom most of them had duly voted for.

In any case, this unedifying clash revealed that there were indeed oligarchs within the PCI, that, being one of them, Occhetto did not enjoy sufficient prestige, and that in order to break the hold of the oligarchs he had to take a Caesaristic route. But this was to no avail since the 'oligarchs' continued to condition the progress of the PCI and its majority towards a renewal of the party, using the blackmail of a schism.

Once the ambitious attempt to open up the party to the so-called submerged or diffused left had failed, the congress could not but ratify the balance of forces between the sponsors of the three different motions (by now full-blown factions) and witness the preannounced split of a tiny group of parliamentarians. What was worse, however, was that the factional struggle was translated into the composition of the elective bodies. Thus, a cumbersome National Council made up of 547 members, 390 men and 157 women, replaced the Central Committee (less than 400 members) and an Executive Committee of 118 members replaced a similar but less inflated body, and both were elected along rigorously factional lines. Two slimmer structures were also created: a *Coordinamento Politico* (Political Co-ordinating Committee) whose 19 members were proposed by the secretary and elected by the Executive Committee, in accordance with the logic of factionalism, and a rather homogeneous politico-managerial staff of eight members chosen by the secretary.

By far the most significant organisational innovation had been made before the turmoil caused by the change of name and emblem of the party. After a long incubation, which went back to the Florence Congress of April 1986, the party had decided to create a shadow government. There were two particularly important motivations mentioned by the party secretary in his inauguration speech of 19 July 1989. First, there was the need to get rid of the consociational tendency still alive in Italian politics and to work instead for the presentation of clear programmatic options. Second, was the imperative to alter the relationship between parties and institutions, returning the parties to their role of programmatic formulation. 'The birth of the shadow government means above all a different manner of living and of organising our party, a different manner of being present and active in the social and institutional life of Italy'.[5] Two major functions were attributed to the shadow government: visibly to represent the communist parliamentary opposition and to counteract governmental proposals effectively in order to show that the PCI was indeed a credible candidate to replace the existing government.

This is not the place to undertake a detailed evaluation of the philosophy[6] and the activities[7] of the Communist shadow government. Clearly inspired by the British experience, it was meant in a exaggerated way to incorporate too many peculiarities of the Italian political system and of the PCI itself. In spite of its previous criticism of the excessive number of 'real' ministers, the Communist shadow government was itself a hypertrophic structure: 21 ministers plus one co-ordinator, the shadow Prime Minister being, rightly, the secretary himself. It was carefully composed of a certain number of parliamentarians (18), more deputies (11) than senators (7), and non-parliamentarians (3), of men (16) and women (5), of Communists (16) and Independents (5). A few months after its inauguration, it became all but paralysed when four shadow ministers rejected Occhetto's proposal to change the party, and one never committed himself. Later, two other shadow ministers, though favourable to Occhetto, resigned over serious, specific programmatic disagreements. Finally, the secretary himself sank the shadow government by appointing his own substitute.

The short life of the shadow government has been plagued by several additional problems. It has not succeeded in obtaining enough decision-making power *vis-à-vis* the party apparatus. Moreover, it has never been fully accepted and recognised as authoritative by the Communist parliamentary caucuses. Therefore, it created a sort of triple command structure: the shadow ministers themselves, Communist functionaries in charge of some issue areas, and Communist parliamentary leaders. While a certain success was enjoyed by the image created and by the very idea that the PCI was characterising itself as a credible, responsible alternative to existing governments, its practice left a lot to be desired.

Summing up, the legacy of 15 months of political struggles within the PCI is not encouraging. A smaller party divided into rigid factions with a subterranean struggle of the centre against the right, a leadership still in search of authority and prestige, a crippled shadow government, a wait-and-see attitude, if not outright disillusion, among the potential outside supporters, who were originally the main target of the renewal effort. Has the party at least proceeded to renew its programme convincingly enough to pursue some of its goals with relative confidence?

In a rightly famous Central Committee report, 'La crisi italiana e le prospettive dell'alternativa',[8] the then vice-secretary Occhetto declared an end to consociational politics and the beginning of an alternative politics to be based on programmatic elaboration, confrontation and affinity. He urged the transformation of Italian politics away from alliances based on alignments and in favour of alliances based on the congruence/consonance of programmes. He stressed the 'primacy of the programmes'. No wonder that under his secretariat the process of programmatic renewal has acquired an even greater momentum. It had, however, to deal with some obstacles, ingrained habits, and structural and political problems. The next section will put these in perspective.

BEYOND TRADITIONAL POLITICS

The Italian Communist Party has been from many points of view the outstanding representative of the best and the worst of traditional politics. It has represented the classic case of the class-mass party of Otto Kirchheimer's suggestive analysis. Indeed, there are good reasons to regret its passing, to adopt Kirchheimer's judgment, 'as we already regret the passing of other features in yesterday's stage of Western civilization'.[9] To be more precise, the Italian Communist Party was a class-mass party, with strong internal discipline, defending the interests of the lower classes, with a national perspective, and defending the Italian Constitution and its parliamentary form of government (including the proportional electoral system). Almost all this seems to have changed or is being consciously revised.

There are three major areas in which the PCI has produced fundamental programmatic renewal in the 1980s: gender relations; environmental politics; institutional and constitutional issues. To these, one might add international politics whose revision started in the 1960s and was well advanced by the end of the 1970s. Let us begin by dealing with the most complex topic of gender. No doubt the starting point might be a positive paradox. The PCI has always been a 'male chauvinist' party in the style of its politics, less so in substance. But it has always been, like other left-wing parties in Europe, more than willing and capable to elect women to important party and parliamentary positions. So much so that its female parliamentary representatives have been far more numerous than those of any other Italian party, in spite of the fact that there are still less women in the communist electorate than men. Female emancipation remained the declared goal of the PCI on the inescapable assumption that full emancipation and liberation would come only with a socialist revolution, or later with a profound transformation or, at least, with the coming to power of the Communist Party.

The feminist movement challenged all this and, though accommodated only slowly within the PCI, produced important changes. Above all, this meant the recognition that men cannot represent women; that both constitute a 'partiality'; that the gender difference is a positive resource; and that, as Occhetto's motion to the March 1990 Congress put it, 'women are a founding actor of the constituent phase of the new political formation'.[10] Or, as Occhetto stressed in his 'declaration of intentions', it is indispensable 'to go beyond a male society: human society is equally open to both genders'.[11]

All components of the party expressed support for women's demands and battles: positive action, equality of wage and working conditions, an important bill on 'the time of women', a bill against rape. The debate among communist women moved from the issue of quota representation to full equality of access to party and elective offices; from separatism represented by the attempt to have a motion for women only ('Our Liberty is in Our Hands') to full dignity within the three factions' motions, the women having realised that their political differences were more significant than their shared gender; from the *pensiero della differenza* ('thought of the difference') to the elaboration of the conditions for full participation and integration within the party.[12]

The debate remained rather obscure, somewhat specialised, often incomprehensible to the outsider, not productive of political mobilisation or votes. Indeed, the gap between the electoral behaviour of men and women in favour of the PCI was not at all reduced. The extreme positions of communist women, put forward by their representative in the Secretariat, Livia Turco, were finally severely criticised by a famous, highly-respected communist journalist, a representative of the old generation, who had fought through difficult times in favour of equality, against separatism and isolation, for the obliteration of differences.[13]

By now the PDS is truly 'a party of women and men'. The remaining differential in terms of the female presence in party and elective offices is not due to any discrimination. It is due simply to the differentiation of interests. Italian women have made it in several important professions such as journalism, the judiciary and medicine. If and when Italian politics becomes attractive, many more women will participate and the PDS will look like an easily available vehicle for them. It will then depend on its policies whether it will succeed in gaining a greater political consensus from women in general.

The second area in which the PCI-PDS has fundamentally reappraised its policies and made a profound programmatic renewal is the area of the environment. While some environmentalists and architects have actively and successfully collaborated with the party in the past (namely, in the 'red show-case' of Bologna, in preserving the historic centre), the PCI was obviously characterised as the party of industrial development. The party of the working class had, as a matter of necessity, to be in favour of policies entailing the numerical growth and political strengthening of its social base. As late as the Florence Congress of 1986, a small majority of the delegates voted for pursuing a programme of nuclear energy development.

Only after the Chernobyl accident did the party officially reverse its position. The party programme is now against any revival of the Italian nuclear energy system, which was almost completely shut down after the voters' approval of a package contained in three referenda held in November 1987. The party favours an 'ecological reconversion of productive activities'.[14] It is willing to take into account all the policy constraints that environmental protection implies, even where and when this might cost votes, as with a major property development in Florence, initially supported by the PCI, and later opposed obliging the PCI to abandon the ruling municipal coalition. Finally, it has appointed as shadow minister for the environment, Chicco Testa, a Communist deputy and former President of the Environment League.

It is difficult to say whether the PDS will be perceived as a red-green party because of the intense competition coming from single-issue green groups, movements and lists. Among other things, there are internal differences between a sort of environmental fundamentalism agitated for by the left wing and the moderate approach, not opposed under specified conditions to the production of nuclear energy, taken by one sector of Napolitano's followers. All the motions to the Bologna congress shared a strong environmentalist emphasis. For several supporters of the secretary's motion, the issue of nuclear energy in Italy is not at all dead, and 'safe and clean nuclear energy' may still be a goal worth pursuing. For most supporters of Motion 2, environmental considerations may not be overriding when it comes to the protection and the guarantee of jobs for the industrial working class.

Understandably enough, on this issue of 'industrialism vs. environmentalism', in Italy and within its class-mass party as in other Western democracies, traditional politics clashes head on with the new politics. While the new party, the PDS, might incline more towards the new politics, the issue promises to remain disturbing if not devastating. Notwithstanding these differences, the PCI-PDS has certainly come a long way from its pro-industrial positions to its present environmentalist declarations and policies. Certainly, this is one area in which the positions taken by the German Social Democrats have considerably, almost decisively, influenced those of the PCI-PDS.

The third field in which the communists and now most of the leaders of the PDS have proceeded to a profound though difficult renewal is that of constitutional and institutional issues. The Italian political and constitutional system has been criticised for its imperfect functioning and unsatisfactory performance from many quarters and for more than a decade. Up to relatively recent times, the communists defended both the Constitution with its weak form of parliamentary government, and the political system based on proportional representation and a plurality of parties. Following the initiative of Achille Occhetto, the need for fundamental institutional reforms has been widely accepted.[19] Indeed, the report by Occhetto, then vice-secretary, to the Central Committee of November 1987, 'La crisi italiana e le prospettive dell'alternativa', and above all his report, as secretary, 'Proposte per la riforma del sistema politico e istituzionale', in October 1988,[15] represented major and coherent turning points. For the first time, the communists attributed the malfunctioning of the Italian political system not just to the governing coalitions, but to the inadequacy of Italian institutions themselves and, obviously to a much lesser extent, to their own behaviour.

Occhetto indicated a strong preference for new institutions and mechanisms which could move the Italian system away from consociationalism and towards a transparent and effective government/opposition confrontation and dynamics. For the first time, an authoritative communist leader dared publicly and openly to criticise the Italian electoral system based on proportional representation. The reform he advocated, and henceforth rather consistently emphasised, would lead to an electoral system capable of producing, or at least, facilitating a competition among candidates, coalitions and programmes. Moreover, and most important, the voters would be empowered to choose among these competing coalitions so as to elect the government and possibly even the Prime Minister.

By so doing, Occhetto and many communists accepted the challenge launched by the socialists and reacted against it. The PSI Secretary General Craxi has proposed the direct election of the President of the Republic and, subsequently, has designed a new form of government for Italy: a presidential republic.[16] The Italian institutional debate revolves around these two opposite projects: a reinforced form of parliamentary government, streamlined in its government/parliament relations and endowed with a more sensitive electoral system capable of manufacturing majorities, versus a presidential republic similar to the United States model, or the French model (the socialists have not been very precise about the final product). Thus, institutional proposals and projects radically differentiate the PDS from the PSI.

At times included in the proposals for institutional reforms, and subordinated to them, but more often presented as a preliminary requirement, is the issue of a new form of citizenship or of citizens' rights. This issue is common to many left-wing European parties, and to most liberal scholars on both sides of the Atlantic. What is peculiar to the version all too frequently utilised by the PDS is the heavy insistence on these rights as claims, expectations and aspirations; for instance, the right to a clean environment, rather than entitlements requiring the performance of a duty by some individual civil servant, or authority, in order to be satisfied. For most of these claims, what is detectable is the persistence of an adversarial culture more than of a political culture willing and capable of governing the contradictions and of guiding the difficult processes through which a new citizenship, in terms of rights and duties, will be achieved.

In a country such as Italy there are two major obstacles to the achievement of a new citizenship. The first one is represented by *partitocrazia*, a degenerated form of party government without alternation. The exaggerated presence of parties in all sectors of the politico-administrative and socio-economic life suffocates the citizen. The second one is a perverse relationship between politics and administration in which nobody assumes personal responsibility and the citizen is effectively deprived of his most important rights. Through this perverse relationship the governing parties nourish their clientelistic and patronage networks themselves providing the services needed by the citizens, even those they are legally entitled to, or by showing their ability and power to make the bureaucracy comply.

This overall issue is obviously related to the type of political economy the 'new' communists have in mind and want to shape as well as how they plan to reform the welfare state, Italian style. Occhetto's supporters, and even more so Napolitano's, are now explicitly stating that in Italy it is not a matter of 'more market and less State'. It is a matter of a better market, hence an anti-trust law and a better state, hence a reform of the bureaucracy. The State should not own more companies and manage them directly. On the contrary, it should draft guidelines, regulate behaviour, and evaluate performance. In theory, there is widespread agreement within the PDS on these goals, in particular on the need for a clear-cut distinction between politics and administration. In practice, however, especially among traditional communists and southern deputies and party leaders, the request for a state presence and intervention, for state subsidies and other non-market, public resources, in a word 'statism', is certainly not going to die easily.

So long accustomed to believe that 'public is beautiful' or, anyway, that 'private is bad', many communists like several of their northern

European social democratic fellows have a difficult time adjusting to these new ideas and practices. It is evident that the party is divided along these lines not simply between old and new communists, but between northern and southern communists (in this case, Rome is southern) and between party leaders and PCI local office-holders. A new culture is being produced, but its penetration throughout the communist body has so far been slow and uneven. As to the welfare state, the PDS obviously opposes its dismantlement and argues in favour of it being restructured through a more precise definition of the services to be provided and the public to be taken care of. This point might not be too original in the light of other left-wing European experiences and solutions, even though welfare states carry their own national peculiarities and their reform requires much attention to detail. One of the best Italian sociologists working in this field is now on Occhetto's personal staff of advisers.[17] If not a guarantee of positive results, this is an encouraging signal.

The interim conclusion of this section on institutional and constitutional revision is that the new party has made long strides toward a modern approach and reformist solutions. However, it remains somewhat divided, even nourishing irreconcilable positions. It has not yet produced a convincing, broadly acceptable political synthesis. It may be obliged to do so, quickly and under pressure, if and when the socialists get their way and obtain a referendum on institutional reform and, more precisely, on direct election of the President of the Republic. Under such circumstances, Occhetto's proposal of an electoral system capable of directly electing the government would prove to be the only viable alternative.

Except for Armando Cossutta and his tiny faction, which remained adamantly pro-Soviet to the point of criticising perestroika, the communists have fundamentally agreed among themselves on international politics and their role in Europe. The party had moved far away from the Soviet Union already under Berlinguer who gradually, increasingly, and definitely cut the PCI's ties with the Soviet Union in the 1970s: witness the sharp criticism of the Soviet war in Afghanistan, a strong pre-emptive statement against the threat of Soviet involvement in the Polish crisis, and full acceptance of the process of European unification and of the unavoidable reality of NATO. At the same time, Berlinguer punctiliously defended and wanted to preserve the Italian Communist identity. Occhetto and Napolitano have taken a long additional step. Jointly, though with different emphases, they have launched an active policy of collaboration with all left-wing European parties, especially with socialist and social-democratic parties. They have established a good relationship with all of them, particularly with the German Social-Democrats, with the more or less avowed goal of joining the Socialist International.

The German Social Democrats are considered a privileged interlocutor for several reasons. First, because of Germany's importance on the European political and economic scene. In the past, more precisely in 1976, when the communists were at the height of their electoral and political success, the German government, at the time headed by the Social Democrats, did not conceal its hostility to communist participation in the Italian government. The transformation of the PCI may facilitate the lifting of that sort of informal veto. Second, the SPD is seen as the model of a powerful mass party facing political, organisational, and programmatic problems not dissimilar from those of the PDS. Finally, the lesson of Bad Godesberg may still loom large for the PDS so much so that one of the most widely respected experts recently recruited directly by Occhetto, the economics professor Michele Salvati, has committed himself to a programmatic renewal of the PDS that will take it beyond Bad Godesberg.[18]

With varying degrees of confidence, all Communists believe that a stronger United Nations role in international affairs is advisable. And all are in favour of the process of European unification, though the 'traditional' Communists harbour many reservations concerning the actual dynamics and the democratic nature of the process. Occhetto and especially Napolitano are very much in favour of actively participating in the Socialist International while the others would prefer to keep their options open. In the end, joining the Socialist International might well prove to be the litmus test of the depth of changes wrought in the foreign policy of the PCI and produced by the PDS.

Some unsolved, or new, contradictions in the behaviour of the PCI soon-to-become PDS appeared when the 1991 Gulf War started. The PCI opposed any military intervention. It voted against Italian involvement and eventually asked for a unilateral withdrawal of the small Italian contingent (ships and aircraft). A prominent streak of lingering anti-Americanism, a bias for Third World countries, and a surprising level of support for unconditional Catholic pacifism (including the Pope's) characterised the statements by Occhetto and some of his close collaborators. Once more it was Giorgio Napolitano's task, as a shadow minister of foreign affairs, to soften the tone, to emphasise continuing support for European and UN initiatives, and to avoid losing contact with the positions taken by other European socialist parties. The birthmark of opposition to the military consequences of the UN resolution signalled to many sectors of informed Italian public opinion that the

PDS has not yet completed its programmatic renewal in international politics, traditionally the crucial test for access to government in Western European countries.


TENTATIVE CONCLUSIONS

The most important reason why a party should renew its programme is that it hopes to find new allies, new supporters and new voters. A programme is the visiting card of a political party.[19] If the combined effect of the programmatic renewal and the change of name and emblem was meant to acquire new political and social allies, then one must say that this effect has not yet been achieved. Occhetto's ambitious goal – to federate all the progressive forces of the left, and exclude the socialists – has failed. And it remains unclear whether and how it can be revived. In the meantime, the Socialist Secretary-General Bettino Craxi has changed the name of his party at a stroke by adding to *Partito Socialista* the label *Unita' Socialista*, clearly suggesting that the PSI is the natural harbour where the unity of the left can and ought to be achieved. Mutual relationships between the PDS and the PSI have not improved at all since Craxi's long-term goal is to absorb the 'former communists', as he has called the PDS.

Togliatti's strategy always carefully distinguished between political and social alliances. Political alliances could be made with several political organisations and parties on the basis of anti-Fascism, in order to protect and enhance Italian democracy. Social alliances could be based not so much on anti-capitalism but on anti-monopoly attitudes and interests. Naturally, the PCI was the best placed organisation at the intersection of these alliances and the industrial working class was the cornerstone of both the political and the social strategies. The need for the politically anti-Fascist and socially anti-capitalist industrial working class to find allies meant first of all identifying the progressive middle strata as important reference groups; and second, it necessitated the transformation of anti-capitalism into opposition against capitalist monopolies but not small industries and entrepreneurs.

In recent times, if political allies have been difficult to find for a communist party in transition, social allies have seemed even more elusive. The industrial working class is shrinking and organisationally is not capable of sustaining the political efforts of the PDS. No longer sharply demarcated, class lines have become much more complex in Italian society and, in consequence, the PDS faces far greater problems in developing a strategy of social alliance. Since industrial workers are no longer the most important foundation for the PDS strategy and all class bonds are diluted, then the best strategy might be to appeal to the citizens through specific issues such as better services, improved performance by the public administration, and a clean environment. The PDS programmatic renewal aims exactly at reaching those citizens. The issue is therefore raised of what kind of party the PDS wants to become. In the eyes of many observers, the PDS seems to be pursuing the path of a radical party of the left, inclined to support and to draw its strength from opposition movements of all kinds: Catholic pacifists, Greens, libertarians. Not only is this strategy a clear break with the Italian 'Communist' past and tradition. In addition to being controversial within the PDS, it is not what other left-wing European parties are doing.

I concluded an analysis of the difficulties of the PCI written in August 1985 with these words:

> the real problem might be that the PCI has to revise its political culture, reform its organization, redefine its strategy of alliances and cease to be a traditional Communist party (which it has not been for some time anyway) without thereby becoming a traditional socialist party.[20]

The challenge has been inevitably and squarely confronted in 1990. The completion of the task still lies ahead. In some areas the party organisation is resilient and pervasive. Nevertheless, it will not be easy to build an organisationally stronger party than the traditional PCI of the 1960s and 1970s. Indeed, it may well be that Italian society has gradually and almost totally outgrown its parties and party system. Programmatic renewal, though significant, is not sufficient to build a strong party. Unless the PDS quickly identifies social and political allies, it runs the risk of finding itself with a reduced institutional presence, less political power, and limited policy influence.[21] The price of its delayed and still incomplete transformation may be high.

## NOTES

Many thanks to my friends and colleagues of the Bologna Center of the Johns Hopkins University Patrick McCarthy and especially John Harper for reading, criticising and improving my paper.

1. All these events are carefully analysed by Stephen Hellman, 'The Difficult Birth of the Democratic Party of the Left', in Stephen Hellman and Gianfranco Pasquino (eds.), *Italian Politics: A Review*, Vol. 7 (London: Pinter, 1992), pp. 68–86.
2. Gianfranco Pasquino, *Organizational Models of Southern European Communist Parties* (Bologna Center of Johns Hopkins Univ., Occasional Papers, No. 29, 1980).
3. See Richard Gillespie's essay in this volume.

4. For an excellent analysis blending these elements see Stephen Hellman, *Italian Communism in Transition: The Rise and Fall of the Historic Compromise in Turin, 1975–1980* (NY-Oxford: OUP, 1988).
5. Presidenza del Governo Ombra, *Il Governo ombra* (Rome: n.d. but 1990).
6. Gianfranco Pasquino, Oreste Massari and Antonio Missiroli, *Opposizione, governo ombra alternativa* (Rome-Bari: Laterza, 1990).
7. Michele Carducci, 'Un nuovo modello di organizzazione dell' opposizione parlamentare: "Il governo ombra" del PCI', *Politica del diritto*, Vol. 21 (1990), pp. 619–56.
8. Achille Occhetto, 'La crisi italiana e le prospettive dell' alternativa', report to the Central Commitee, 26–27 Nov. 1987, now in Pasquino (ed.), *La lenta marcia nelle istituzioni: i passi del Pci* (Bologna: Il Mulino, 1988), pp. 313–60.
9. Otto Kirchheimer, 'The Transformation of the Western European Party Systems', in Joseph La Palombara and Myron Weiner (eds.), *Political Parties and Political Development* (Princeton, NJ: Princeton UP, 1966), pp. 177–200.
10. Documenti per il Congresso staordinario del PCI, *Il Comitato centrale della svolta/1: Il comitato centrale della svolta/2: Le mozioni. Il regolamento La lettera della donne. La Carta della FGCI* (Rome: l'Unita', 1990).
11. Achille Occhetto, 'Dichiarazione di intenti', supplement to *l'Unita'*, 10 Oct. 1990. See also 'Materiali della Conferenza programmatica nazionale', *Critica marxista*, Vol. 28 (1990).
12. Several of these points are presented in Maria Luisa Boccia and Isabella Peretti (eds.), 'Il genere della rappresentanza', supplement to *Democrazia e diritto* 27/1 (1988).
13. Miriam Mafai, 'Le vedove di Lenin e la deriva femminista', *MicroMeqa*, No. 4 (1990), pp. 7–15.
14. Giovan Battista Zorzoli, 'Sulla riconversione ecologica delle attivita' produttive', *Critica marxista*, Vol. 28 (1990), pp. 431–43. See also 'Dopo Chernobyl. Potere popolare e scelte nucleari', supplement to *Democrazia e diritto* 25/3 (1986).
15. Both are collected in Pasquino (ed.), *La lenta marcia nelle istituzioni: i passi del Pci*, pp. 313–36 and 433–8.
16. Direzione PSI Ufficio Centrale Stampa e Propaganda, *Un riformismo moderno un socialismo liberale. Tesi programmatiche* (presented to the Conferenza programmatica del PSI, Rimini, 22–25 March 1990) (Imola: Grafiche Galeati, 1990).
17. Massimo Paci, 'Stato sociale e democrazia economica', *Critica marxista*, Vol. 28 (1990), pp. 97–110.
18. Michele Salvati, *Interessi e ideali, Interventi sul programma del nuovo Pci* (Milan: Feltrinelli, 1990).
19. This point is well argued by Michele Salvati, *L'Italia verso il Duemila. Analisi e proposte per un programma di legislatura* (Rome: Editori Riuniti, 1992).
20. Pasquino, 'Mid-stream and under Stress. The Italian Communist Party', in Michael Waller and Meindert Fennema (eds.), *Communist Parties in Western Europe: Decline or Adaptation?* (Oxford: Basil Blackwell, 1988), pp. 26–46.
21. Indeed, in the general election of 5–6 April 1992, the PDS vote, at 16.1 per cent of the total, was 10.5 points below the previous PCI vote. *Rifondazione Communista* obtained 5.6 per cent of the total vote.

# A Programme for Social Democratic Revival?

## RICHARD GILLESPIE

The evidence presented in this volume amply demonstrates the existence of a European 'wave' of social democratic programmatic renewal effort during the 1980s, the sweep of which was if anything broader than the previous renewal wave in the 1950s. In the past decade a renewal process, involving some form of real programmatic discussion, was notably absent in the case of the more autocratically-managed parties (PASOK in Greece and Craxi's Socialists in Italy), in the French case of a highly 'presidentialist' socialist party, and in Portugal where the Socialist Party experienced marked leadership instability. Yet the wave was powerful enough to engage the energies of parties in Germany, Sweden, Great Britain, Spain, Norway and the Netherlands, as well as in Austria in the early 1980s.

In view of this, it is perhaps surprising that the studies presented here suggest only a modest degree of cross-fertilisation between the parties under consideration. No single party served as an automatic point of reference for the other parties – as the SPD had in the past: the social democratic movement had outgrown its father-figure and its press had declined. Despite an increase in cross-national institutional collaboration in response to the existence of the European Community, socialist parties remain rather more insular than their ideologies suggest. Their widespread interest in programmatic renewal in the 1980s derived not from an awareness of new ideas in other parties, so much as a need to respond to general European trends, as well as to national catalysts.

Electoral failures played a major part in stimulating programmatic reconsideration in Norway, the Netherlands, Germany and Great Britain, but not in Sweden and Spain. However, electoral slippage did help to provoke debate in Sweden and to reinforce the case for renewal in Spain once the process had already been initiated. That said, Spain is a unique case in this regard due to the massive lead enjoyed by the PSOE over its closest electoral rival: although that lead experienced gradual erosion in the late 1980s, it remained so substantial that one must regard the Spanish experience as one forced less by necessity than permitted by an unusually privileged position in a national party system.

In all of the parties examined here, there is ample evidence of shared concern over the challenges posed by economic globalisation, ecological degeneration, the political advance of neo-liberalism, the decline of the traditional social base of left-wing parties, and the rise of an achievement culture in which social solidarity had little or no place. In most places, socialist parties found that their electoral rivals had responded to new cultural attitudes and political concerns rather more quickly than they themselves; but not so in Sweden and Spain where governing socialist parties looked to renewal in order to set or influence the future policy agenda and pre-empt rival initiatives.

Although the slogan was *programmatic* renewal, some parties were more strictly or more seriously concerned with policy reconsideration than others; some aspired to a more comprehensive kind of renewal, while in others strategic considerations were paramount. The latter phenomenon was naturally more prevalent where coalition-making was the means of entry into government. From Germany in the 1950s where Bad Godesberg had much to do with the social democratic pursuit of coalition partners, to the Netherlands in the 1960s where renewal represented a reaction against coalition, this element remained present in the 1980s with, for example, the Norwegian Labour Party's renewal process being marked by a need for allies to the right and even the Italian PDS having coalition aspirations. In contrast, the strategic aim of the PSOE was to consolidate its own dominance of the party system by further colonising the political centre.

In all the cases of renewal, the party leadership initiated the process and managed to keep it more or less under control. Intellectuals were consulted particularly in Scandinavia, the Netherlands and Spain. There is weaker evidence of programmatic debate among the rank and file. In the case of the PSOE, this can be attributed to stage management: the party apparatus discouraged the expression of internal party policy differences, for one of the objectives of the process was to attract and involve outsiders on the basis of offerings carefully prepared by the party leadership. The German party also consulted the representatives of interest groups, desiring as it did to renew its image as a *Volkspartei*, but its genuine attempts to promote rank and file debate failed. It may be that many of the issues discussed demanded too much expertise from the ordinary party member, although in the Dutch case a very strong desire to govern also served to greatly restrict the debate.

One might have expected relatively strong leadership control over the renewal process to have ensured a more satisfactory result than the sometimes chaotic debates surrounding renewal in the 1950s. In none of the major social democratic parties was the opposition to renewal so strong that it threatened to subvert the process. The trade unions which stood to lose so much from the questioning of traditional collectivism and from the new environmental concern in the end proved reluctant to play a spoiling role; as Andrew Taylor shows, they recognised that even a less sympathetic socialist party would still be their closest available political ally.

However, renewal processes did suffer in places from the existence of party factionalism – in the Italian PSD after the formal abandonment of democratic centralism, and in Spain arising from rivalry between neo-liberal ministers and the party apparatus. In the Italian case, Occhetto's renewal initiatives became seriously bogged down in factional disputes, while in Spain, where the debate was strongly regimented by the faction controlling the party apparatus, the whole value of the renewal process was called into question when that faction subsequently lost power in a cabinet reshuffle.

Regardless of the internal party situation, the management of the party renewal process proved hazardous in most countries. It was one thing for a social democratic leadership to maintain control over a party debate and another for it to exploit the results of debate for electoral gain. Ideally, the instigators wanted to tuck renewal exercises tidily into intervals between elections, yet practical realities often dictated that renewal processes would be more protracted than desired (particularly in the SPD), while elections sometimes loomed up sooner than desired. These often had to be fought on issues not envisaged in the debate, such as German unification, Swedish entry into the EC, or the performance of socialist parties in government rather than their proposals for the future.

The extent to which programmes were modified in the name of renewal varied considerably. At one extreme, one finds relatively inno-vative parties, such as the Swedish party, which came up with some quite imaginative ideas on how to meet ecological challenges, appeal to women and respond to social individualism; in the middle, parties such as the Norwegian managed only minor programmatic adjustments; while at the more conservative extreme, one finds the Spanish, who produced a mere manifesto at the end of a three-year process (although arguably this failure mattered far less than elsewhere because of the political shortcomings of the PSOE's electoral rivals). In most cases the result was a question of new emphases, most commonly on ecological and gender-related issues. It was a far cry from the SPD's erstwhile promise to 'redefine social democracy' and to reconcile the values of social solidarity and individual achievement.

It is tempting to write off the recent renewal process in view of the European election results of the early 1990s. A fairer assessment, however, would need to accept that programmatic renewal did at least initially facilitate coalition formation in the Netherlands and in Norway. Moreover, it must be acknowledged that no political party in the early 1980s envisaged the degree of upheaval in Europe that was to ensue within the next few years, and that brought new issues onto the electoral agenda. Besides, programmes play a relatively modest role in deciding the outcome of elections. Their importance to political parties has been in decline for several decades, as Carl Hodge notes: they have ceased to be regarded, even by most party activists, as blueprints for social transformation once the party is elected to office.

Results hinge much more upon a selection of perceived issues, the successful projection of party images, the record of the outgoing government and public confidence in party leaders. Yet the party programme remains useful, as Gianfranco Pasquino puts it, as a 'visiting card', a means of acquiring new allies, supporters and voters. There is no big new idea inscribed upon the new social democratic cards, but there are at least a series of programmatic ideas designed to appeal to a broader range of social groups than have traditionally supported the left, and the adoption and articulation of these ideas may also help prevent new rivals from entering the party system. As regards the electoral disappointments, it is clear that they would have been greater without the renewal effort.

The air of disappointment that has surrounded social democratic renewal so far is also a product of the immensity of the problems with which these parties are grappling. It is much more difficult for programmes emanating from nationally-based parties to appear credible when increasingly the problems and proposed solutions are global and long term. Yet locked into a 'catch-all' logic as they are, some of the disappointment surrounding programmatic renewal must be put down to party leaderships that remain over-preoccupied with the short term. For all the talk of articulating a socialist response to the 1990s, the year 2000 or indeed the twenty-first century, socialist party leaderships still tend to have the next general election as their most meaningful horizon. Excessive instrumentalism in considering programmic change may have prevented a more profound policy regeneration in several parties discussed here. On the other hand, by the late 1980s at least, it must be acknowledged that the dramatic upheavals in Europe themselves encouraged reactive behaviour rather than long-term strategic thinking and planning.

Overall, it seems evident that further reconsideration of social democratic programmes will be necessary in the 1990s as parties are confronted by major issues relating to migration, territorial redivision and the development of supranational entities, on top of the perennial questions. It may be that parties will have to find mechanisms for much more open-ended, if not permanent, programmatic renewal if they are to do more than simply adapt *a posteriori* to developments in a rapidly changing world. Already there are some signs of attempts at continuity, for example, in new provisions for future party congresses normally to focus in detail on partial programmatic reviews, on the basis of studies prepared by specialists, rather than attempt to debate whole programmes, without adequate preparation, in the space of a few days. However, there is a danger that socialist parties that become immersed in the detail of public policy as a result of programmatic compartmentalism will lose much of their old moral vitality. If their basic values fall victim to technocratic domination, they risk losing their capacity to *inspire* a political revival.

# Notes on Contributors

**Richard Gillespie** is Senior Lecturer in Politics at the University of Warwick. He is the author of *Soldiers of Perón: Argentina's Montoneros* (1983) and *The Spanish Socialist Party: A History of Factionalism* (1989) Dr Gillespie has written more recently on Spain's external relations, with special reference to Europe and the Mediterranean.

**Knut Heidar** is Professor of Political Science at the University of Oslo. His publications include *Norske Politiske Fakta 1884–1982* (1983), *Parti-demokrati på prøve* (1988) and co-author, *Vesteuropeisk Politikk* (1993).

**Carl Cavanagh Hodge** is an Assistant Professor of Political Science at Okanagan College, University of British Columbia. He has published articles in the *European History Quarterly, Governance* and *West European Politics*.

**Stephen Padgett** is Jean Monnet Lecturer in European Politics in the Department of Government, University of Essex. He is co-author of *Political Parties and Elections in West Germany* (1986) and *A History of Social Democracy in Postwar Europe* (1991). He has also written widely on the German Social Democratic Party, and on political economy and policy-making in the Federal Republic. He is co-editor of the journal *German Politics*.

**Gianfranco Pasquino** is Professor of Political Science at the University of Bologna and Adjunct Professor of Political Science at the Bologna Center of the Johns Hopkins University. Co-editor of *Polis*, his most recent books are *La Repubblica dei cittadini ombra* (1991) and *La nuova politica* (1992).

**William E. Paterson** is Salvesen Professor of European Institutions and Director of the Europa Institute, University of Edinburgh. His most recent co-authored books are *Government and the Chemical Industry in Britain and Germany* (1988), *Governing Germany* (1991) and *A History of Social Democracy in Postwar Europe* (1991). Besides numerous books and articles on German politics, the European Community and comparative European politics, he is co-editor of the journal *German Politics*.

**Diane Sainsbury** is Associate Professor of Political Science, University of Stockholm. Her most recent publications include 'Analysing Welfare State Variations', *Scandinavian Political Studies* (1991) and 'Swedish Social Democracy in Transition', *West European Politics* (1991), also published in Jan-Erik Lane (ed.), *Understanding the Swedish Model* (1991).

**Eric Shaw** is Lecturer in the Department of Political Studies, Stirling University. He is the author of *Discipline and Discord in the Labour Party* (Manchester University Press, 1988) and is at present completing a study of the Labour Party since 1979.

**Andrew J. Taylor** is Principal Lecturer in Politics at the University of Huddersfield. He is author of *The Politics of the Yorkshire Miners* (1984), *Trade Unions and the Labour Party* (1987) and *Trade Unions and Politics: A Comparative Introduction* (1989), and is completing a study of the Conservative Party's relationship with the unions in the twentieth century.

**Steven B. Wolinetz** is Professor of Political Science at Memorial University of Newfoundland. The author of a frequently cited article on the catch-all thesis, he is currently working on a book on tripartism in the Netherlands.

# Index